Fodor's EXPLORING

PORTUGAL

FODOR'S TRAVEL PUBLICATIONS
NEW YORK • TORONTO • LONDON • SYDNEY • AUCKLAND

WWW.FODORS.COM

Published in the United States by Fodor's Travel Publications, Inc.
Published in the United Kingdom by AA Publishing.

Fodor's and Fodor's Exploring are registered trademarks of Random House, Inc.

ISBN 0-679-00711-3
ISSN 1098-7460
Second Edition

Fodor's Exploring Portugal

Author: **Tim Jepson**
Cartography: **The Automobile Association**
Cover design: **Tigist Getachew, Fabrizio La Rocca**
Top inset: **AA Photo Library**
Front cover silhouette: **Bob Krist**

Printed and bound in Italy by Printer Trento srl.

How to use this book

ORGANIZATION

Portugal Is, Portugal Was
Discusses aspects of life and culture in contemporary Portugal and explores significant periods in its history.

A–Z
Breaks down the country into regional chapters, and covers places to visit, including walks and drives. Within this section fall the Focus On articles, which consider a variety of subjects in greater detail.

Travel Facts
Contains the strictly practical information for a successful trip.

Hotels and Restaurants
Lists recommended establishments in Portugal, giving a brief summary of attractions.

ADMISSION CHARGES
Standard admission charges are categorized in this book as follows:

Inexpensive	under 400$00
Moderate	400$00–700$00
Expensive	over 700$00

ABOUT THE RATINGS
Most places described in this book have been given a separate rating. These are as follows:

▶▶▶ Do not miss

▶▶   Highly recommended

▶   Worth seeing

MAP REFERENCES
To make each particular location easier to find, every main entry in this book has a map reference to the right of its name. This comprises a number, followed by a letter, followed by another number, such as 76C2. The first number (76) refers to the page on which the map can be found, the letter (C) and the second number (2) pinpoint the square in which the main entry is located. The maps on the inside front cover and inside back cover are referred to as IFC and IBC respectively.

Contents

**Tim Jepson has
traveled through
Europe for 20 years.
He has written several
guides for Fodor's,
including Exploring
guides to Italy,
Florence & Tuscany,
and Canada.**

My Portugal

It's always gratifying when favorable first impressions
turn out to be the right ones. On my first visit to Portugal
I was captivated by the country and its people, from the
friendliness of the flight attendants on my Air Portugal
flight to the old-world charm of the farmhouse where I
spent an enjoyably rustic week in the Alentejo. Little on
my subsequent trips has altered my first opinions, despite
the fact that Portugal is now one of the fastest-changing
countries in western Europe.

That first farmhouse, some 15 years ago, had neither
electricity nor running water. Its floors were pressed
earth and rough stone, the plumbing nonexistent, the
heating a vast smoking fireplace. The nearest town was
Portalegre, where one Saturday morning I remember
scouring the shops—which then resembled those
of Soviet Russia in their paucity of produce—and securing what appeared to be the town's only cabbage.

Somehow those privations didn't matter, seeming to
symbolize the old-world outlook and traditional ways of
life that constitute part of Portugal's wonderfully
ramshackle charm. At the same time, however, it can't
have been much fun being a Portuguese peasant. So now
I have mixed feelings on the recent changes brought
about by EU membership, changes that have introduced
roads, services, education, and a better standard of living
to much of the country.

These are obviously all to the good, even if modernization is beginning to take the edge off Portugal's more
quaint old ways. But while the country is changing, its
charm remains, and Lisbon is still one of Europe's most
likeable cities. The charm survives, too, in Coimbra, Évora,
and Guimarães, historic towns as rewarding as any in
Europe, as well as in the country's plethora of pretty
villages—Monsaraz and its little bullring is my own
personal favorite. If you are visiting for the first time, I hope
your first impressions are as pleasant as mine, and if you're
coming back, I trust you'll find nothing in a changing
country to keep you from returning time and time again.
Tim Jepson

Portugal Is

Nothing defines a country as powerfully as its people. A large part of Portugal's considerable charm can be laid at the door of the Portuguese, in whom Latin passion, sociability, and natural exuberance is mixed with an enchanting combination of reserve, hospitality, and deep-rooted melancholy.

NUMBER The first thing to say about the Portuguese people is how few of them there are: Portugal's population numbers only around 10.5 million, although an estimated 200 million people across the globe—principally in Brazil—speak Portuguese as their first language.

The next thing is how ethnically diverse they are: over the centuries

Times are changing, but the old ways still prevail in much of the country

the blood of Germanic and Iberian tribes, ancient ancestors of the Portuguese, has been mixed with that of the Romans, Phoenicians, Moors, and Carthaginians, not to mention the peoples from Portugal's former African and Asian colonies, including Angola, Mozambique, Macau, and East Timor. Yet although skins may be either light or dark, and eyes the blue of Celt or the brown of Moor, the Portuguese character is remarkably uniform and self-contained. Their cosmopolitan ancestry has also, for the most part, made the Portuguese mercifully tolerant and free of discrimination.

LONGING National stereotyping is always a dangerous game, but in Portugal, as in any country, certain traits stand out as defining national characteristics. The Portuguese, for example, like to think of themselves as the least Latin of the Latin countries. They are quieter and more reserved than their Spanish and Italian neighbors, and their exuberance is tempered by a famously intangible sense of *saudade*, a word that loosely translates as "longing" or "nostalgic yearning." A faintly melancholic strain seems to underpin the Portuguese character, closely allied to a feeling that Portugal's past, once so great, can somehow be resurrected and that their country will again stand tall on the world stage. The Portuguese, despite impressions to the contrary, are fiercely patriotic, and also place great importance on respect—hence the wealth of titles and courtesies employed in greetings and dealings with officialdom.

HOSPITALITY The Portuguese are highly dignified in manner, and set great store by appearances. This is one reason why children, rich or poor, are invariably well turned out, and why old folk look spruce for their afternoon get-togethers in the village square. Dignity and reserve, however, mask open-handed hospitality, for the Portuguese are more than usually generous and friendly. For this they must thank the Arab part of their heritage, with its tradition of courtesy to the stranger, together with the customs found in many Latin countries where poverty has somehow sharpened the sense of hospitality. The old ways are breaking down in Portugal, as they are almost everywhere, but one of the pleasures of a visit to the country—especially in the more rural areas—remains the warmth of the welcome extended to visitors.

❏ An estimated 47 percent of Portuguese men sport a moustache. ❏

Pilgrims at Fátima, Portugal's greatest shrine: deep-rooted religious certainties still hold sway in many of the country's rural areas

CHANGE The new millennium finds the Portuguese in a state of flux. As Portugal changes, swept forward in a modernizing rush by a tide of European Union money, so the Portuguese, it seems, are changing as well. Old women in the countryside still wear black, old men still gather in the village square, but in the cities, towns, and beach resorts the young are largely indistinguishable from their European counterparts. The march of materialism, and with it the aspirations of a relatively enriched people, has done much to alter in the matter of a few years attitudes and traditional ways of life that had remained unchanged for centuries. Religious certainties and age-old traditions still hold sway in a few rural redoubts, but for the rest the Portuguese are, for better or worse, an increasingly secular people ever more inclined towards the mainstream of European life.

Portugal is a deeply rural nation, still wedded strongly to the land despite the tumultuous changes that have convulsed the country over the last two decades. For those who work the soil, its landscapes, although beautiful to look at, are unyielding, and as a result Portuguese agriculture remains among the most backward in Europe.

12

VARIETY Portugal is a small country, but one whose narrow bounds contain a huge variety of landscapes. In the far north, the crag-topped and barren mountains, scented with wild-flowers, are the domain of the wind and lonely shepherds. Further south, the high sierras give way to rippling green hills, pictures of pastoral perfection framing age-old small-holdings, whitewashed villages, and sun-dappled vineyards. Farther south again, in a great belt that stretches across a third of the country, lie the arid, sun-drilled plains of the Alentejo, a checkerboard of wheat fields and huge cork plantations. In the deep south, the Mediterranean takes stronger hold, cistus scenting the maquis-covered hills, almond and orange trees blossoming on the Algarve's mild-weathered margins.

The midday sun beats relentlessly down on the fields of the Algarve

❏ Portugal covers some 34,404 square miles (89,106sq km), roughly three quarters the area of England or almost all of Indiana. ❏

DIVISIONS Most of northern Portugal forms part of the Meseta, the ancient mountainous block that embraces the greater part of the Iberian peninsula (its upland plains and mountain ranges extend across central Spain). Portugal is further linked to Spain by its two main rivers, the Tagus and the Douro, both of which cross the country but rise in Portugal's Iberian neighbor. The Tagus, Portugal's longest waterway, also marks the rough boundary between north and south. To the north, the climate is cooler, the farms smaller, and the people more conservative. The land is also higher (90 percent is over 1,300 feet, or 400m), save on the coastal margins, whose plains, marshes, and flatlands fringe most of the country. At the same time, the coast embraces the beaches and frac-tured coves of the Algarve, the long duned-backed lagoons of the Atlantic, and the soaring windswept cliffs and headlands of Cape St. Vincent.

NATURE Portugal's fauna is as varied as its landscapes, its position mean-ing that it boasts species common to European, Mediterranean, and North African habitats. The wolf prowls the high mountains of the Serra da Estrela, while the rarest of all European big cats, the lynx, is still said to inhabit the wilder reaches of the Alentejo. Northern European

mammals such as the rabbit, fox, and hare are all common, although many are subtly distinct local subspecies.

Portugal's position relative to Africa also ensures a large number of birds, for the country lies astride the major migration routes of many central and Western European species. Similarly, position plays a crucial part in determining the country's flora, which also embraces species from widely differing habitats. In the northern interior, which generally speaking is lush, green, and damp, some 86 percent of all plants, trees, and flowers are European. In the south, however, the figure is just 29 percent, with some 46 percent of Mediterranean origin.

> ❑ Almost half of the Portuguese people either live or work in the countryside. ❑

AGRICULTURE Inspirational to look on, the land is unforgiving as a means of earning a living. And with agriculture and rural labor such hard task masters, it is no accident that emigration has long been a fact of Portuguese life (see pages 88–89).

That said, a vast proportion of the Portuguese still live or work on the land, with only two of the country's cities—Lisbon and Porto—boasting populations above 100,000. Half the country is classified as agricultural land (a third is forest), while a quarter of Portuguese workers are classified as farmers. Yet Portuguese agriculture, despite the European Union's best efforts, remains desperately inefficient. The reasons are many: half of all farmers are now aged over 55, illiteracy rates are high (33 percent among farmers), and many farms are so small as to be uneconomical (half cover 2.5 acres—1 hectare—or less). More encouragingly, however, Portugal accounts for half of the world's cork production (see pages 200–201), while its wines—over and above port—are rapidly achieving greater international renown.

13

> ❑ Agriculture, fishing, and forestry account for 10 percent of Portugal's gross domestic product. ❑

Sheep farm in the Algarve hills

Portugal's long Atlantic coast, booming ports, and great maritime traditions mean the sea and seafaring have long figured large in Portuguese life, from the itinerant Phoenician sailors who first settled around Lisbon to the coves and broad sandy beaches that first lured tourists— and their money—to the Algarve.

HOLIDAYS Portugal for most of us means sun, sea, and sand. While past visitors were lured by low prices and a benign climate, today's tourists are tempted by the string of rocky coves, cliffs, sandy shores, and translucent waters of the Algarve, now a byword for beaches, golfing vacations, and reasonably priced resorts.

It was not always thus, Portugal's present open-armed welcome to vacationers being in marked contrast to the Salazar years, when

Portugal's coastline is a mixture of sandy beaches, towering cliffs, and wild, windblown headlands

the dictator actively discouraged the potentially "corrupting" influence of outsiders. As late as 1960, the year in which Faro's international airport opened, the Algarve offered just 1,000 tourist beds. In 1988 the figure was 58,500, while by 1995 the figure had risen to 82,000 thanks to EU grants and booming foreign investment.

❑ Of the roughly 22.5 million visitors to Portugal in 1995, more than a third, 9.7 million, were tourists, 60 percent of whom went to the Algarve. ❑

14

DISCOVERY Portugal's sea coast embraces far more than the mild-weathered resorts of the Algarve, however, and Portugal is increasingly trying to promote some of the lesser-known stretches of its more westerly littoral. The next big pull will be the westernmost limit of the Algarve, a previously undeveloped region around Sagres and Cabo de São Vicente. This was the cradle of Portugal's maritime associations, the area in which Henry the Navigator planned and launched the voyages of discovery that laid the foundations of an empire (see pages 226–227). It was here, too, at the site of one of Europe's key strategic points—a jutting hinge guarding the Atlantic approaches—that some of the continent's greatest sea battles have been fought over the centuries (see panel on page 224).

BEACHES Farther north and nearer the colder waters of the Atlantic, the resorts of the so-called Costa de Lisboa (the littoral south of Lisbon) are also going from strength to strength. Closer to the capital, the Costa del Sol (Estoril coast) provides Lisbon's seafront playground, far enough from the city's busy port—one of Iberia's most important—to be free of pollution. Royalty and Europe's 19th-century moneyed classes once wintered here, seduced by a wonderfully mild microclimate. Today, their elegant old-world hotels are the preserve of northern European visitors in search of "a beakerful of the warm south." Farther north still, on the unspoiled Costa de Prata ("Silver Coast"), the Atlantic grows more inhospitable: the water is colder, the wind is stronger, and the waves are more relentless. However, there are some superb beaches here, often backed by dunes and pine woods, as well as amiable resorts such as Figueira da Foz and Praia de Mira. On Portugal's northernmost coast, the Costa Verde ("Green Coast"), lie still wilder and more dramatic seascapes, along with some excellent if bracing beaches.

FISHING The sea in Portugal is not all about tourists and tradition. Fish and

Fishing has been the major activity of many Portuguese coastal towns for centuries

fishing have long been mainstays of Portuguese life. Few coastal towns are without their pastel-painted fishing boats or rust-streaked trawlers, fishing still providing a vital economic lifeline despite a world of falling stocks and tight quotas. A large proportion of Portugal's fish goes straight to the home market—the Portuguese are voracious fish-eaters—one reason why Portugal must take its share of the blame for overfishing. It was the country's traditional passion for salt cod (*bacalhau*) that helped to wipe out the cod stocks on Newfoundland's Grand Banks, a fishing ground trawled for centuries by the Portuguese. It is a sign of the times that Portugal must now import a quarter of its fish, including its great traditional standbys of sardines (from Russia) and salt cod (from Norway).

The role of the state is a more pertinent issue in Portugal than in many Western European countries, for Portugal was not only subject to a dictatorship which collapsed as recently as 1974, but also endured a fragile decade of democracy that was only finally secured through membership of the European Union in 1986.

16

HISTORY Portuguese politics has been a mess for centuries. Order of sorts was established during the middle part of this century, but at the cost of Salazar's dictatorship (see pages 42–43), and although the 1974 Carnation Revolution rid the country of oppression (see pages 44–45), it unleashed a decade of profound social and political upheaval. There were 16 governments, for example, in the first 13 years after the revolution. And it was to be 12 years before a civilian, Mário Soares, was entrusted with the job of president (army candidates, the revolution notwithstanding, had occupied the post in the 60 years before 1986).

Democracy's fragile hold was strengthened in 1986 by Portugal's membership of the EEC (now the EU). A year later, after a decade of minority government, the Social Democrats under Cavaco Silva won a working majority in parliament. Silva then embarked on a controversial but largely successful program of privatization, while in 1982 (and again in 1989) the more radical dictates of the 1974 revolution were replaced by a more conciliatory constitution. Portugal's political progress, together with its democratic credentials, was symbolized by its presidency of the EU in 1992.

❑ The five blue shields at the heart of the Portuguese flag symbolize the five wounds of Christ. The seven castles around the central white shield represent seven fortresses retaken from the Moors during the Reconquista (see pages 30–31). ❑

GOVERNMENT Since the 1974 revolution, Portugal has enjoyed a republican political system. A president is elected by the people, who have universal suffrage, every five years, and may then be reelected for another consecutive term (but no more). The president then nominates the prime minister, basing his choice on the party (or parties) holding a majority in parliament. Parliament consists of a single chamber of between 240 and 250 members, each of whom is elected by the people every four years. Changes to the constitution in 1982 to some extent limited the president's powers, although he still maintains the right to veto certain laws passed in the parliamentary

Local politics: the attractive-looking town hall at Faro

chamber. A slightly different system prevails in Madeira and the Azores, both of which are semiautonomous regions with their own elected assemblies.

REGIONS For most visitors to Portugal, and as far as this and many other guidebooks are concerned, the country still divides into the areas that for centuries defined its principal regions. From north to south these are the Minho, Trás-os-Montes, the Douro, the Beiras (Alta, Baixa, and Litoral), Ribatejo, Estremadura, the Alentejo (Alto and Baixo), and the Algarve. Today, these regions have lost their administrative distinctions as the country has officially been divided into districts: 18 on the mainland, three in the Azores, and one in Madeira. Many of the country's bureaucracies operate at this district level, most notably those concerned with the provision of public health and education.

At a more local level, power is devolved to a municipal council, or *concelho*. There are 305 in all, housed in the local town hall (the Paço do Concelho) and run by a committee of councillors (the Câmara Municpal). The committee is headed by the president and town mayor, who is elected (along with the councillors) every four years. At a lower level still—roughly the equivalent of a New England town—there are 4,200 *freguesias*, responsible for recordkeeping and minor administration in villages or different areas of large towns.

❑ "Portugal has lost, one hopes for ever, its image as a country stopped in time and history." President Mário Soares (1988). ❑

17

The Portuguese parliament in session in Lisbon

Social issues such as health and education have a special importance in Portugal, a country that has been wracked by poverty for centuries and which has only relatively recently—with the help of European Union funding—begun to turn around some of the worst illiteracy and infant mortality rates in Europe.

18

BIRTH In a trend that is reflected across much of southern Europe, the Portuguese are marrying less than they used to and are having far fewer children. In 1975 there were 103,125 marriages in a population of around 10 million; by 1989 the figure was down to 73,195, almost three-quarters of them conducted in church. But if the church statistic seems to suggest adherence to the old ways, other figures indicate a loosening of the traditional ties of faith and convention. Abortion has been available since 1984 (although not "on demand"), family planning is permitted by law, and contraception is available from the age of 18. Divorce rates are soaring and birth rates—surprisingly for a previously rock-solid Catholic country—are falling. The old days when

Portuguese parents might have ten or more children are now largely gone. In 1980 there were 16.2 births per thousand head of population; ten years later this figure was 11.5 per thousand. Just as tellingly, 14.5 percent of the 120,000 babies registered in 1990 were born out of wedlock.

❑ *Pobreza não é vileza* ("Poverty is a not a crime")—Portuguese saying. ❑

DEATH But while these figures suggest changing social attitudes, other more worrying figures reflect the degree to which poverty is still a fact of daily life (and death) in Portugal. Some 3 million Portuguese, or around 30 percent of the population, live below the poverty line (as defined by the European Union). Infant mortality rates, a depressingly reliable indicator, are around 7.9 deaths per thousand. This is an improvement on past figures, but Portugal still ranks close to the bottom of the European league. Some 7–8 children per thousand die in their first year of life, and about the same number before they reach the age of five. However, according to latest figures, about 94 percent of the population have running publicly piped water, up from 66 percent in the late 1980s. The availability of housing, also once a huge problem, is now less acute than a decade ago. In 1991 about 65 percent of Portuguese lived in their own homes, and many

Top: Capela dos Ossos, Igreja do Carmo, Faro. Left: Portugal's birth rate has fallen in the last 20 years

hundreds of thousands of homes across the country are believed to have been built illegally.

> ❑ The mortality rate on Portuguese roads is the highest in Europe—on average, there are around 2,000 deaths a year. ❑

EDUCATION Portugal is making great strides in many areas, and most of the more damning statistics are gradually being turned around. It's a long, hard road, however, and one in which education provides the greatest obstacles. Portugal's problems in this area, like so many, stem from the Salazar dictatorship, when illiteracy was deliberately used as a vehicle of social coercion: people who were poor and ill-educated, so the thinking went, were cheaper for the state and easier to keep in their place.

Since 1975 the number of people tying the knot in Portugal has dropped by over a quarter

Today, the illiteracy rate is around 15 percent—or a staggering 1.5 million people.

Many of these are elderly (especially women) or middle-aged men who left school early or emigrated in the chaotic aftermath of the Salazar years.

Only 40 percent of Portuguese children have secondary education (that is, a total of nine years of schooling); the EU average is 70 percent. Although universal education is now available, and the number of teachers has risen dramatically in recent years, poverty forces many children, especially in the semi-industrialized rural north, to leave school to work at an early age in ill-paid manual jobs.

Laws and EU regulation on such matters are sadly ineffectual.

If the 1974 revolution changed the face of Portugal's political landscape beyond recognition, then the country's membership of the European Economic Community in 1986, and the influx of new money it brought, unleashed a period of economic growth that in the space of a decade has transformed the lives of most Portuguese.

20

POVERTY Portugal has known periods of wealth beyond imagination—notably during the Age of Discovery and following the influx of gold and diamonds from Brazil—but for most of its recent history it has been a quite different story. While its southern Mediterranean neighbors, Italy and Spain, pulled themselves up after World War II, Portugal remained an essentially agricultural country, its peasants wedded to the land or forced into emigration, the age-old recourse of the agrarian poor (see pages 88–89). Under the Salazar dictatorship, a handful of people controlled what wealth the country had. The poor remained

Boats in a Lisbon marina, symbols of new prosperity

impoverished, and not only impoverished but ignorant and illiterate, for education and welfare were withheld from the masses as a means of social control and economic cost-cutting.

> ❏ "Portugal needs to do in ten or twenty years what other countries achieved in a century."
> Prime Minister Cavaco Silva (1990). ❏

WATERSHED Things are different now. Over the last decade Portugal has witnessed an economic rebirth of staggering proportions. True, it has been from a desperately low base, but the flow of new money and foreign investment has changed the face of the country. The transformation began in earnest in 1986, when Portugal was admitted to the European Economic Community. Almost at once, EEC funds flooded in to finance dramatic changes in the country's industrial, financial, and economic infrastructure; roads, railroads, agriculture, education, irrigation projects, airports, the telephone system, industry all benefited. In 1986 Portugal received 49.5 billion escudos ($320 million). Over the next two years the total reached a staggering 380 billion escudos ($2.5 billion), or 3.2 percent of the country's GDP, and in 1993 the figure had climbed to 4 percent. By 1988, unemployment fell to 6 percent, the lowest of any EU member except Luxembourg, and, with cheap labor providing a powerful incentive for overseas companies, foreign investment boomed.

The impressive Expo '98 in Lisbon's Parque das Nações

❏ Per capita income in Portugal rose from $2,100 in 1985 to over $10,500 in 1995. ❏

REALITY Yet, despite these remarkable changes, problems remain. Portugal still has frightening illiteracy and infant mortality rates (see pages 18–19). And, although more people have telephones, televisions, and all the other material manifestations of improved living standards, in the farthest reaches of the Minho and Trás-os-Montes—not to mention the *bairros de lata*, or shanty-town suburbs of Lisbon and Porto—here are areas of eye-opening poverty where the economic renaissance is still obviously absent.

❏ Portuguese workers earn anything up to five times less than workers in France or Germany. ❏

COMPETITION Portugal's honeymoon period as a European Union member came to an end in 1995, the year in which the EU began to cut back on the largesse that had eased the country's passage into the mainstream of European economic life. Although Portugal will remain a net recipient of funds for years to come, the country will henceforth have to face the harsh realities of the global marketplace without financial feather-bedding.

FUTURE To its credit, Portugal is making light of its potential problems, and is looking ahead to forthcoming challenges with remarkable optimism. Its enterprising and forward-looking spirit was embodied in the vast Lisbon Expo held in 1998, the 500th anniversary of Vasco da Gama's pioneering voyage to the Indies, and in the hosting of the Euro 2004 football competition. Some critics feel that much is being lost in the rush to modernism and obeisance to the free market. Once-pristine coastlines have surrendered to the advance of concrete, the environment has come off second-best to industry, and the architectural glories of Lisbon and elsewhere have succumbed to the wreckers' hammer and drill. In looking forward, Portugal must also—if only occasionally—now learn to look back.

Portugal is a country that is tailor-made for fun and festivities, as well as ritual and more solemn observance. Its powerful Catholic traditions ensure a wide variety of religious festivals, pilgrimages, and saints' days, while its long rural traditions result in ancient village festas, *age-old markets, and long-running agricultural fairs.*

RELIGION Ritual and religion play important parts in Portuguese life, mingling with more secular everyday activities in a way that can be difficult for non-Catholics or non-Latin cultures to appreciate. Immersion in religious culture is most obviously reflected in the country's huge number of religious festivals, processions, and pilgrimages.

Many Portuguese, for example, visit the graves of dead relatives on All Saints' Day (November 1), a day in the Portuguese calendar that has added resonance, for it was on November 1, 1755 that Portugal was ravaged by the "Great Earthquake."

A street procession in Tomar's Festa dos Tabuleiros

Many Portuguese also embark on the famous pilgrimage to Fátima, Portugal's greatest religious shrine, scene of two vast annual congregations on May 13 and October 13 (see pages 172–173). Viana do Castelo is the focus of another large pilgrimage in August, this time in celebration of Nossa Senhora da Agonia, while September in Lamego secs a large pilgrimage in honor of Nossa Senhora dos Remédios. Another town, Nazaré, honors Nossa Senhora da Nazaré (Our Lady of Nazareth), also in September.

> ❑ In 1736 it was estimated there were only 122 working days in the Portuguese year, the rest being taken up with religious festivals. ❑

SAINTS Virtually every town and village has an Easter parade, of which the best known is probably the Ecce Homo procession in Braga. Most places also have one or more local saints, each of whom must be duly and suitably celebrated. The most notable of these are Lisbon's so-called Festas dos Santos Populares, in which saints Peter, Anthony, and John are commemorated in three riotous festivals in the space of two weeks in June. These same saints feature in countless *festas* across the country, but especially in Braga (St. John), Vila Real (St. Peter and St. Anthony), and above all in Porto, whose main festival of the year, on June 24, is devoted to St. John. Other towns with much revered saints and festivals to match include Miranda

do Douro, which honors St. Barbara in August; Amarante, which celebrates St. Gonsalo in June; and Guimarães, where the town remembers St. Walter in August.

FESTIVALS If you can't make the big festivals of Porto and Lisbon, the chances are you will stumble across one of the minor festivals that take place in virtually every Portuguese village at some time during the year. Many of these are held to give thanks for the harvest or a local delicacy, their present-day religious veneer underlaid by traditions that probably date back to pagan times. Other festivals, especially in the north, have folk or agricultural origins, while many involve a local saint being

Houses decked out in festive mood

23

wheeled out as an excuse for a party. Procedure in these local *festas* or *romarias* is usually the same: the local band plays, fireworks are lit, and food and wine are consumed to excess. A figure of the saint is carried in procession, and a special mass is held to lend religious decorum to the proceedings.

Soccer is a national obsession. Above: the Stadium of Light, home of Benfica

SOCCER If Fátima and feast days are the natural expression of Portugal's religious fervor, then soccer—along with TV soap opera—is the most vocal and popular manifestation of the country's secular preoccupations. While bullfighting has its devotees (see pages 178–179), soccer is the unquestioned national sport, absorbing swathes (largely male) of the population for months of the year. While today's players do not evoke the magic of names like Eusebio, the great star of the 1960s, Portugal still produces winning teams on the European stage. Benfica and Sporting are the two great Lisbon teams, although both are currently overshadowed (much to the intense chagrin of the Lisboetas) by the swashbuckling achievements of FC Porto, the country's third big team. The progress of these and other teams is followed obsessively, and it is no surprise that sports journals are the most popular of all Portugal's national newspapers. Soccer fever will reach an even higher pitch in 2004 when the country hosts the prestigious four-yearly, pan-European international soccer competition.

Portugal Was

S. FRANCISCVS.

Before Portugal emerged as a nation state in the 12th century, its history was largely that of the Iberian peninsula as a whole. Open frontiers and a lack of defining mountain ranges between today's Portugal and Spain allowed for the free passage of migrants, armies, and cultural and technological change.

PREHISTORY Portugal's oldest-known human artifacts are a series of paleolithic cave paintings in the Beira Alta, dating the country's earliest indigenous civilization to around 20,000 BC. Burial sites and other archaeological fragments indicate the arrival of more advanced cultures around 8000 BC, many of whom settled in the Tagus Valley before spreading to remote parts of the Alentejo and Estremadura. Thousands of years then elapsed before the arrival of the Greeks and Phoenicians (around 900 BC), both of whom established trading posts on the Iberian coast (including one that was on the site of modern Lisbon).

Around 700 BC it was the turn of the Celts, who came across Europe and settled in the Minho and other parts of northern Portugal. There they established artistic and cultural traditions that endured for centuries, building a series of forti-fied villages, or *citânias*, some—notably Briteiros (see page 102)—of remarkable sophistica-tion. Around 250 BC the Celts were joined by the Carthaginians, a North African race whose imperial ambitions brought them increas-ingly into conflict with the power of Rome.

Top: Roman mosaic at Conimbriga
Right: Roman inscribed column at Chaves

ROMANS Carthage was eventually crushed by Rome (in the so-called Punic Wars), despite the best efforts of Carthaginian generals such as Hannibal, who in 220 BC passed through Iberia en route for the Alps and his assault on the Italian penin-sula. Just ten years later the Romans themselves turned to Iberia, conquer-ing much of southern Spain and Portugal in a series of lightning campaigns. In central Portugal, however, their progress was slower, and in particular in the region occu-pied by the Lusitani, a tribe of Celtic origin (they were named after Lusus, a companion of Bacchus, Portugal's legendary first settler). Under the leadership of Viriatus, Portugal's first national hero, the Lusitanians waged a long guerrilla campaign against the Romans. Defeat finally came in 139 BC, and only then after Viriatus had been betrayed and murdered by paid assassins.

COLONIZATION Under Julius Caesar an army of 15,000 completed the job of conquest in 60 BC. Four centuries of romanization then followed, a period which left an indelible impression on the region. Only Portugal's remote Celtic north remained impervious to Roman influence. Colonies were founded, importantly at Olisipo (Lisbon), Ebora (Évora), and Pax Julia

26

(Beja) and roads, bridges, and aqueducts were built, many of which remained in use until comparatively recently. Vast agricultural estates developed in the south, forerunners of the modern-day *latifúndios* (see page 187), and land was planted with vines, wheat, olives, and barley, all introduced by the Romans. Rome's most permanent legacy, however, was the Latin language, which evolved into Portuguese over a period of 400 years.

The Temple of Diana at Évora, one of the few surviving memorials to four centuries of Roman rule

❏ Christianity reached southern Portugal around the end of the 1st century; by the 3rd century there were bishoprics at Faro, Braga, Évora, and Lisbon. ❏

VISIGOTHS After the fall of Rome (in the 5th century) four "barbarian" tribes descended on Iberia: the Vandals, Visigoths, Alans, and Swabians (or Suevi). Of these, only the Visigoths and Suevi made a lasting impression. The Suevi, originally from eastern Germany, arrived first, settling in the area between the Douro and Minho rivers. There they established courts at Braga and Portucale (Porto), literally the "area around the port." Around 585 the Suevi and their territories were absorbed by the Visigoths, who retained control of Iberia for a century. Their rule had little lasting effect, however, particularly in Portugal, which lay far from their imperial capital of Toledo in Spain. The power of the Visigoths was eclipsed around 700, when one of the factions within their increasingly splintered hierarchy appealed for help from a new source of power—the Moors.

❏ Portuguese tuna paste, still considered a delicacy, was admired by the Phoenicians, appreciated in classical Athens, and exported to ancient Rome. ❏

The Moors, a term of convenience for a variety of North African peoples, held sway over much of present-day Spain and Portugal for almost 500 years. The period was one of remarkable tolerance and enlightenment in which commerce, agriculture, science, and learning all benefited from the civilizing influence of "infidel" rule.

28

MIXTURE The North African invaders who crossed the Mediterranean in 710 are now known as the Moors. The name suggests a homogeneous people with a single-minded unity of purpose, but they were in truth a disparate band of fellow travelers, made up of Arabs, Syrians, Persians, Moroccan Berbers, Egyptian Copts, and even a sprinkling of Jews. Within a decade of their arrival, and despite their diverse origins, the Moors had occupied most of the Iberian peninsula, penetrating as far as the mountains of the Asturias in northern Spain. In "Portugal" their influence was largely concentrated in the south; the present-day town of Aveiro (south of Porto) marked the northernmost extent of their power. Beyond that, in the mountains and old Swabian redoubts, Christian and Germanic ways of life continued their precarious hold. These redoubts would later form the germ of

resistance to the Moors and, almost as importantly, the seed of what would later become Portugal.

KINGDOMS Moorish power in the Iberian peninsula focused on Córdoba (in present-day Spain), which in time became the Moors' great imperial capital. In Portugal, however, it centered increasingly on the al-Gharb, or "Western Land" (present-day Algarve). As the years went by, different Moorish factions assumed power, reflecting the ebb and flow of dynastic power in North Africa. As a result, the al-Gharb emerged as a separate Moorish kingdom in the 9th century, distinct from al-Andalus, the Muslim protectorate that covered most of modern Spain. Al-Gharb lacked nothing by way of

Top: the battle for Lisbon's castle depicted in tiles. Below: the restored Moorish castle at Sintra

splendor, however—its capital Shelb (Silves) was reputed to have been ten times richer than Lisbon.

❑ That most Christian of names, Fátima, is actually of Moorish derivation. ❑

CULTURE It is worth remembering that the Moors ruled much of Portugal and Spain for some 500 years (from 711 to 1249). This is the same length of time that in Britain separates the reigns of Henry VIII and the present queen, and in North America divides Columbus's voyage of discovery from the first lunar landing. Much can happen in five centuries, something to consider when examining the effect Moorish culture exerted on the "Portuguese." Much of the Moors' legacy survives to the present day, even in something as basic as language: the Moorish word *almude*, for example, still means 25 liters of wine, and an *arrôba* is still a much-used measure for cork or fruit (it is roughly equivalent to 33 pounds, or 15kg).

Other legacies also survive, but they are so deeply woven into the texture of modern life that they often pass unnoticed. Brick paving, roofed chimneys, and tiled walls, for example, arrived with the Moors, as did astrolabes, compasses, and a revolutionary form of shipbuilding. Science and learning flourished, and the works of the ancient Greek philosophers, among others, found a new audience via Arabic translations. In the economic sphere, agriculture was the greatest beneficiary: irrigation was improved and crop

rotation pioneered; rice, cotton, oranges, and lemons were introduced; and grain began to be milled, replacing the method of pounding it in mortars (a hopelessly inefficient procedure). New urban centers developed, and with them craft and other industries, the produce for which found an outlet in a plethora of newly pioneered trade routes. On top of this, Christians and Jews were allowed freedom of worship and their own civil laws. Nevertheless, many Portuguese were waiting for the chance to turn on their conquerors.

29

The Moors introduced to Portugal not only their costumes but also innovations in art

Although 500 years of Moorish rule improved Portugal's lot, Christian forces, active almost from the time the Moors first arrived, eventually embarked on a campaign of reconquest that ultimately created the oldest nation state in Europe—Portugal—and saw the crowning of the country's first king.

SEEDS The Christian overthrow of the Moors, the Reconquista, began almost from the moment the invaders set foot in Europe. In 718, according to myth, just eight years after the Moors' first Iberian incursion, a small band of Visigoths thwarted the advance guard of a Moorish expeditionary force at Covadonga (in the Spanish Asturias). From this nugget of resistance, one of many in the northern mountains, was born a small independent region initially no more than a few miles wide. As the Moors were pushed southwards over the next 200 years, this territory grew into a domain that extended across Léon, Galicia, and the old Swabian territory of Portucale (the area between the Douro and Minho). In time, this region became a kingdom and gained a ruler—the king of Léon and Castile. Among his tasks was the job of appointing governors to run that part of his territory known as Portucale.

HANDOVER In the middle of the 11th century the king of Léon and Castile was Ferdinand I. In 1057 he succeeded in driving the Moors from Lamego, a year later he cleared them from Viseu, and in 1064 he forced them from the city of Coimbra. His successor, Alfonso VI, had rather less luck, largely because his reign coincided with the arrival in Iberia of the Almoravids, a forceful Moorish clan intent on fresh conquest. In 1087 Alfonso VI therefore sent out an appeal for help in confronting the "infidel." Among those who answered the call was Raymond of Burgundy, who was offered the hand

of Urraca, Alfonso's daughter and heir, as a reward for his assistance. Raymond's cousin, Henry of Burgundy, who had also rallied to the cause, married Tareja (Teresa), Alfonso VI's illegitimate daughter. Part of Tareja's dowry included the land of Portucale, of which Henry eventually became ruler.

AFONSO HENRIQUES In 1109 Tareja and Henry had a son, Afonso Henriques. Five years later, when Henry died, Tareja became regent in his place. When Afonso was 19, however, he seized power

Warrior king: Dom Afonso Henriques

from his mother, who was dispatched into exile in Galicia. Eleven years later, in 1139, Afonso secured a famous victory against the Moors at Ourique, an event that bolstered his growing authority and enabled him to cast off the bonds of vassalage owed to the king of Léon and Castile (by then Alfonso VII). In the same year Afonso declared himself "King of Portugal," turning Portucale from a Castilian earldom into an independent kingdom (the first, and oldest, of Europe's present nation states). In 1143, after Castile reluctantly recognized his title (in the Treaty of Zamora), Afonso was acclaimed king at Santa Maria de Almacave in Lamego. Later that year, in return for 4oz (113g) of gold a year and a vow of loyalty, the papacy also bestowed its approval on the newly independent "Portugal."

Don Afonso Henriques prays before his victory at Ourique

RECONQUEST Thus was founded the House of Burgundy (1128–1383), Portugal's first royal dynasty. Afonso did not rest on his laurels, however, and in 1147 he resumed his campaign against the Moors, driving them from the strategically important city of Santarém. Lisbon, the great prize, fell in the same year. At Afonso's death in 1185, only the Algarve and the Alentejo remained in Moorish hands. His son, Sancho I (reigned 1185–1211), regained some of the outstanding territory, only for most of it to be recaptured, while Sancho II (reigned 1223–1248) was able to recover the Alentejo and the eastern Algarve. However, it was only with the capture of Faro in 1249 under Afonso III (reigned 1248–1279), Sancho II's brother and successor, that the Moorish presence was finally erased. The way then lay open for one of Portugal's greatest kings.

❑ Afonso Henriques made first Guimarães and then Coimbra his capital. Afonso III transferred the title to Lisbon in 1260. ❑

The Capela dos Reis, or Kings' Chapel, at Braga contains the tombs of Portugal's earliest rulers

❑ Portugal came into being, according to Oliveira Martins, the great 19th-century historian, "thanks to the valiant, mediocre, tenacious, brutal and perfidious character of Afonso Henriques." ❑

For the most part, Afonso Henriques' successors were a pretty sorry lot, successful in ridding Portugal of the Moors, but halfhearted in most other respects. However, one remarkable man, Dom Dinis (reigned 1279–1325), son of Afonso III, proved to be a shining exception and one of the greatest kings in Portuguese history.

STABILITY When Dom Dinis took the throne in 1279, aged just 18, Portugal was still finding its feet. Much of the country had been split between the Church, nobility, and religious orders (notably the Knights Templars), a division of spoils necessitated in the fragile days of reconquest by the need to defend and establish the fledgling state. A parliament, or *Cortes*, consisting mainly of nobles and clergy, had been summoned in Coimbra as early as 1211, and to this Dinis added a municipal structure (a Roman legacy) in towns and cities. With political and social structures bedding down, however, a new threat appeared on Portugal's horizon, and one that would dominate its foreign policy for much of the next 700 years.

ACHIEVEMENTS The new threat was Castile, heart of modern Spain. Alarmed by a unified Portugal, which seemed to threaten its power, Castile adopted a bellicose approach to its new neighbor. Dom Dinis, for his part, built some 50 fortresses along his borders, many of which survive to this day. At the same time he negotiated with Castile to produce the Treaty of Alcanices (1297), a document in which Castile formally recognized Portugal's frontiers. He also founded the University of Coimbra, championed agricultural improvements, replanted forests, wrote accomplished poetry, promoted trade (by creating 40 local

João I of Portugal secures his famous victory over the Castilians at the Battle of Aljubarrota in 1385

32

England's Duke of Lancaster dines with Portugal's king: the two royal families were joined by marriage

fairs), and brought the Church under stricter royal control.

SUCCESSION Dinis's successors would not prove quite so accomplished. After a series of lesser kings, the House of Burgundy reached its nadir with the feckless Fernando I (reigned 1367–1383). Like many of his predecessors, Fernando had married into the Castilian ruling house to promote peace between Portugal and its potential enemy. His three marriages, however, produced no male heir. His only heiress, Beatriz, followed family tradition at the age of 12 by making a marriage of convenience with Juan I, king of Castile. The terms of this match stated that Beatriz would become "queen of Portugal" and Juan her "consort," thereby raising the prospect that a Castilian king might rule Portugal—something the Burgundian kings had been trying to avoid for 200 years. When Fernando died, Juan immediately "ordered" the Portuguese to proclaim Beatriz their queen, and in a further provocation he added Portugal's coat of arms to his own royal standard.

REVOLT The prospect of a Castilian king was not distasteful to many Portuguese noblemen and clergy, who saw several potential advantages in such an alliance. However, absorption by the hated Castilians was less pleasing to the merchants and to the mob, who cast around for someone to champion their cause. Such a figure was soon found in the guise of João of Avis, the illegitimate son of Dom Pedro, Fernando I's father. A popular revolt ensued, and after two years of confusion João was declared king by the Portuguese *Cortes*.

JOÃO I Castile immediately invaded Portugal, only to be defeated by João I at the Battle of Aljubarrota (1385), a victory that secured Portuguese independence for two centuries and marked one of the defining moments in the country's history (see pages 168–169). João then set about searching for an alliance to challenge Castile and reinforce the House of Avis, Portugal's new monastic dynasty. He found it in the Treaty of Windsor (1386), the basis of an alliance with England that would endure until the 20th century. The union was sealed with his marriage to Philippa of Lancaster, daughter of John of Gaunt, granddaughter of Edward III and sister to the future Henry IV.

❑ The House of Burgundy produced nine kings and endured 255 years. ❑

The marriage of João I to Philippa of Lancaster laid the foundations for the greatest period in Portugal's history, not least because the union—by all accounts a happy and loving one—produced a crop of gifted children, one of whom, Henry, would initiate the voyages of discovery that eventually fostered Portugal's worldwide empire.

BEGINNINGS Portugal was always destined to be a maritime power. It occupied a position at the mouth of the Mediterranean, with ports on its southern coast facing across to North Africa and ports on its western coast looking out across the Atlantic—not for nothing have some of Europe's greatest sea battles been fought off its shores. Once peace was signed with Castile (1411), João was free to set his sights beyond these watery horizons. In the first instance this meant North Africa, whose attraction was land, together with the chance of defeating local pirates (long a thorn in the

Spices: an Eastern treasure

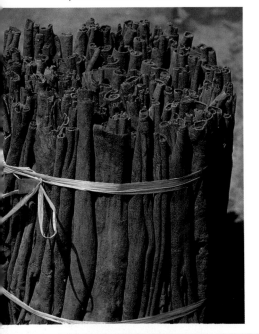

Portuguese flesh) and of securing definitive control of the Straits of Gibraltar.

In the long run the policy was a failure, for North Africa was never taken. However, in the short term it secured a famous victory when the fortified Moroccan city of Ceuta fell to a 200-ship Portuguese task force on July 25, 1415. Among the captains that day was Henriques, one of João's three sons, better known to posterity as Henry the Navigator (see pages 226–227). Fired by his brief maritime experience, Henry later settled in Sagres, a windblown cape on Portugal's southwesternmost tip. There he founded a school of the greatest navigators, cartographers, and shipbuilders of the day, and went on to promote a series of voyages, each of which probed further into the unknown waters off the West African coast.

DISCOVERY Madeira was discovered in 1419, followed by the Azores in 1427. In 1434 Gil Eanes rounded Cape Bojador (in present-day Morocco), the "edge" of the known world at the time, thus surmounting one of the great psychological barriers of the age. By 1460, the year of Henry's death, the Cape Verde Islands had been discovered, along with much of the West African coast. After a lull, exploration picked up again under Dom João II (reigned 1481–1495), one of the House of Avis's more forceful kings. In 1482 Diogo Cão reached the Congo, bringing the Angolan coast under Portuguese control, and gold from the region yielded unheard-of wealth. Further riches shortly flowed

Pioneering genius:
Vasco da Gama

into Portugal from Brazil. In 1487, in another exploratory leap, Bartolomeu Dias rounded the southern tip of Africa, later christened the Cabo da Boa Esperença, or "Cape of Good Hope."

EMPIRE Portugal was to miss out in 1492, however, when it rejected the advances of Christopher Columbus, who instead took his expeditionary proposals to Spain. It made amends in 1498, during the reign of Manuel I (1495–1521), when four ships under Vasco da Gama sailed beyond the Cape of Good Hope, thus achieving the maritime Holy Grail—a sea route to the Indies. The monopoly of Venetian and Ottoman traders in the East was broken at a stroke, and wealth began to accrue instead to

Portuguese merchants, who started to trade huge quantities of silks, spices, metals, and other precious commodities.

MANUEL More was to come. In 1500 Pedro Álvares Cabral, badly misjudging the route to the East, discovered Brazil. Portugal's fortunes reached their zenith. The wealth of the richest nation in Europe began to make itself felt in art, and particularly in the flamboyant Manueline architecture of the period (see pages 166–167).

Farther afield, imperial expansion continued apace and forts were built across Asia to protect Portugal's new shipping lanes: outposts appeared at Goa (1510), Hormuz (1515), Macau (1557), and elsewhere. Another trade, the slave trade, begun in Henry's day, grew to huge proportions. Almost as quickly as it had begun, however, Portugal's economic miracle fizzled out.

> ❏ The modest cargo of pepper returned by da Gama's pioneering voyage paid for the expedition three times over. ❏

Lisbon's "Monument of the Discoveries" commemorates Portugal's great explorers

Profligacy, mismanagement, and bad luck led to Portugal's dramatic economic collapse, ending its short-lived period of glory. When the last Avis king, Sebastião, was killed in battle, bankruptcy and a vacuum in the succession left the way clear for a Spanish takeover. The dark cloud of Spanish rule hovered over Portugal for some 60 years.

DECLINE The reasons for Portugal's fall from grace were many. First, its far-flung empire and the vast network of outposts needed to defend it proved as much of a drain as a boon to national finances. Second, entrepreneurs spurned investment at home, preferring to seek easy profits abroad. As a result, Portugal began importing more than it exported—and paying for foreign goods with colonial gold. State coffers emptied faster than they filled, agriculture and industry stagnated, and traditional crafts and skills were forgotten. Many Portuguese left the land for the cities (Lisbon boomed) or left Portugal altogether, settling in Brazil, Madeira, or West Africa. The country's population dropped from 2 to 1 million. Other nations (notably the Italians) pioneered new routes to the East, provoking a drastic fall in the price of spices and other commodities that had once been precious.

❏ "At the scent of this cinnamon, the kingdom loses its people." Portuguese poet Sá de Miranda lamenting the effects of imperial greed. ❏

DISASTER Against this background, Manuel I's Avis successor, João III (reigned 1521–1557), attempted in vain to keep the country on an even keel. In a move that would have dire consequences, however, his sister, Dona Isabel, married Charles V of Spain, thus providing the justification for the claim of their son, Philip II of Spain, to the Portuguese throne

Doomed king: Sebastião's death eventually allowed Spain to take the Portuguese throne

some 50 years later. João himself had ten children, of whom only one survived, Dom Sebastião (reigned 1557–1578). A wilful and difficult man, he took it into his head to resurrect the glorious days of the crusades. Thus he proceeded to confront the Moors at the Battle of Alcácer-Quibir (1578)—and in the process he and 8,000 of his followers were killed. Surviving royal heirs (Sebastião died childless) proved few and far between, and the next in line, Cardinal Henrique, lived just two years. Philip II of Spain, Sebastião's cousin, was made of sterner stuff, however. Seizing his chance, he defeated the remnants of the shattered Portuguese army at Alcântara, and in 1581 declared himself Felipe I of Portugal.

37

> ❏ Philip II of Spain is reputed to have said of Portugal: "I inherited it, I bought it, I conquered it." ❏

Dona Isabel, Portuguese princess, whose marriage to Charles V of Spain later validated Spanish claims to the Portuguese throne

SPAIN Spanish rule would last 60 years. In the short term it brought benefits—wheat to replace domestic shortages, ships to protect Portuguese trade, and an end to centuries of crippling border disputes—but in the long term it proved a disaster. Spain's enemies were now Portugal's enemies, which meant trade with traditional partners such as the English and Dutch soon declined. And while Philip II had attempted a modicum of reconciliation, his son, Philip III (reigned 1598–1621), visited Portugal just once (in 1619), and Philip IV (reigned 1621–1640) ignored it almost altogether—at least until he needed Portuguese recruits to put down a rebellion in Catalonia. His attempt to conscript the Portuguese proved the final straw. While Philip was distracted by the revolt, a small clique of conspirators ejected the Spanish governor from Lisbon and proclaimed a new Portuguese king— João IV (1640–1656).

The new monarch was the former Duke of Bragança, scion of one of the country's most powerful noble families, an ancient dynasty whose royal connections stemmed from an illegitimate son of João I of Avis. João's claim was tenuous—he was a great-nephew of João III—but it was good enough. His descendants, the House of Bragança, would rule Portugal until the fall of the monarchy in 1910.

> ❏ The day of Portugal's independence from Spain in 1640 (December 1) is still celebrated as a national holiday. ❏

The discovery of gold and diamonds in Brazil ushered in Portugal's second great period of wealth, the fruits of which largely disappeared after the "Great Earthquake" of 1755. A dictatorial first minister, the Marquês de Pombal, rose to prominence, followed by the scourge of Europe—Napoleon.

38

WEALTH João IV managed to set Portugal back on its feet, securing among other things a new alliance with Britain through the marriage of his daughter, Catherine of Bragança, to Charles II. The reign of the third Bragança incumbent, Pedro II (reigned 1683–1706), was bankrolled by the discovery of gold in Brazil, and that of his profligate son, João V (reigned 1706–1750), by the flood of diamonds from the same source. João, however, squandered a fortune, lavishing huge sums on the vast convent at Mafra (he spent so much that royal coffers couldn't even pay for his funeral). His son, Dom José (reigned 1750–1777), was not so much profligate as apathetic and half-witted. Eager only to ride, gamble, and attend the opera, he willingly left affairs of state to the infamous Marquês de Pombal.

DESPOT Pombal's name is one of the most resonant in Portuguese history. Associated with cruelty and repression on the one hand, he was on the other known for renewing and modernizing whole areas of Portuguese life. His hold on power was cemented when he oversaw the reconstruction of Lisbon in the aftermath of the earthquake of 1755, a tumultuous event that all but destroyed the capital and countless towns across the south of the country. Later he moved on to reorganize Portugal's education, economy, bureaucracy, tax system, and trading practices. He abolished slavery and expelled the Jesuits, long influential in Portuguese education. He emasculated the Inquisition and stripped the nobles of their privileges, while dissenters (of whom

The despotic Marquês de Pombal

there were many) were ruthlessly dispatched—whether peasant or prince. For example, when Porto's innkeepers objected to state interference in the Douro wine trade, 17 were summarily hanged and another 160 sent to the galleys.

> ❏ "The prisons and cells were the only means I found to tame this blind and ignorant nation."
> Marquês de Pombal ❏

NAPOLEON On the accession of José's heir, Maria I (reigned 1777–1816), Pombal was arrested and banished to his estates. Many of his reforms, however, survived him. They would also survive the arrival of Napoleon, whose Europe-wide campaigns embroiled Portugal in what became known as the Peninsular Wars.

Napoleon threatened to invade Portugal unless it supported his naval blockade of Britain, an unlikely

Wellington (above) was victorious at the Battle of Buçaco (below)

scenario given the traditional ties of friendship between the two countries. In 1807 a French army under General Junot marched on Lisbon. Britain, having secured naval supremacy with the victory of Admiral Lord Nelson at the Battle of Trafalgar (in 1805), sent assistance to its ally in the shape of 21,000 men and generals Beresford and Wellesley (who was later made the Duke of Wellington).

Twice the French invaded and twice they were driven back. Wellington, fighting a guerrilla war of ferocious intensity, eventually secured a decisive victory at Buçaco (1810).

COUP After Napoleon's defeat Portugal effectively became a British protectorate, with Beresford as governor. The Portuguese royal family, long since removed to Brazil for their own safety, proved unwilling to return. Only the army remained active, and it was a group of officers, taking their lead from liberal advances in Spain and France, who in 1820 summoned an unofficial *Cortes* to demand sweeping constitutional changes (Beresford was out of the country at the time). Dom Joao VI (1792–1826), Portugal's somewhat timid king, returned from Brazil, professing himself ready to accept the changes. His wife, on the other hand, the forthright Dona Carlota, and his younger son, Miguel, would have nothing to do with them. These divergent views were soon reflected across Portugal, and the country was plunged into civil war and a century of political restlessness.

Despite Dom Pedro IV's accession to the throne and the modest victory for liberalism it symbolized, the integrity of Portuguese politics, together with the performance of the country's economy, declined alarmingly during the 19th century, dragging the monarchy down with it and paving the way for the establishment of a republic.

40

PROBLEMS In 1826 João VI died and his son, Pedro IV, was proclaimed king. However, Pedro was already emperor of Brazil, by then an independent country. Preferring the Brazilian title, he abdicated the Portuguese throne in favor of his daughter, Dona Maria, on two conditions: first, that she marry his brother, Miguel (who had been opposed to the army's constitutional demands of 1820–1822; see page 39); and second, that the pair accept a constitutional charter, a less radical bill of rights than the program demanded in 1820, but a liberal statement of intent nonetheless. Miguel accepted, but no sooner had the agreement been signed than he reneged on its terms, assuming absolute powers and embarking on a purge of liberal opinion. Battle ensued—the so-called "War of the Two Brothers"—with Pedro returning from Brazil (where he been deposed) to fight for the Portuguese crown. In 1834, with British help, he secured it and Miguel was dispatched to permanent exile in Austria.

CHAOS Portugal's moment of repose did not last long. In 1834, in an attempt to raise much-needed funds, the liberal-dominated *Cortes* abolished the country's religious houses: almost a quarter of Portugal's cultivated land changed hands in the process. Pedro died at the same time, leaving the throne to his teenage daughter, Maria II (reigned 1834–1853), who quickly came into conflict with more radical elements pushing for the adoption of the old 1822 demands (at the expense of her father's charter).

These divisions, which soon came close to provoking civil war, were reflected in a succession of short-lived governments. Politicians came and went at an alarming rate. None ever tackled the economic and political crises that lay at the heart of Portugal's deepening malaise.

Manuel II, Portugal's last king, died in exile in Britain in 1932

OVERTHROW In the 1850s a flurry of public works in the form of roads, railroads, and the other trappings of a "modern" state provided a brief respite from economic turmoil. The reputation of the monarchy, however, was steadily worsening. Morally and financially bankrupt, it was also humiliated on the international stage by Britain and

Manning the street barricades during the battle to overthrow the monarchy in 1910

Germany's dismissive attitude to Portugal's imperial ambitions in Africa. As living standards fell and public indignation grew, many thousands emigrated, and strikes, unemployment, and public demonstrations became the order of the day. Republican sentiments increasingly took hold, culminating in the assassination of Dom Carlos (reigned 1889–1908), whose attempts at authoritarian rule had only increased discontent. On October 5, 1910, the monarchy was overthrown by a joint coup of the army and navy. The new king, Manuel II, found refuge in Britain, where he died in 1932.

❑ "Portugal, the week I was in Madrid, had three revolutions and four changes of government in a day, and they haven't got daylight saving either, or they could have squeezed in another revolution."
Will Rogers (1926) ❑

REPUBLIC The new republic was a shambles. Between 1910 and 1926 there were 45 different governments, numerous coups, and endless violent confrontations provoked by diehard monarchists.

Portugal's belated entry into World War I in 1916 exposed the country's moribund economy to further strain (by 1923 the escudo was worth a twentieth of its 1917 value). There was yet another coup in 1926, which at first appeared like any other. The political wheels ground on, and General Oscar Carmona, a monarchist, emerged as president. In 1928 he made another innocuous appointment, installing Dr. António de Oliveira Salazar, a professor of economics at Coimbra University, as the new cabinet finance minister. The new appointee would rule Portugal for the next 40 years.

António Salazar is probably the least well known of Europe's 20th-century dictators, ranking behind Franco, Hitler, and Mussolini. But he was a dictator nonetheless, and ruled Portugal as such for almost 40 years, stifling the country's political, cultural, and economic development in the process.

CHARACTER Salazar was born on April 28, 1889 (eight days after Hitler), the son of a farm manager. Smart, diligent, and devout, his future seemed to lie with the Church. In 1908, however, he startled his parents, in particular his fiercely ambitious mother, by announcing he would not be studying for the priesthood. Instead he enrolled at Coimbra University, joined an elitist Catholic organization, and by 1914 had graduated in law. By 1918 he had become an academic, writing modest articles on bookkeeping. In 1921 he briefly entered parliament before the chaos of Portuguese politics drove him back to academia. Over the next five years his reputation as an economist blossomed, mainly

❑ Portugal remained neutral in World War II, but signed a pact of friendship with Franco and flew flags at half-mast when Hitler died. ❑

through arrogant self-promotion, and in 1926 he was asked to help deal with the country's chaotic finances. A few days later he resigned as his conditions for accepting the post remained unfulfilled.

POWER In 1928 Salazar was approached again. This time his terms were met—total control over every aspect of government and civil service spending. Within a year, a 330 million escudo deficit had been turned into a budgetary surplus, the first since 1913 (the books would remain balanced until 1974).

Members of a revolutionary uprising are led to the negotiating table in Porto in 1927

Within five years Salazar appeared indispensable, and in 1932 he was appointed prime minister, a position he retained until 1968. Within a short time he extended his power to all areas of Portuguese life, exerting authority in his Estado Novo ("New State") with methods and ideology similar to—if marginally less brutal than—those of Franco, Hitler, and Mussolini. Censorship was absolute and education strictly controlled. Government members belonged to one party, the União Nacional (National Union), while propaganda (Salazar was a poor speaker)

> ❑ It is estimated that under Salazar just ten great families owned Portugal's leading 170 firms and controlled 53 percent of the country's wealth. ❑

endlessly promoted the ideals of Deus, pátria, and família (God, country, and family). Foreign influences, even foreign investment, were actively discouraged, and although tourism was encouraged belatedly in the 1960s it was strictly controlled.

CONTROL Broadly speaking, Salazar clung to power by keeping the right people happy, skillfully juggling the demands of the army and Church with those of the monarchists and urban middle classes. The poor, by contrast, were kept ignorant and illiterate, not only to save money but also as a form of social control. Agriculture stagnated and social welfare was almost nonexistent, and while industry did develop it was sporadic. Growth was measured at 9 percent annually in the 1950s and 1960s, but from a very low base. In cultural and social terms Portugal was dull and reactionary, the masses, in the words of one critic, kept in their place with a diet of "*fado*, Fátima, and football."

PORTENTS In specific terms the regime retained control through the use of the feared PIDE, a police force initially trained by the Gestapo, and

> ❑ Portugal under Salazar, in the words of Prime Minster Mário Soares, was "as tidy and quiet as a cemetery." ❑

through a network of concentration camps and some 100,000 informers. However, it failed to exert control in Portugal's overseas colonies, where the eruption of a series of bloody wars of independence would eventually topple the regime. Angola was the first in 1961, with Mozambique and Guinea-Bissau soon to follow.

Salazar, a ferocious imperialist, poured men and money into the disintegrating empire. Conscription was introduced, adding to the waves of emigration increasingly depriving Portugal of its pool of cheap labor.

43

António Salazar, dictator of Portugal for almost 40 years

The status quo was gradually beginning to change. Then, in 1968, Salazar toppled from his deck chair while on holiday, hitting his head and subsequently suffering a stroke. The dictator, suddenly incapacitated and feeble, lived another two years, but was removed as premier. No one dared tell him.

Four years after Salazar's death in 1970, the tensions produced by Portugal's wars in its African colonies ushered in the so-called "Carnation Revolution," a joyful and practically bloodless affair masterminded by disaffected army officers that finally rid the country of almost half a century of dictatorship.

AFRICA Salazar's demise had almost no immediate effect. His successor, Marcelo Caetano, slackened the dictatorial reins, but in truth remained wedded to the ways of the old guard. Limited democratization changed little at home and still less in the colonies, where bloody wars of

44

António de Spínola (right), an old-school general who paved the way for revolution

independence continued with unabated ferocity. Caetano was to write of these conflicts: "Night and day this problem is in my mind… Constantly I seek ways to relieve the sacrifices of the Portuguese people." None of these "ways," however, went so far as to seek dialogue or reconciliation. Men (100,000 in all) continued to be shipped off to fight, often against their will, but with little noticeable effect on the increasingly successful guerrilla insurgents. The Portuguese army, in the words of one historian, "began to wonder whether the colonial wars were good for its image after all."

ACTION These doubts eventually came to be expressed at higher and higher levels. The buck finally stopped with António de Spínola. A more unlikely figure as the catalyst for revolution would be hard to imagine: a cavalry officer of the old school, the monocled 64-year-old general had fought for Franco during the Spanish Civil War and received training from the Nazis, with whom he had seen action on the Russian front. At the same time, he was tough and respected, and as military governor of Guinea-Bissau (1968–1973) he had attempted to combat revolt with social reforms as well as military might. His experience in Africa, however, convinced him that Portugal's wars there could not be won, a thesis he propounded in *Portugal and the Future*, published in Lisbon in February 1974. Caetano, on reading the book, later wrote that when he finished it "I understood that the military coup which I could sense had been coming was now inevitable."

FALSE START Others read the book and saw the signs, among them some 200 middle-ranking army officers, the so-called "Young Captains," men who had not only come to see the futility of the African wars but also, in many cases, sympathized with the sentiments that provoked them. Low pay and a flawed promotion system increased their disaffection. In the early months of 1974 the officers organized "picnics" in the Alentejan countryside, plotting future strategy away from the eyes of the secret police. On March 14 Caetano sacked General Spínola, along with Costa Gomes, the chief of staff, both of whom had refused to endorse Portugal's colonial policy. Two days later troops loyal to Spínola moved towards Lisbon, only to be intercepted en route. It was an isolated and uncoordinated incident.

REVOLUTION On April 25, 1974, however, almost half a century of dictatorship melted away. One of the

The 1974 revolution was almost bloodless. The soldiers, who occupied Lisbon unopposed, stuck red carnations in the ends of their rifles

most peaceful revolutions in history moved smoothly into place. It began, characteristically, with a song, "*E Depois do Adeus*" ("And After the Farewells"), a prearranged warning of imminent action broadcast on a radio music program at 11:55 PM on the 24th. At 12:29 AM another song signaled the start of the coup, the prophetic "*Grândola, Vila Morena*," which began: "Grândola, dusky town, land of brotherhood, it is the people who hold sway within your walls… ." By 3 AM all units were in place. At 8:30 the next morning the Movimento das Forças Armadas (MFA, or Armed Forces Movement) broadcast its actions to the country. Crowds took to the streets, as surprised by events as the rest of the world (even the CIA, it is said, didn't know what was happening).

Portugal's revolution was almost bloodless. Four secret policemen were killed as they fired into a Lisbon crowd, and one overexcited on-looker fell from a balcony. Its aftermath, in the way of most revolutions, was less happy, although from its confusion Portugal was to emerge as a fully fledged democracy.

AFTERMATH High spirits and near anarchy followed the revolution. General Spínola, although not directly involved in the coup, formed a Junta of National Salvation on April 26 with MFA backing, and on May 15 he was inaugurated as president. Censorship was lifted, elections were promised, and the secret police disbanded. Politics seethed with activity. Parties formed and disbanded overnight, and the communists—the only group to maintain any form of opposition under Salazar—moved into positions of power. Workers, their hopes raised, embarked on waves of strikes. Bread ran short, transport foundered, and administration at all levels fell apart.

Mário Soares, prime minister in the postrevolutionary government

❑ After the revolution even Portugal's prostitutes formed a union, showing their support for the "Young Captains" by offering a 50 percent discount to all ranks below lieutenant. ❑

CHANGE Dissent and disagreement soon followed, and the first to go was Spínola. A reactionary at heart, he was opposed to early independence for Portugal's colonies (which was nevertheless granted) and in March 1975 he attempted a coup of his own, an uprising that proved stillborn (he fled to Spain). A Supreme Revolutionary Council (CRS) was formed, headed by the more radical army officers of the MFA. Shortly afterwards, banks and insurance companies were nationalized. The first moves towards land reform then began, with many of the south's vast estates turned into collective or cooperative ventures overnight. A year after the revolution, true to its word, the MFA organized elections, which proceeded peacefully despite the tumult convulsing the country. The Socialist Party (PS) won 37.9 percent of the vote, while the communists—for all their ideological vigor—gained just 12.5 percent.

COUP However, a democratically elected assembly changed nothing, and if anything it made matters worse. The north, always more conservative, began to grow appre-hensive at the rate of change, while

46

others believed the ideals of 1974 were being compromised. Another coup ensued, this time the work of left-wing army officers. It, too, failed, ushering in a period when moderation and pragmatism began to prevail. In 1976 the MFA agreed to withdraw from its "supervisory" role in politics. In April of the same year a constitution was ratified, and on April 25 the Socialists were returned as the largest party in the country's first constitutional government. The new prime minister was Mário Soares, and the president remained a soldier, General António Eanes.

❏ Portugal had six governments in the two years after the revolution, and ten in the years between 1976 and 1987. ❏

MODERATION Portuguese politics continued along a difficult path for a decade, and no single party achieved an overall majority until July 1987. The years after the revolution, however, followed a general pattern of retrenchment, the movement's more radical aspects gradually being watered down as moderate center-left policies increasingly took hold. In January 1986 Portugal joined the EEC, now the European Union (EU), a move that unleashed an unprecedented period of change (see page 20). Mário Soares, replaced as prime minister by Aníbal Cavaco Silva, leader of the Social Democrats, became the country's new president (the first "civilian" president since 1926), and while EU membership produced a flood of loans and foreign investment, it was at the cost

Freedom of expression after 40 years of dictatorship

of hard-headed and controversial economic measures. The old revolutionary spirits of 1974 may despair, but they can at least rest assured that Portugal, for better or worse, has emerged from its travails with its democracy assured.

❏ In 1989 a poll showed that a quarter of all Portuguese between the ages of 15 and 24 had never heard of António Salazar, the man who had been the country's dictator for 40 years. ❏

A-Z Lisbon

►►► CITY HIGHLIGHTS

►►► EXCURSION HIGHLIGHTS

LISBON The city of Lisbon (Lisboa in Portuguese) is one of Europe's smallest and most atmospheric capitals. Ranged in a jumbled medieval heap over rambling hills, it has the bustling vigor of a busy port combined with the intimacy and friendliness of an old-fashioned town. Washing hangs from ancient balconies, Moorish alleys twist round dark corners, and the Lisboetas fill a thousand cafés and ramshackle restaurants with animated Latin chatter. At night the haunting strains of *fado*, a melancholic music of loss and longing, drifts from dingy dives, while by day elderly matrons walk tiny dogs amid the fading elegance

Pages 48–49: behind the Monument of the Discoveries, the April 25 Bridge crosses the River Tagus

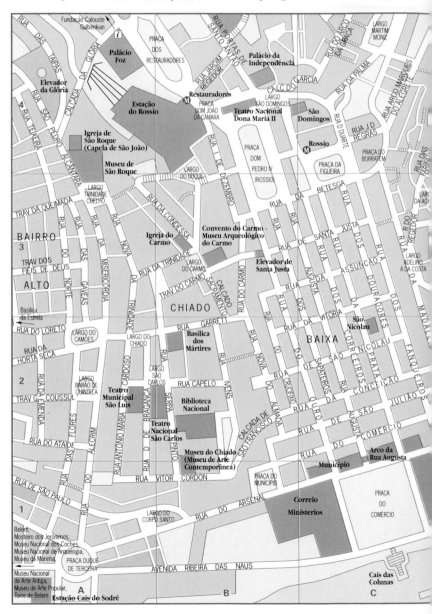

of a former imperial capital. Rattling trams and rusty elevators add to the period feel—like Paris in the 1920s some say—making up in atmosphere what the city rather lacks by way of genuine treasures.

Lisbon is also a changing city, however. Its streets are a hotbed of construction and flashy new facades. In the last ten years a flood of European Union funding and developers with an eye for investment have combined to transform many city streets—and not always for the better. Charm is inevitably sacrificed when glass and concrete replace stone and stucco. At the same time, Lisbon is more

TOURIST INFORMATION
The main tourist office, or Turismo (tel: 21 346 3314. *Open* daily 9–8), is in the Palácio Foz, in the central Praça dos Restauradores. There is also an information office at Portela Airport (tel: 21 849 4323. *Open* daily 6 AM–2 AM).

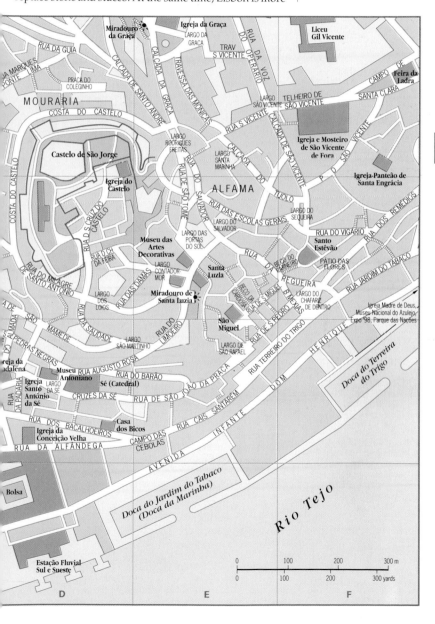

Lisbon

ARRIVING BY AIR

Lisbon's Portela Airport (tel: 21 841 3500) is about 4 miles (7km) north of the center. The easiest way to get into the center is by taxi (taxis are inexpensive in Portugal—see page 70). Alternatively, a shuttle bus leaves every 20 minutes (7 AM–9 PM) for the Praça Marquês de Pombal, Praça dos Restauradores, the Rossio, Praça do Comércio, and Cais do Sodré train station.

ARRIVING BY TRAIN

The main station is Santa Apolónia (tel: 21 888 4025 or 21 881 6242), in the Alfama district, about 15 minutes' walk east of the Praça do Comércio. Buses 9, 39, 46, or 90 go to the Rossio or Praça dos Restauradores. Some local trains stop at the central Rossio station (tel: toll-free 800 20 0904), the Cais do Sodré, about 0.5 miles (700m) west of the Praça do Comércio, or the Barreiro station (tel: 21 207 3118), on the southern bank of the River Tagus (catch a ferry across the river to the Sul e Sueste, or Fluvial, terminal on Praça do Comércio).

ARRIVING BY BUS

The most important terminal is in Avenida Casal Ribeiro (tel: 21 354 5775), north of the city center. The nearest Metro station is Saldanha.

PRAÇA DO COMÉRCIO

Lisbon's grandest square was laid out following the 1755 earthquake. Its airy waterfront space and classical buildings were intended as a gateway leading from the sea into the ordered Pombaline streets of the Baixa and the rest of the city. At its heart stands an equestrian statue of José I, king at the time of the earthquake and the subsequent rebuilding.

confident and sophisticated than it once was—not to say more prosperous. Nightlife, shopping, and restaurants, for example, have improved immeasurably. But, despite development, enough of the "old" Lisbon survives to make the city a likeable and rewarding stopover, and its museums and monuments are rich enough to warrant at least two or three days during any Portuguese visit.

HISTORY Romantics tell you that Ulysses founded Lisbon. In fact, the Phoenicians were probably the first to settle the area, attracted by its fine natural harbor, its easily defended site, and its bountiful agricultural hinterland. Around 1200 BC they built a fortress on the site of the present-day Castelo de São Jorge, christening the settlement Alis ubbo, meaning "Serene Harbor." They were followed by the Greeks, Carthaginians, and Romans, the latter arriving in 205 BC and renaming the colony Olissipo. The Romans were dislodged by the Barbarians, who gave way in turn to the Moors, the last remaining in the city— by then known as Lissabona or Lishbona—for some four centuries. The "Portuguese," under their first king, Afonso Henriques, took the city in 1147 with the help of soldiers bound for the Second Crusade. However, it was not until 1255, when Afonso III left Coimbra, that it was chosen as the country's capital.

Lisbon's fortunes then followed those of Portugal itself, enjoying periods of untold magnificence during the great Age of Discovery (see pages 34–35). The vast wealth generated by the colonies financed the building of countless monuments, notably in Belém, and pushed the city's population from 65,000 in 1527 to around 165,000 in 1620. Nemesis came in the form of the 1755 earthquake, which destroyed two thirds of the city and killed 40,000 Lisboetas. Most of the population was at mass during the quake (the calamity struck on All Souls' Day), and the damage from the disaster was further exacerbated by fires sparked by thousands of church candles. Rebuilding was coordinated by the future Marquês de Pombal, the king's dictatorial minister, who championed the revolutionary grid of streets and squares that now characterizes the city center. Later, the Duke of Wellington was to build his strategy during the Peninsular Wars around a successful defense of the city. As the capital of neutral Portugal in World War II, Lisbon was a hotbed of intrigue and espionage. In 1910 it witnessed the overthrow of the monarchy, and in 1974 it saw the start of the Carnation Revolution. Today, as money pours in, Lisbon's changing face is the most obvious manifestation of Portugal's belated reentry on to the European stage.

ORIENTATION Lisbon is a confusing city to view from afar, a great jumble of districts and different levels ranged across a profusion of hills. The areas that count, however, are distinct and easily explored. Imagine you are a visitor arriving by sea, the approach for thousands over the centuries. You land at the waterfront **Praça do Comércio**, one of the city's main squares (see panel). Ahead of you, stretching north, is the well-ordered grid of streets known as the **Baixa**, or lower town, home to offices, restaurants, and many of the city's best shops. At the northern end of this grid lies the **Rossio**, Lisbon's other main square (see panel), flanked by two other large piazzas—the Praça da Figueira and Praça dos Restauradores (see panel). From here one of the city's main boulevards, the **Avenida da Liberdade**, runs north, useful to know only in that it leads to the Gulbenkian, one of the city's top museums.

Returning to Praça do Comércio, and with your back to the River Tagus, the city's three other key districts lie to your right and left. Rising to the right (eastward) is a hill surmounted by the Castelo de São Jorge, Lisbon's ancient heart, and below it, woven into a warren of atmospheric old streets, is the enticing **Alfama** district. To your left (westward) are two distinct areas: the elegant shopping district of the **Chiado**, half-way up the hill above the Baixa's grid; and atop the hill the **Bairro Alto**, or upper town, the principal focus for Lisbon's bars and restaurants. From west to east, these three districts, along with the Baixa, stretch for no more than a mile (2km), and from Praça do Comércio north to the Rossio is just over 0.5 miles (1km). Old Lisbon, therefore, is a compact area to explore—though the gradients make it tough for walking.

There are four reasons, at least if time is short, for straying further afield: the Gulbenkian Foundation to the north (see pages 55–56); the church of Madre de Deus and National Tile Museum to the east (see page 56); the site of Expo '98 and its outstanding Oceanarium, one of several attractions in the Expo park (see page 63); and, not to be missed, the waterfront suburb of Belém, 2.5 miles (4km) west of the old center. The latter was the medieval point of departure and arrival for the great voyages of discovery, and contains many of Lisbon's essential sights: the Torre de Belém, the Mosteiro dos Jerónimos, the Museu de Marinha (Maritime Museum), the Museu de Arte Popular (Folk Art Museum), and the city's most-visited sight, the Museu Nacional dos Coches (National Coach Museum).

Finally, few people visit Lisbon without making an excursion to Sintra, a town of fabled natural beauty and fascinating royal palaces (see pages 67–68).

THE ROSSIO
Despite its rather dowdy appearance, the Rossio, or Praça Dom Pedro IV (the figure atop the square's central column), at the northern head of the Baixa's grid is the bustling heart of modern Lisbon. Banks and other anonymous buildings mean it lacks architectural grandeur—only the Dona Maria II national theater (1840) on its northern side has any distinction—but it is full of some popular old-world cafés where you can sit outside and watch the world go by.

PRAÇA DOS RESTAURADORES
The third largest of Lisbon's central squares takes its name from the men who in 1640 led the revolt against the Spanish and "restored" Portugal to Portuguese rule. The city's tourist office (see panel on page 50) occupies the 19th-century Palácio Foz on the square's western flanks.

53

Mosaic map below the Padrão dos Descobrimentos

MUSEU DAS ARTES DECORATIVAS
The lovely Decorative Arts Museum (Largo das Portas do Sol 2) features some of Portugal's finest furniture and some of its most covetable decorative artifacts. It contains beautiful rugs, carpets, tapestries, and embroidered shawls, together with exquisite pieces of silver, porcelain, and glass (tel: 21 888 1991. *Open* Tue–Sun 10–5. *Admission: moderate.* Bus 37. Tram 12, 28).

Castelo de São Jorge and the port area

▶▶▶ **Alfama**   *51E3*

The Alfama district, gathered around and below the Castelo de São Jorge (see opposite), is the oldest and most atmospheric area of the city. This warren of almost Arabic streets and alleys is an excellent place to wander at random (following a planned itinerary is difficult), although the restorers, restaurants, and a rash of trendy shops are beginning to take the edge off its historic appeal. During your exploration try to visit the churches of **São Miguel** (Largo São Miguel) and **Santo Estevão** (Largo de Santo Estevão), the former renowned for its gilt, woodwork, and *trompe l'oeil*, and the latter for the view from the corner of its little square.

Other outstanding **viewpoints** in the Alfama district— and there are several—include the Miradouro da Santa Luzia (with several nice cafés) and Largo das Portas do Sol, both close to the fascinating **Museu das Artes Decorativas**, which is housed in a tile-adorned 17th-century palácio (see panel). The best of the **streets** are the impossibly narrow Beco do Carneiro (just west of Santo Estevão) and the old-world Beco de Cardosa; the Pátio das Flores, which is filled with pretty little houses; and the Rua de São Pedro and Rua dos Remédios, the district's bustling main thoroughfares. For an impression of the historic Alfama, seek out the gloriously old-fashioned Largo de São Rafael, like much of the area remarkably unchanged over the last 200 years. The downside of this picturesque area is that you should always keep an eye open for pickpockets.

►► Castelo de São Jorge and Olissipónia (Castle of São Jorge) 51D4

Rua Costa do Castelo (tel: 21 887 7244)
Open: daily 9–9. Olissipónia daily 10–6. Admission free
Tram 12, 28. Bus 37

Lisbon's dramatically sited castle probably marks the point where the city first took root. Possibly a Phoenician stronghold, it was fortified by the Romans and then the Visigoths, falling to the Moors in the 8th century. Most of the surviving walls date from the period of Moorish domination. The loss of the castle (to Afonso Henriques in 1147) marked a turning point in the Moors' withdrawal from Portugal, although the siege and its bloody aftermath reflected badly on Henriques' so-called Christian allies. Promising booty and glory, the king had waylaid groups of crusaders en route for the Holy Land, persuading them to join him in the 17-week siege of the fortress. On the Moors' surrender, the British and French crusaders ran amok, pillaging and killing the citadels' Christian and Moorish inhabitants alike. Ironically, the castle, which is dedicated to St. George (São Jorge), is said to be named in honor of the Anglo-Portuguese pact of 1371.

Today, the much-restored castle merits a visit for the superlative **views►►►** from its parade ground and turreted battlements. The panorama stretches over the rooftops of the city and across the waters of the River Tagus. Its outer walls shelter the little medieval quarter of Santa Cruz, while the main entrance is watched over by a statue of Afonso Henriques. Most of the old interior has been turned into gardens, a lovely place to spend a restorative hour or so enjoying the views and wandering along the shady tree-lined terraces.

Also worth seeing is **Olissipónia**, a multi-media exhibition that offers some intriguing insights into Lisbon and its history.

►►► Fundação Calouste Gulbenkian (Calouste Gulbenkian Foundation) 50A4

Avenida de Berna 45a (tel: 21 782 3000)
Open: Wed–Sun 10–6, Tue 2–6. Admission: inexpensive, free on Sun. Bus 16, 26 or 56; 31 or 46 from the Rossio. Metro to Palhavã (Praça de Espanha) or São Sebastião

The Lisbon headquarters of the Gulbenkian Foundation (closed at time of writing) contain one of the greatest museums in Portugal. Financed by the legacy of Calouste Gulbenkian, an Armenian oil tycoon (see panel), the foundation not only cares for Gulbenkian's private art collection, which was bequeathed to Portugal, but also sponsors a wide range of cultural, educational, and charitable activities. Occupying beautiful modern buildings, it is divided into two sections, one dealing with European art and artifacts, and the other with ancient and oriental exhibits. Ideally you should make two visits, one to each section, perhaps taking a break in between in the foundation's lovely gardens or the large Parque Eduardo VII to the south. Neither collection is especially large, but virtually every exhibit is outstanding in its own way.

55

Islamic art at the Gulbenkian

CENTRO DE ARTE MODERNA

The Gulbenkian's modern art gallery lies just south of the main gallery in the midst of the foundation's sculpture-strewn gardens. It is entirely given over to modern Portuguese art, a genre that displays little historic cohesion—many of Portugal's finest artists have trained abroad or followed the broad developments of European and North American art. This said, there are some dazzling pieces of work, the chief names to look out for being Almada Negreiros, Vieira da Silva, and Amadeo de Sousa-Cardoso. (Rua Dr. Nicolau Bettencourt, tel: 21 795 0241. *Open* Wed–Sun 10–6, Tue 2–6. Metro to São Sebastião, Palhavã (Praça de Espanha). Bus 16, 26, 31, 46, 56.)

The **European section** is arranged more or less chronologically and, where possible, by schools and nationality. There are also numerous rooms devoted to the decorative arts, including tapestries, silverware, furniture, and furnishings, as well as to painting and sculpture. It opens with several delicately worked medieval French ivories— French art and artifacts was one of Gulbenkian's particular passions. Later French work includes paintings by Manet, Dégas, Renoir, and Henri Fantin-Latour, together with 169 pieces of jewelry by art nouveau star René Lalique. The Dutch and Flemish are also well represented, with canvases by Rubens (including a famous portrait of his sensuous second wife, Hélène Fourment), Van der Weyden, van Dyck, Ruisdael, and Frans Hals.

Pride of place goes to Rembrandt's celebrated *Portrait of an Old Man* and *Alexander the Great*, for which his son is reputed to have posed. British painters include Turner and Gainsborough, while among the Italians the outstanding works are by Ghirlandaio and the Venetian Francesco Guardi.

The **ancient and oriental section** opens with a small but exquisite room devoted to the chronological development of Egyptian art up to the Roman era. There follow displays of Greek, Roman, and Mesopotamian artifacts, with particularly outstanding collections of Hellenic coins and Armenian ceramics and manuscripts. Gulbenkian paid much attention to oriental art, and in particular to pottery and silk and wool carpets (some of the loveliest items in the gallery), as well as a wide range of glass, fabrics, and ancient manuscripts. The Far Eastern artifacts include exceptional pieces of Chinese porcelain and valuable Japanese lacquerwork.

►► Igreja Madre de Deus/Museu Nacional do Azulejo (Church of Madre de Deus/ National Tile Museum) 51F3

Rua Madre de Deus 4 (tel: 21 814 7747)
Open: Wed–Sun 10–6, Tue 2–6. Admission: moderate. Bus 18, 42, 104, 105

Like Belém to the west, this church and museum combination, which lies a good 2 miles (3km) east of the Baixa, is one of the few sights in Lisbon worth leaving the city center for. The convent church, founded in 1509 by João II's widow, Leonor, was rebuilt following the 1755 earthquake (only a single Manueline doorway remains from the earlier building). The interior is one of the richest in Lisbon, adorned with paintings, glowing gilded woodwork, and swathes of Dutch and Spanish *azulejos* (tiles). The decoration reaches its pinnacle in the crypt, dominated by a shimmering gilded altar, and in the beautiful chapter house.

The church's cloister and other monastic buildings house the **Museu Nacional do Azulejo** (**National Tile Museum**), a must for anyone enraptured by Portugal's penchant for decorative tiles. The displays, full of outstanding *azulejos* from different periods, trace the genre's development from the Moorish-influenced tiles of the 15th century through to the present day. The highlights are the Manueline cloisters, still decorated with their original 16th-century tiles, and a huge 125-foot-long (38m) tile picture depicting Lisbon's waterfront before it was devastated by the 1755 earthquake.

►► Igreja-Museu de São Roque
(Church-Museum of São Roque)   50A4

Largo Trindade Coelho (tel: 21 323 5000)
Open: Tue–Sun 10–5. Admission: church free, museum inex-
pensive. Bus 58, 100. Metro to Baixa–Chiado

A deceptively plain facade masks the church of St. Roch, built by the Jesuits at the end of the 16th century. Within the church, however, is a fine wooden ceiling and a succession of sumptuously decorated baroque side chapels. Chief among the latter is the astounding **Capela de São João** (last chapel on the left), believed, size for size, to be one of the most expensive church chapels ever built (estimates put the cost at the time at $350,000). Commissioned by João V in 1742, it was designed by Vanvitelli, the papal architect, and constructed in Rome. There it was blessed by Pope Benedict XIV (in return for a "gift" of 100,000 cruzados) before being shipped in three boats to Lisbon, where its jumble of priceless materials—amethyst, lapus lazuli, ivory, porphyry, and Carrara marble—was reassembled in 1750. Alongside the church, accessed from a door in the south aisle, is the church museum, worth seeing for its collection of embroidery, paintings, vestments, and ecclesiastical plate (in particular two vast torch holders).

CONVENTO DO CARMO
The 14th-century Gothic Carmelite church just a couple of minutes' walk south of the Igreja de São Roque was—until toppled by the 1755 earthquake—the largest church in Lisbon. Today, its evocative and spectacular ruins shelter the appealing Museu Arqueológico do Carmo (closed at the time of writing for restoration). It contains a wonderfully eccentric and hotchpotch collection, the highlights of which include redoubtable Gothic and Romanesque tombs, South American mummies, beautiful *azulejos*, shrunken heads from Peru, Brazilian jewelry, and Bronze Age pottery.

57

The sumptuous baroque splendor of the Igreja de São Roque

Painting and sculpture were slow to take hold in Portugal. Early works of art were confined largely to monolithic sculpture, while later art and artifacts owed much to the influence of artists from Italy and the Low Countries. Only during Portugal's Manueline heyday did home-grown art really begin to make its mark.

BAROQUE

The baroque flourished in Portugal, spurred on by the rush of wealth unleashed by the discovery of gold and diamonds in Brazil. Woodcarving rather than stonecarving became popular, much of it gilded with Brazilian gold. The result was the welter of altars, frames, ceilings, and other sculptural forms that adorn so many Portuguese church and palace interiors. Foreign influences, notably Italian, were again strong, especially at Mafra (see page 69), where the vast convent stimulated a school of sculpture whose members included leading Italian baroque practitioners such as Alessandro Giusti (1715–1799).

Baroque decoration in Coimbra's University library

Early art Among Portugal's earliest artifacts are the *berrões* of the Trás-os-Montes, roughly carved granite bulls and boars fashioned by early Celtic tribes (4000–2000 BC). Of mysterious purpose, they were probably ritualistic rather than artistic creations, designed for use in fertility rites, or as funerary headstones or boundary markers. Save for a few mosaics at Conimbriga, Faro and elsewhere, indigenous Roman art is rather thin on the ground, many of Portugal's classical statues having been imported from elsewhere or carved by foreign sculptors. Original Visigothic and Moorish art is similarly scarce, although the decorative influences of the latter pervade Portuguese arts and crafts to this day. Only with the arrival of the Gothic towards the end of the 12th century did Portugal begin to find a distinctive artistic voice of its own.

Sculpture This voice first made itself heard in sculpture, where decorative architectural carving gave way to more intricate funerary art. During the 14th century funerary sculpture developed in Lisbon, Évora, and Coimbra, eventually becoming diffused in northern Portugal, and in Porto and Lamego in particular. It reached its climax with the tombs of Inês de Castro and Pedro I in Alcobaça (see above and page 164), and the monument at Batalha to Dom João I and Philippa of Lancaster (see page 170).

Late in the next century, Renaissance sculpture blossomed under Nicolau (Nicolas) Chanterène, whose Italianate style found supreme expression in the great west door of Lisbon's Mosteiro dos Jerónimos (see pages 60–61) and the pulpit and tombs of Coimbra's Mosteiro de Santa Cruz (see page 146). At the same time, a Portuguese twist was being added by Manueline sculptors, of whom the most distinguished were Mateus Fernandes, responsible for work at Batalha, and Diogo de Arruda, whose window at Tomar (see page 183) is one of Portugal's artistic masterpieces.

Painting Portugal came to painting comparatively late, its artists initially inspired almost entirely by the work of outsiders. "Portuguese" painting was almost nonexistent until around 1428, when the Flemish artist Jan van Eyck was tempted to Portugal to paint the Infanta Isabel, only daughter of Dom João I. Van Eyck may well have inspired Portugal's first great painter, Nuno Gonçalves (1475–1541), creator of Lisbon's São Vicente altarpiece, one of the country's undoubted masterpieces (see pages 62–63). In any event, Flemish painters subsequently

The Deposition from the Cross: *from the Cook Triptych by Vasco Fernandes*

proved immensely influential, their work reaching Portugal as a result of the close trading ties between Iberia and the Low Countries. Two Flemish painters who moved to Portugal, Frei Carlos and Francisco Henriques (their Portuguese names), were responsible for some of the country's finest late 15th-century works, their detailed narrative and glorious coloring being copied by a host of largely anonymous indigenous painters (best seen in Lisbon's Museu de Arte Antiga; see pages 62–63).

Portuguese School Renaissance ideas from Italy and elsewhere were eventually assimilated by native painters, who were emboldened by the rash of commissions resulting from Portugal's increased prosperity in the 16th century. Painters such as Vasco Fernandes, or Grão Vasco ("Great Vasco"), pioneered a truly Portuguese School of painting, recognizable by its realism, delicacy, and rich coloring, as well as its naturalistic backgrounds, faintly idealized figures, and accurately drawn and expressionistic faces. Vasco painted extensively in Viseu, home to one of Portugal's major Renaissance schools of painting. He was accompanied by artists such as Gaspar Vaz, who moved from Lisbon, site of the country's other great schools and a city whose leading Renaissance names included Garcia Fernandes, Gregório Lopes, and Cristóvão de Figueiredo. Portuguese innovation, however, was curtailed following the Spanish takeover of 1580, but reemerged with the baroque flowering of the 18th century (see panel opposite).

LATER PAINTING
Painting slumped in Portugal after the Renaissance, its 17th-century torpor relieved by just two great artists: Domingos Vieira (1600–1678) and Josefa de Óbidos, also known as Josefa de Ayala (1630/4–1684), best known for her portraits and still lifes (see pages 176–177). Leading names in the 18th century were Vieira Lusitano (1699–1783) and Domingos António de Sequeira (1768–1837), the latter being particularly renowned for his drawings and portraits. The great names of Portuguese 19th-century art were Sousa Pinto (1856–1939), a noted pastel artist, and Silva Porto (1850–1893) and Marquês de Oliveira (1853–1927), both of whom were influenced by Naturalism.

MODERN ART
Portugal's artistic tendency to follow rather than lead is evident among its modern artists, many of whom have tended to leave Portugal to train or work abroad, their subsequent work reflecting the broader influences of European artistic movements. Thus Santa Rita (1889–1918) was much influenced by the Italian Futurists; Almada Negreiros (1893–1970), one of the greatest of Portugal's modern artists, worked in the Cubist tradition; and Paris-trained Amadeo de Souza-Cardoso (1887–1918) found refuge in Cubism and Expressionism.

MUSEU NACIONAL DE ARQUEOLOGIA

The rather threadbare National Archaeological Museum (tel: 21 362 0000. *Open* Wed–Sun 10–6, Tue 2–6. Closed Mon. *Admission: moderate*) occupies the 19th-century east wing of the Mosteiro dos Jerónimos. Its displays move chronologically through Portugal's long history, beginning with prehistoric carvings and funerary stones, Iron Age weapons, granite sculptures (the famous *berrões* of the Minho and Trás-os-Montes), and a fine collection of mosaics and other Roman antiquities. The Treasury, with its collection of gold and jewelry, is one of the museum's more interesting corners.

MUSEU DE MARINHA

Located in the west wing of the Mosteiro dos Jerónimos and the nearby Galliot Pavilion is the Maritime Museum, one of Europe's leading collections of maritime artifacts (tel: 21 362 0019. *Open* mid-Jun–end Sep, Tue–Sun 10–6; Oct–mid-Jun, Tue–Sun 10–5. Closed Mon. *Admission: inexpensive; free Sun morning*). Charting Portugal's long and distinguished links with the sea, it features a host of beautiful model boats spanning several centuries, together with a collection of uniforms, maps, navigational instruments, and a handful of real ships. One of the highlights, located in a special annex, is a reconstruc-tion of the ornate state rooms of the royal yacht *Amélia*, built for Carlos I, the monarch assassinated in Lisbon's Praça do Comércio in 1908.

►►► Mosteiro dos Jerónimos (Jerónimos Monastery) 50A1

Praça do Império, Belém (tel: 21 362 0034; e-mail: mjeronimos@mail.telepac.pt)
Open: Tue–Sun 10–5. Closed Mon. Admission: monastery free; cloister moderate Jun–Sep, inexpensive Oct–May. Tram 15 from Praça do Comércio. Bus 27, 28, 29, 43, 49, or 51

The Jerónimos Monastery is one of the most captivating buildings in Portugal. Located in the suburb of Belém, it can be visited in conjunction with other Belem sites such as the Torre de Belém (see page 65), the Museu de Arte Popular (see panel on page 64), and the Museu Nacional dos Coches (see pages 63–64). While in the vicinity of the monastery you may also want to spend time in two museums housed in the monastery complex: the interesting **Museu de Marinha (Maritime Museum)** and the less alluring **Museu Nacional de Arqueologia (National Archaeological Museum)**—see panels.

HISTORY The first building on the site was a small monastery—the Ermida do Restelo or Capela de São Jerónimo. It was built by Henry the Navigator in 1460, and was designed to offer solace to the seafarers who used Belém as one of their key points of departure. The new monastery, a Jeronymite foundation, was begun by Manuel I in 1502, this time in commemoration of Vasco da Gama's successful voyage to the Indies (see page 35). In 1497, before embarking on the voyage, da Gama and his men staged a vigil in Henry's monastery church. There they took confession and received a general absolution, a spiritual safeguard should they die on their voyage.

The new monastery was partly funded by a 5 percent tax levied by Manuel on all the precious stones and spices flowing into Portugal from Africa and the Indies (except for cinnamon, pepper, and cloves, which were the subject of a royal monopoly). The building increasingly distracted Manuel, who turned his attention from the abbey at Batalha (see page 168) to concentrate on his new pet project. Between 1502 and 1517 the master of works was Diogo da Boitaca (or Boytac), a Frenchman who instigated the predominantly Gothic tone of the monastery. He was replaced by João de Castilho, a Spaniard, who with his collaborators introduced Manueline and Plateresque forms to the building. De Castilho was then joined by Nicolau Chanterène, who championed new Renaissance forms. The work lost a little of its impetus, however, when a new king, Dom João III, was enthused by building work at the Convent of Christ at Tomar (see page 182). This led to a loss of funding in 1551, although most of the building had been completed by this time, two further leading architects, Diogo de Torralva and João de Ruão (Jéronimos of Rouen), having introduced a more classical flavor to the monastery complex.

CHURCH The main entrance to the monastery church, the **Igreja de Santa Maria**, is the magnificent **south door**, the work of Boytac and João de Castilho. The wealth of decoration centers on a statue of Henry the Navigator (the bearded figure between the doors), while the canopy above is crowned by the Cross of the Order of the Knights of Christ. The west door, the work of Chanterène, focuses on statues representing Manuel I and his second wife, Maria (to either side of the door), accompanied by their respective patron saints. Above the doorway are niches containing the four Evangelists, buttresses with figures of the Apostles, and scenes representing the Annunciation, the Nativity, and the Adoration of the Magi.

Inside the church the stonework and soaring aisles are breathtaking. Detailed carving adorns countless surfaces, reaching its zenith in the glorious **fan vaulting** that over-arches the nave. The baroque transept contains the tombs of minor royal scions, while the chancel contains the tombs of Dom Manuel I and Dom João III, together with their queens. Vasco da Gama's funerary monument lies beneath the gallery at the entrance to the church, although most people hurry past it, anxious to reach the monastery's superlative **cloister** (entered close to the left transept).

One of the country's great architectural set pieces, the two-storied cloister features a feast of Manueline and Renaissance carving, the lower story (predominantly the work

Grace and symmetry in the cloisters of the Mosteiro dos Jerónimos

A Japanese "Namban" paneled screen showing a Portuguese ship

JAPANESE SCREENS
Multipaneled Japanese screens form one of the more unusual highlights of the National Museum of Ancient Art. Their panels depict the arrival of the Portuguese on the island of Tane-ga-Shima (Tanegaxima) in 1543. The Japanese christened the strange new arrivals *Namban-jin*, or "barbarians from the south," and the art that resulted from the meeting of the two cultures was known ever after as "Namban." The Japanese were fascinated by the Portuguese, and in particular by their moustaches, odd clothes, and the decidedly unoriental size of their noses. Buttons, which were unheard of in Japan, also attracted their attention. As a result, noses and buttons receive particular pictorial emphasis in the panels.

of João de Castilho) being particularly outstanding. A door leads from the later and more restrained upper story (1544) to the upper choir, which features a lovely set of decorated choir stalls (1560).

▶▶▶ Museu Nacional de Arte Antiga (National Museum of Ancient Art) *Off 50A1*
Rua das Janelas Verdes 95–Jardim 9 de Abril (tel: 21 396 4151) Open: Wed–Sun 10–6, Tue 2–6. Closed Mon. Admission: moderate. Tram 15, 18. Bus 7, 40, 49, 51, 60
This museum contains one of Portugal's finest art collections, and is second only to the Gulbenkian among Lisbon's leading museums. "Ancient" in this context is a misnomer, for the collection for the most part comprises works of art that reflect the development of Portuguese painting from the 11th century onward. Most of the exhibits were taken from churches and monasteries when the latter were suppressed in 1833. Located in Lapa, a suburb 1.2 miles (2km) west of Praça do Comércio, the museum is housed in two connected buildings—the 17th-century palace of the Counts of Alvor and a modern annex built over the site of a former Carmelite convent.

PAINTINGS By far the most famous painting is the polyptych of the *Panéis de São Vicente de Fora* (the altarpiece, or **Adoration of St. Vincent**), probably painted by Nuno Gonçalves between about 1465 and 1470. Amazingly, the work was only discovered in 1882, having languished dirty and dismembered in the attic of the defunct church of São Vicente. Its six panels show some 60 figures (among whom are a variety of superbly realized historical characters) paying homage to St. Vincent (depicted twice), the patron saint of Lisbon.

In the center left-hand panel, for example, stand the figures of Henry the Navigator, Afonso V (in green), and the widowed Duchess of Bragança (in white headdress). Other characters represent fishermen, Cistercian monks, a Moorish knight, a Jew, a beggar, scholars, and members of the army, Church, and royal family. Gonçalves is thought to have painted himself as the top left-hand figure in the left of the two central panels.

Other noted Portuguese paintings in the gallery include the so-called Cook triptych, the work of Grão Vasco, and an *Annunciation* by Frei Carlos. The latter work exemplifies the debt of Portuguese painting to Flemish art, a result of trade between Portugal and the Low Countries. Other exceptional works include Hieronymous Bosch's extraordinary *Temptation of St. Anthony*, a *Madonna and Child* by Memling, and Albrecht Dürer's *St. Jerome*, together with paintings by Jan van Eyck, Poussin, Hans Holbein, Courbet, Raphael, and Velázquez.

DECORATIVE ARTS As is the case at the Gulbenkian, however, painting is complemented by the decorative arts, for the gallery also houses numerous artifacts accumulated over the centuries from Portugal's overseas colonies and elsewhere. Among these are one of Europe's finest collections of silver tableware, Flemish tapestries, glassware, Italian ceramics, ecclesiastical vestments, and a noted monstrance from the Mosteiro de Belém, reputedly made with the first gold brought back from the Indies by Vasco da Gama. Also look out for the gorgeous **carpets**, the famous Japanese **Namban screens** (see panel opposite), and the chapel from the former convent on the site, distinguished by its gilded work and *azulejos*.

The Adoration of St. Vincent *by Nuno Gonçalves, in the Museu Nacional de Arte Antiga*

63

▶▶▶ Museu Nacional dos Coches (National Coach Museum)   50A1

Praça Afonso de Albuquerque-Rua de Belém, Belém (tel: 21 361 0850)
Open: Wed–Mon 10–5:30. Closed Tue. Admission: moderate, free Sun morning. Tram 15 from Praça do Comércio. Bus 27, 28, 29, 43, 49, or 51

This complex (closed until March 2001), bursting with historical coaches and carriages, is the most popular sight in Lisbon and is one of the most important collections of its type in the world. Located in the suburb of Belém, the museum, founded in 1904 by Queen Amélia, is housed in the former riding academy and stables of the Palácio de Belém, a royal palace begun around 1726 by Dom João V. Today, the palace proper (closed to visitors) is the official residence of the Portuguese president.

Carriages were never merely modes of transport, but were used to proclaim the wealth and ostentatious taste of their owners. This was particularly true of royal and state carriages, where decorative splendor was part and parcel of royal showmanship. This said, the museum's most sumptuous coaches are probably the trio of gilded carriages built in 1716 for the Marquês de Frontes, Portugal's ambassador to the Holy See. Although they were built in Rome, the beautiful baroque coaches are decorated with allegorical scenes representing Portuguese military triumphs and voyages of discovery.

If the museum has a fault, it is that there are almost too many coaches, the endless repetition of splendid carriages dulling the scintillating impression created by the first displays. There would have been still more to admire, however, had Dom João VI not taken many with him when he moved to Brazil in 1807. By this date coaches

PARQUE DAS NAÇÕES
The main legacy of Lisbon's Expo '98 has been the exhibition's wonderful park (tel: 21 891 9333; www.parquedasnações.pt. *Open* Sun–Thu 9:30 AM–1 AM, Fri–Sat 9:30 AM–3 AM. *Admission free*. Metro Oriente) and some of the impressive attractions created for the event. The best of these is the spectacular Oceanarium, the largest in Europe (*Open* daily 10–6. *Admission: expensive*), but you should also see the Virtual Reality Pavilion (*Open* Tue–Sun 1–7), which includes the Journey to Oceania experience (*Admission: expensive*) and the Virtual Reality Oceanarium (*Admission: inexpensive*; combined ticket available for both attractions). Other sights include a ride on the Lisbon Cable Car (*Open* Mon–Fri 11–9, Sat–Sun 10–9:30. *Admission: moderate*) and the Vasco da Gama Tower (*Open* daily 10–8. *Admission: moderate*).

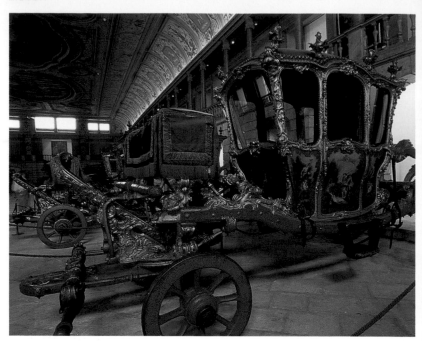

Traveling in style: a coach at the Museu Nacional dos Coches

MUSEU DE ARTE POPULAR
One of the most exhaustive museums of its type in the country, the Museum of Folk Art provides a province-by-province look at Portugal's rich heritage of folk art, crafts, customs, and traditions. Although the setting is low on atmosphere, the exhibits are fascinating, and run the gamut of rural furniture, costumes, ceramics, paintings, and a wide range of miscellaneous ephemera. The museum lies almost adjacent to the Monument of the Discoveries (see panel opposite) on Avenida de Brasília (tel: 21 301 1282. *Open* Tue–Sun 10–12:30, 2–5. Closed Mon. *Admission: inexpensive.* Tram 15. Bus 9, 27, 28, 43, 49, 51).

were less splendid than in days gone by, largely as a result of injunctions introduced by the Marquês de Pombal at the end of the 18th century. Designed as austerity measures, his sumptuary laws forbade the use of ornate fabrics and expensive metals. This had the effect of reducing expensive imports, but also deliberately made it harder for public coaches to challenge the splendor of royal conveyances.

► **Sé (Cathedral)**   *51D2*
Largo da Sé
Open Mon–Sat 10–5. Admission free. Tram 12, 28. Bus 37
Lisbon's cathedral was begun around 1150, not long after the city had fallen to Afonso Henriques, Portugal's first king. It was the city's first church, built, legend has it, over the site of a former mosque. Like similar cathedrals in Évora, Coimbra, and Porto, it retains a fortress-like appearance, its Romanesque plan having survived major earthquakes in 1344 and 1755 (not to mention the attentions of restorers over the years). Its architects are believed to have been Robert and Bernard, the French duo also responsible for the cathedral in Coimbra. Inside, there is relatively little to see as much rococo and baroque decoration has been stripped away over the years. The principal treasures are a font in which St. Anthony of Padua is said to have been baptized in 1195, and the 14th-century ambulatory, whose radiating chapels contain a variety of appealing Gothic tombs. Two separate small admission charges admit you to the care-worn 14th-century cloister, built to a Cistercian Gothic design, and to the baroque sacristy, which contains relics, sacred images, reliquaries, and the famous gem-encrusted José I monstrance.

▶▶▶ Torre de Belém (Belém Tower)   50A1

Avenida de Brasília (tel: 21 362 0034)
Open: Tue–Sun 10–5. Closed Mon. Admission: moderate.
Tram 15. Bus 27, 28, 29, 43, 49, 51

The Torre de Belém, a true masterpiece of Manueline and Moorish-tinged Renaissance architecture, is perhaps the closest thing Portugal has to a national monument.

It is a Unesco World Heritage building. Bold, self-confident and wonderfully capricious, the five-story tower stands as a monument to the country's maritime triumphs, its walls appropriately still lapped by the sea on three sides.

The tower was built between 1515 and 1520, the last five years of Dom Manuel I's reign. This makes it one of Portugal's few thoroughbred Manueline buildings, since most others have been added to piecemeal over the centuries. Its much-traveled architect, Francisco de Arruda, had previously been employed on military projects in North Africa, hence the Moorish motifs that enliven the tower. Chief among these are the little domes crowning the battlements and tiny side sentry boxes, together with the arcaded windows and graceful little Venetian-style loggias adorning the main tower. Each of the crenellations on the upper and lower set of battlements is decorated with the Cross of the Order of Christ (the cross also reappears in the tracery of the individual loggias below). The armillary sphere, symbol of Manuel I, is also much in evidence.

You enter the tower through a jutting bastion with a small internal cloister, below which lie storerooms that were used as dungeons at the beginning of the 19th century during the reign of Dom Miguel. Steps then lead to the upper battlements, which provide breezy views of Belém and the open sea.

PADRÃO DOS DESCOBRIMENTOS
The vast seafront Monument of the Discoveries at Belém (Avenida de Brasília, tel: 21 301 6228. *Open* Tue–Sun 9:30–6:30. *Admission free*) makes a fitting modern counterpart to the Torre de Belém. Built in 1960, it commemorates the 500th anniversary of the death of Henry the Navigator (see pages 226–227). The jutting triangular pediment represents the prow of a ship, while the trio of curving forms above symbolize billowing sails. Henry stands at the head of the crowd of figures on the prow, a ship in his hands. A lift takes you to the top of the monument, where you can look down on a mosaic depicting a compass and map of the world, together with the dates of various discoveries.

65

The Torre de Belém, a monument to maritime triumphs

Walk

Lisbon: the castle and Alfama

See map on pages 50–51.

View over Lisbon from the Castelo de São Jorge

This 2.2-mile (3.5km) walk (2–3 hours, depending on how many places of interest you visit on it) makes a good introduction to the city and is worth following early on in your trip.

From **Praça dos Restauradores**, where you can visit the tourist office, walk south past the famous facade of the Rossio railway station. Then walk the length of the **Rossio**, Lisbon's main square, before following the pedestrianized Rua Augusta through the **Baixa**. Look at the **Praça do Comércio**, then return into the Baixa and turn right on Rua da Conceição. Cross Largo da Madalena and climb to the **Sé (Cathedral)▶**. Follow the street uphill left of the cathedral as far as Santa Luzia and its viewpoint. Be certain to take in the wonderful **Museu das Artes Decorativas▶▶▶** across the road (see panel on page 54). From the museum, turn right (the way you came), take the first right (Travessa de Santa Luzia) uphill,

bearing right and following signs to the "Castelo de São Jorge."

Enter the **castle▶▶** and walk right round under its walls—there are lovely **views▶▶▶** of the city below—before emerging eventually at a green iron gate and the Largo de Minho de Deus (down to your left). Turn left into the shabby square and find Rua da Santa Marinha at its top (north) side. Follow this to the church of São Vicente. Take the street to the left of the church into Campo de Santa Clara. Walk towards the small garden and palm trees, then go right to come round behind the church of Santa Engrácia. With your back to the facade, drop left past the brown-tiled house ahead. Turn right on Rua dos Remédios at the bottom, right again on Rua São Estêvão, and then bear left on Rua São Miguel, one of the most atmospheric streets in the **Alfama▶▶**. Return to the cathedral and Baixa via Rua de São João de Praça.

Excursions

The lush, romantic landscapes and sumptuous royal palaces of Sintra, lauded over the centuries by poets and kings, provide by far the most tempting excursion from Lisbon. Less well known is the convent and palace at Mafra, one of the masterpieces of Portuguese baroque.

▶▶▶ Sintra   *158A1*

This is not a single town or a single sight. On first acquaintance the various palaces and interconnected villages can be slightly disorientating. The "town" divides into three basic areas: Estefânia, the modern district round the train station; Sintra-Vila, the main town; and São Pedro de Sintra, the area's former village (1.2 miles, or 2km, to the east). The key things to see are three palaces: the Palácio Nacional de Sintra and Quinta da Regaleira, located in Sintra-Vila; and the Palácio Nacional da Pena, which lies in parkland about 2 miles (3km) south of Sintra-Vila. Between the two lie the ruins of a Moorish castle, the Castelo dos Mouros. The parkland surrounding the Palácio da Pena is worth exploring, the best target being the viewpoint of the Cruz Alta. To the west of Sintra lie two more sights: the Convento dos Capuchos (closed for restoration), an old Capuchin monastery (see panel on page 68), and the gloriously romantic gardens of Monserrate.

SINTRA Moorish potentates probably had a summer palace in Sintra as early as the 8th century, although the present royal **Palácio Nacional de Sintra▶▶** dates to the reign of Dom João I in the 15th century. It continued to be used as a royal retreat until the end of the 19th century. The building's long history has resulted in a number of architectural styles, with Gothic and Manueline uppermost, although it is the glorious decor of the many state rooms—and the *azulejos* in particular—that provide the palace's main charm. The building lies at the center of the town on

PRACTICALITIES
The tourist office for Sintra is in Sintra-Vila at Praça da República 23 (tel: 21 923 1157); it also offers full- or half-day tours of the various sights.
 Trains for Sintra depart from the Estação do Rossio in Lisbon roughly every 20 minutes. The trip takes 45 minutes. Buses from the city are extremely slow. Numerous organized tours operate to Sintra (ask at the Lisbon tourist office; see panel on page 51), but to get the most out of a visit you should explore under your own steam (and probably stay overnight). Try to arrive early or late in the day to avoid the large summer crowds. You can walk between many of the sights, but while distances are not excessive the gradients are steep. In summer a bus connects the Palácio de Sintra to the Palácio de Pena from the main square of Sintra-Vila. Taxis are also available, but demand is heavy.

67

The Palácio Nacional de Sintra

QUINTA DA REGALEIRA
This house and its grounds are relatively modern—they were created at the turn of the 20th century—but represent a blend of folly, fantasy, alchemy, and romance. They are the work of Antonio Augusto Carvalho Monteiro and his architect, Luigi Manini, who created a blend of Gothic, Manueline, and Renaissance architecture, along with ornate and extravagant details. The grounds, with their wells, grottoes, and follies, are full of secrets, while the main house—the Palácio dos Milhões—is fascinating. Visits must be arranged in advance (tel: 21 910 6650; e-mail: regaleira@mail.telepac.pt. *Open* 4–12; guided tours daily. *Admission: expensive*).

Decorative motif at Sintra

CONVENTO DE SANTA CRUZ DOS CAPUCHOS
This former Capuchin monastery lies around 3 miles (5km) southwest of Sintra-Vila just off the N247 road to Cabo da Roca, a tremendous 500-foot (150m) cliff that marks the most westerly point of continental Europe. Set in dramatic craggy scenery, the convent was begun in 1560, falling into disuse in 1834 following the suppression of the monasteries. Today, its seclusion and slightly forlorn air add to its charm, while the tiny cells, many lined with cork stripped from the surrounding trees, remain as extraordinary as ever. Ring the custodian's bell to be shown around (closed for restoration at the time of writing).

Largo da Rainha D. Amélia (tel: 21 910 6840. *Open* guided tours Thu–Tue 10–5. *Admission: moderate*).

After visiting the palace, head south towards the Palácio da Pena—a picturesque drive—halting to walk up to the **Castelo dos Mouros►►** (tel: 21 923 5116. *Open* Jun–Sep, daily 9–6; Oct–May, daily 9–5. *Admission free*), probably built in the 8th century and taken by Afonso Henriques with the help of Scandinavian crusaders in 1147. The views from its rocky pinnacles are magnificent.

PENA While the Palácio de Sintra is a monument to the style of centuries, the lofty **Palácio Nacional da Pena►►►** is a wonderfully kitsch memorial to the dubious decorative tastes of one man. Built over the ruins of a 16th-century monastery, the palace was the eccentric brainchild of Ferdinand of Saxe-Coburg-Gotha, the German husband of Dona Maria II. With the help of German architect Baron Eschwege, he devised a madcap medieval pastiche, gilding the interior with a profusion of hangings, otiose stucco, leaden furniture, and other extravagant decorative flourishes. Views from the palace terraces are sublime, while the delightful park and gardens are full of exotic plants and trees. For even better views you can walk (or drive) via a marked path to **Cruz Alta►►** (1,736 feet, or 529m), the highest point in the Serra de Sintra hills (tel: 21 910 5340. *Open* palace mid-Sep–Jun, Tue–Sun 10–5; Jul–mid-Sep,

Tue–Sun 10–6:30. Park Jun–Sep, daily 10–6; Oct–May, daily 10–5. *Admission: moderate, park free*).

MONSERRATE The Pena park, like much of the countryside around Sintra, is a bewitching mixture of verdant woodland and swathes of mimosa, bougainvillea, camellias, and other exotic plants and flowers. Little, however, outshines the beautiful **gardens at Monserrate►►** (2.5 miles, or 4km, west of Sintra on the N375), a green oasis in which you could spend the best part of a day in idle wandering and romantic musings. William Beckford, a wealthy and eccentric Englishman, rented a house here in 1793, adding an English garden and several landscape follies to its existing grounds. Some 50 years later another Englishman, Sir Francis Cook, built a house (closed to the public) and more exotic gardens were added (*Open* summer, daily 10–5; last entry 4. *Admission free*).

▶▶▶ Mafra   158A2

The Palácio de Mafra

Until 1711 Mafra was an undistinguished little village. Today, it is an undistinguished little town, but it is now home to the vast **Convento-Palácio de Mafra▶▶** (tel: 261 81 7550. *Open* Wed–Mon 10–4:30. *Admission: moderate*), one of the largest baroque palaces in Europe. It was begun in 1717, the result of a vow made by Dom João V, who in 1711, after three childless years of marriage, pledged to build a monastery if he and his queen, Maria Ana of Austria, could be blessed with a child. A daughter, Bárbara (later queen of Spain), was born within a year. The design for the monastery was entrusted to Friedrich Ludwig, a German architect, but most of the work and decoration was carried out by a team of Italian builders and craftsmen. Financial backing was provided by the gold and diamonds recently discovered in Brazil.

Initially the plan was for a monastery of 13 monks. However, João decided it should challenge St. Peter's in Rome and the Escorial monastery in Spain, and the result was a project on a quite staggering scale. By the time the building was completed in 1735, it housed 300—even the consecration ceremony took eight hours.

Today, part of the gargantuan complex is used by the military, but you are still able to view the basilica and many of the old state apartments. The former, tucked behind part of a 720-foot-long (220m) facade, is an elegant if slightly lifeless affair. Its highlights are the external statues, which depict the founders of religious orders in creamy Carrara marble, and the pinky-white expanse of the 230-foot (70m) cupola. Some of the apartments (visited with a guide) are dull, while others are decorated in styles whose only appeal lies in their wonderfully kitsch excess. Many are worth seeing, however, in particular the magnificent 40,000-volume library and the king's and queen's pavilions, modestly situated at opposite ends of the palace.

PRACTICALITIES
Mafra lies around 25 miles (40km) northwest of Lisbon. Empresa Mafrense buses run from the city roughly hourly, departing from Largo Martin Moniz northeast of the Rossio. The travel time is 90 minutes. Alternatively, you could visit the convent in conjunction with a trip to Sintra: hourly buses for Mafra leave from outside Sintra's train station.

OVER THE TOP
Mafra's convent generated a plethora of staggering statistics. Some 50,000 civilian laborers worked on the project over 13 years, and the average number of workers on site each day was 15,000. Around 7,000 soldiers were employed to oversee the workforce. Some 7,000 carts were used to shift rubble and materials.

Lisbon

Old-world splendor in a Lisbon hotel

TOURIST PASS

A *Passe Turístico* (Tourist Pass) is available for unlimited travel over either four days or seven days on buses, trams, the Metro, and *elevadores* (see panel below). It is available on production of a passport at the booths near the Santa Justa *elevador* (close to the Rossio), in Praça da Figueira and the Restauradores Metro.

TOURIST STREETCARS

During the summer there are usually a couple of streetcars, often wonderfully restored old models, that run specially for visitors. Normally a guide provides a running commentary. One route is known as the *Circuito Colinas*, or "Hills Circuit," and the other the *Circuito Tejo*, or "Tagus Circuit." Both depart from Praça do Comércio. For details, contact the tourist office or tel: 21 361 3000.

ELEVATORS

Lisbon's many hills have prompted an unusual form of public transport, the Santa Justa elevator (*elevador*), in Rua do Ouro in the Baixa. It takes you to Praça do Carmo in the Bairro Alto, saving a steep climb. Similar steep walks can be avoided by using the funiculars: the Glória (Praça dos Restauradores to Rua São Pedro de Alcântara in the Bairro Alto) and the Bica (Rua de Boavista to Rua do Loreto).

DRIVING

Given the city's atrocious driving conditions, the difficulty of finding a parking space, and the danger of theft, it makes sense to remain carfree until you leave the city. If you must drive, expect traffic jams, especially crossing the Ponte 25 de Abril, and use official central parking lots (if there is any space).

Practicalities

TAXIS Much of central Lisbon can easily be seen on foot. Only the Gulbenkian, the National Tile Museum, and the cluster of sights at Belém require public transportation. Taxis are inexpensive and efficient if you don't want to walk or rely on buses. However, hailing a cab on the street can be difficult (a green light means it is taken), so head for taxi stands around the city (on the Rossio, Praça da Figueira, and elsewhere) or phone for one (tel: 21 815 5061, 21 811 1100, or 21 793 2756). Fares are higher after 10 PM, at weekends, and during public holidays.

BUSES Buses (*autocarros*) are useful for reaching the more outlying sights. Though less exciting than trams (see below), they are often a little quicker. Tickets can be bought on board, but are cheaper if you buy them in advance from a ticket booth. A book of ten tickets (*módulos* or *caderneta*) works out cheaper still. Tickets should be validated in the machines on each bus or tram. You can also buy one- or three-day bus and tram passes, which should be validated the first time you use them: 24- or 72-hour validity starts from that moment. A bus stop is a *paragem*.

STREETCARS Lisbon's famous rattling old streetcars, or *eléctricos*, are one of the city's highlights. You should try to ride one at least once. The most renowned route to travel for its own sake is the 28. The streetcars date from around 1903, when they replaced horse-drawn carriages. So popular have they become with visitors that many were recently returned to Germany, where they were built, and overhauled to squeeze out a few more years' service. Whether they will survive Lisbon's modernizing drive, however, is another matter. Streetcar tickets cost the same as, and are interchangeable with, bus tickets.

METRO Large "M" signs indicate the entrance to Lisbon's subway system (Metropolitano). It is unlikely you will need to use the network—although it is useful for the Gulbenkian—but if you do, tickets can be bought from vending machines or (for slightly more) from ticket booths. A discounted ten-ticket *caderneta* or one- and seven-day Metro-only passes are also available.

Accommodations, food, and drink

WHERE TO STAY There was a time when even a pauper could live like a king in Lisbon's hotels. Portugal's entry into the European Union, however, has produced a rash of new hotels and an all-round hike in prices. This said, some fine hotels still exist, and in the middle and lower price brackets the choice is vast.

Lower-priced hotels are mainly concentrated in the Baixa, and in and around the Rossio between Praça da Figueira and Praça dos Restauradores. These are likely to be noisy unless you can secure off-street rooms. Two of the more evocative districts, the Alfama and Bairro Alto, have relatively few accommodations. In most cheaper places you may have to share bathrooms and toilets. Don't be put off by the staircases in Lisbon's crumbling tenements, home to many of the city's pensions—they are often much dingier than the rooms they lead to.

Upscale options dot the same central districts, but there is more choice in the quieter and wealthier residential districts on the fringes of the city center. Favored locations include the areas east of the Parque Eduardo VII and the Gulbenkian, by the Museu de Arte Antiga, and in the streets to the northeast by the Arroios Metro station.

DRINKING Lisbon's citizens make good use of their many bars and coffeehouses by day and night. One of the oldest and most famous is **A Brasileira**, a former haunt of artists and writers that hides behind a wonderful art nouveau facade at Rua Garrett 120 in the Chiado district. Other grand old cafés include **Nicola** (Praça Dom Pedro IV 26, off the Rossio), the nearby **Suiça** (Praça Dom Pedro IV 96), and the fashionable **Benard** (Rua Garrett 104); all are renowned for their pastries. At night, bars fill with people in search of a predinner drink, although most only really liven up after 11 PM. Key areas for late-night drinking are the Bairro Alto and around Avenida 24 de Julho.

EATING Food is one of Lisbon's great pleasures. Prices are reasonable, the quality high, and the choice of cuisine increasingly cosmopolitan. You can nibble grilled sardines at simple streetside tavernas, sit down to a sophisticated candlelit dinner, or sample some of the more adventurous cooking introduced by exiles returning from Portugal's former colonies. In addition to these, fish and seafood are as excellent as you'd expect from a busy port. The main eating areas are the Baixa; the Chiado, which has some of the city's smarter establishments; and the Bairro Alto, home to the trendier and more exotic restaurants.

RESERVING A ROOM
Accommodations are at a premium at Easter and during midsummer. If you arrive by plane the hotel desk at the airport has information on room availability, but does not make reservations. However, the tourist office in Praça dos Restauradores (see panel on page 51) operates a free reservations service. During busy periods start as early as possible if you're hunting for rooms under your own steam. Later in the day you may have to take what you can and resume your search in the morning. This said, you should usually find something. Note that many pensions are grouped together in single tenements, and that most occupy upper floors, so be prepared to climb a lot of stairs.

71

EATING PRACTICALITIES
Most Portuguese eat relatively late—from around 8 PM onward for dinner. Note that many restaurants close on Sunday evening. Remember, too, that cafés and bars can be a good source of snacks, while markets and small food stores provide endless picnic options. Keep an eye open for the city's *cervejarias*, or beer halls, often wonderfully old-fashioned places where you can eat and drink inexpensively.

Shade and succor in the Praça do Comercio

MARKETS

For a taste of a lively Lisbon market visit the *mercado* in Rua da Atalaia, the daily food market that serves the Bairro Alto district (*Open* Mon–Sat 7–2). Alternatively, head for the larger markets around the Cais do Sodré station—a huge fish market, the Ribeira food market, and the food and drink stands of Rua do Arsenal.

SHOPPING COMPLEXES

The Amoreiras building in north Lisbon is a vast shopping, office, and hotel complex, and forms a key component of the city skyline (take bus 11 from the Rossio or Praça dos Restauradores). It is overshadowed, however, by the Centro Comercial Colombo, Iberia's largest collection of stores, restaurants, movie theaters, amusements, and hypermarkets (Avenida Lusíada, Letras, tel: 21 716 0250. Metro Colégio Milita Luz).

Lisbon's modern Amoreiras complex

Shopping

WHERE TO BUY Lisbon's most interesting stores are concentrated in the Baixa, the grid of streets between Praça do Comércio and the Rossio. Also worth a visit is the Chiado, to the west, a district whose preeminence survived the fire of 1988 that destroyed many of its historical buildings. In the Baixa the main shopping streets are Rua do Ouro, Rua da Prata, and Rua Augusta, while in the Chiado the Rua Garrett is lined with some of the city's more upscale stores. Moving further west, the Bairro Alto, long the focus of the city's nightlife, is increasingly home to designer and other fashion stores. There are many colorful markets (see panel), but some of the largest lie around Cais do Sodré. Lisbon's principal flea market is the **Feira da Ladra** (*Open* Tue and Sat mornings), located on the edge of the Alfama district around Campo de Santa Clara.

WHAT TO BUY The Feira da Ladra may turn up an occasional antique, but for more reliable antiques shops head for Rua Dom Pedro V and Rua de São José. One of the best stores, known for its old tiles, is **Solar** (Rua Dom Pedro V 68–70). Tiles can also be bought at **Sant'Anna** (Rua do Alecrim 95–7), founded in 1741. Pottery and ceramics are both good buys: visit the **Centro do Turismo** (Rua Castilho 61b). For china and glassware try **Vista Alegre** (Largo do Chiado 18), founded in 1841—it is expensive but unbeatable. Lisbon's top jeweler is **W. A. Sarmento** (Rua Aurea 251), known in particular for gold and silver filigree . Other highly priced treasures await you at the **Casa Quintão** (Rua do Alecrim 113–15), celebrated for its beautiful Arraiolos carpets. For something equally typical, but considerably cheaper, try a *fado* recording from **Valentim de Carvalho** (Rossio, Praça Dom Pedro IV 59), a book, video, and CD store, or take home a bottle of port or Madeira from **Napoleão** (Rua dos Fanqueiros 72/6) in the Baixa.

Fado: *music from the heart*

Nightlife

Nightlife in Lisbon can mean anything from a drink in a bar or a meal in a restaurant to an evening spent sipping port (see panel) or listening to the melancholy strains of *fado*. In summer, it means taking to the streets, pausing at pavement cafés, or joining the excitable crowds that drift between bars, clubs, and restaurants. Traditionally, the best bars and clubs are found in the Bairro Alto and the area on and around Avenida 24 de Julho west of Cais do Sodré, but more recently the "Docas de Alcântara," the rejuvenated marina area by the Ponte 25 de Abril, has become trendy. Most bars open around 10 PM, although the action usually only hots up after midnight.

The **Gulbenkian Foundation** (see pages 55–56) hosts regular classical music recitals and ballet performances during its October–June season. Chamber and symphony concerts are also held at the **Teatro Municipal de São Luís** (Rua Antonío Maria Cardoso 40, tel: 21 342 7172). Free concerts are often performed at the Cathedral (Sé), the Igreja dos Mártires, the Basílica da Estrêla, and the Carmo and São Roque churches. Classical concerts are also held at the principal venue for opera and ballet, the **Teatro Nacional de São Carlos** (Rua Serpa Pinto 9, tel: 21 346 5914). The season runs from September to mid-July. Lisbon's many movie theaters show current and vintage films, usually in the original language and with Portuguese subtitles.

Many visitors like to sample one of the city's famous *fado* clubs, in the Bairro Alto and Alfama. Some are now becoming touristy, and in many you have to eat or pay a minimum drinks' bill. Most open around 9 PM, fill up about midnight and close around 4 AM. Some of the best known are **Adega do Machado** (Rua do Norte 91, Bairro Alto), **Parreirinha d'Alfama** (Beco do Espírito Santo 1, Alfama), **A Severa** (Rua das Gáveas 51/7, Bairro Alto), and **Adega Mesquita** (Rua do Diário de Notícias 107, Bairro Alto).

TICKETS AND INFORMATION

You can buy tickets for a wide variety of concerts, films, plays, and shows by calling in person at the Agência de Bilhetes para Espectáculos Públicos on the corner of Praça dos Restauradores. Movie tickets can be booked directly with individual movie theaters. The Gulbenkian Foundation and the tourist office, among other places, have details of forthcoming events, while the latter publishes *Agenda Cultural*, a free monthly listings magazine. If you can manage a little Portuguese, the local *Diário de Notícias* daily newspaper also carries extensive listings.

PORT WINE INSTITUTE

The Solar do Vinho do Porto in Rua de São Pedro de Alcântara 45 R/C (tel: 21 347 5707) is one of Lisbon's best-known institutions (*Open* Mon–Sat 2 PM–midnight). Owned by the Port Wine Institute, it is a large, relaxed, and rather refined bar given over entirely to port. You can order by the glass or bottle from a *lista de vinhos* that includes over 150 different ports. It is located in the Bairro Alto close to the upper station of the Glória funicular.

BULLFIGHTS

Touradas, or bullfights (see page 178), usually take place on Easter Sunday and Thursdays from June to September at the main Praça de Touros do Campo Pequeno (tel: 21 793 2442). The nearest Metro station is Campo Pequeno.

Trás-os-Montes

▶▶▶ REGION HIGHLIGHTS

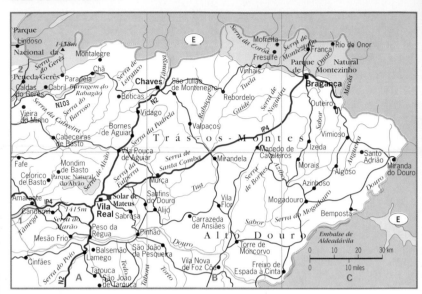

GETTING AROUND

The Trás-os-Montes is best approached from the Douro to the southwest, either from Lamego and Amarante, or from the Minho to the west via a more circuitous route from Braga and the Peneda-Gerês National Park. The N103 links Braga and Chaves, while the IP4 links Bragança and Vila Real. Trains serve only Vila Real, but the bus network serves most centers from the nodal points of Chaves, Bragança, and Vila Real. Services can be infrequent, so read timetables diligently.

CLIMATE

The mountains in the west of the region, buffeted by Atlantic depressions, have the country's highest rainfall (12 inches, or 30cm, per year), while the eastern plains, where a Continental effect prevails, suffer the greatest extremes of temperature (averaging 42˚F, or 5.6˚C, in winter and 76˚F, or 24.6˚C, in summer).

TRÁS-OS-MONTES

The name of Portugal's most isolated enclave, Trás-os-Montes—which means "Beyond the Mountains"—admirably encapsulates the remote other-worldliness of this fascinating area. Lost behind its upland barrier, the region preserves traditions and ways of life that have almost vanished from most of Western Europe. Several local dialects still prevail, all but impenetrable even to other Portuguese, while centuries-old festivals and folk traditions continue to play a living part in day-to-day life. A peasant-based pattern of rustic small-holdings underpins the region's economy, tractors only recently having begun to replace mules and oxen as the principal beasts of burden. Conditions in the countryside are harsh. Weather, in particular, holds the region back—"nine months of winter and three months of hell," goes the oft-quoted local saying. Winters are wet and icy, and summers dry and scorching, twin scourges that compound the curse of the wild and largely unforgiving landscape. It almost goes without saying that emigration has long blighted the region.

This said, things are changing, albeit less quickly than in the rest of Portugal. Both the European Union and World Bank are channeling resources into the region's agriculture and infrastructure. New roads—replacing mule tracks—are pushing through the mountains to link remote towns and villages, while small industrial initiatives are finding a foothold in the larger towns. Money is also trickling into the region with returning emigrants, who increasingly build the house of their dreams—or as much as they can afford—before returning to economic exile abroad.

Not all of the region is equally affected by bad weather and the intractability of landscape. In the south, the so-called *terra quente* ("hot land"), the soils are more fertile and conditions more benign. This allows the growth of fruit trees—apple, pear, orange, cherry, and almond—together with cereal crops and a sprinkling of vines. Almond trees, in particular, are widespread, their coats of spring blossom creating one of the region's most captivating sights (visit during late February–March to enjoy the spectacle). By contrast, in the north, the *terra fria* ("cold land"), life is hard in the extreme. Much of the terrain here consists of high plateaus (around 2,300 feet, or 700m), bounded by mountains (4,250 feet, or 1,300m) and cut by steepsided valleys. Hilltops are bare, and remain the domain of shepherds and their ragged flocks.

Pages 74–75: remote and mountainous Montesinho Park

Wooded hills almost engulf a village in the Trás-os-Montes

PILLORIES

Few towns in Portugal, and particularly northern Portugal, are without their pillory, or *pelourinho*. They first appeared during the 13th century, at about the time centralized and coordinated rule was being established in the country. A pillory became the embodiment of the rights granted to towns to administer justice and punishment, and as such were often built in town centers close to seats of power such as the town hall, parish church, or principal monastery.

They also had a practical purpose, however, and indicted malefactors would be shackled either to a pillory's distinctive hooks or summit cross. As time went by, pillories also became more artistic in intent, often with Manueline details grafted onto the original structure.

WHAT TO SEE Art, culture, and sights in the conventional sense are scarce in Trás-os-Montes, but no other Portuguese region offers quite the same insight into a vanishing way of life. Roads are still poor for the most part, and public transportation labored, meaning that a certain amount of patience is required when exploring the back country. However, if you have a car almost any choice of itinerary should bring its rewards. The area's best-known target is **Vila Real**, visited less for the town itself as for the nearby Solar de Mateus, the baroque palace immortalized on millions of Mateus Rosé bottles. At the same time, Vila Real itself, one of the region's more industrialized towns, provides services and public transportation facilities harder to come by elsewhere. A town to see for its own sake, by comparison, is **Bragança**, distinguished by an evocative castle and an alluring old town center. Much the same goes for **Chaves**, a touch less striking but noted for its spa and pretty riverside setting. The scenery between these two towns is also outstanding.

Where landscape is concerned, the region comes up trumps virtually everywhere. Some of the finest scenery lies in the north, close to Bragança, where a tract of the area's most rugged country is protected by the **Parque Natural de Montesinho**. In the southwest, close to Vila Real, the smaller Parque Natural de Alvão embraces an enclave of rustic hamlets and wild granite hills. The town of **Miranda do Douro** in the east is also worth a visit, particularly in spring, when the surrounding almond groves are laden with blossom.

78

The pillory and ancient granite porca *in Bragança*

▶▶ Bragança 76C2

The capital of the Trás-os-Montes is reputed to have been founded as Brigantio by King Brigo IV of Spain in 960 BC. It was garrisoned by Julius Caesar, becoming Juliobriga, and then disputed by Moors and Christians during the four centuries leading up to Portuguese unification. But if its name seems familiar it's because it was once the fiefdom of the Bragança dukes, the dynasty that provided Portugal's kings from 1640 until the monarchy was abolished in 1910. Their rise began in 1442, when the bastard son of João I, eighth Count of Barcelos, was made Duke of Bragança by the acting regent, Dom Pedro, as a sop to a fractious nobility. Several generations later, in 1640, the eighth duke was made King João IV (see pages 37 and 38). Thenceforth, the heir to the throne was invariably made Duke of Bragança. Incidentally, it was a Bragança scion, the hapless Catherine, who became wife of Britain's philandering Charles II (she is said to have introduced the British to the ritual of afternoon tea).

Today, apartment blocks and new houses blight the town's outskirts, but away from these Bragança retains a peerless medieval center, its huddle of whitewashed houses gathered behind high walls that skirt a formidable keep. Until recently, this tight-bound enclave was a byword for isolation, a situation now changed by the construction of new roads to Mirandela and the south. That said, the town is still one of Portugal's remoter bases, remaining stranded on the road to almost nowhere save Spain. However, for visitors it makes a good base for exploring the Trás-os-Montes and the Montesinho Nature Park in particular (see pages 85–86).

OLD TOWN The wall-bounded old town, known as the **Cidadela▶▶▶**, glowers over its surroundings from a 2,165-foot-high (660m) aerie. The place to start exploring is at its focus, a great fist of a castle called the **Torre da Menagem** (tel: 273 322 378. *Open* Fri–Wed 9–12, 2–5. *Admission: inexpensive*). Rebuilt over earlier foundations in 1187, it was restrengthened in the 15th century by João I

Bragança has been a garrison town since the days of Julius Caesar

79

PRACTICALITIES
Bragança's tourist office (tel: 273 381 273) lies on the northern side of town in the middle of Avenida Cidade de Zamora. Trains no longer run to the town, but most local buses still congregate outside the old station, in the north-western corner of town at the end of Avenida João da Cruz; the town center, Praça da Sé, is just 200 yards (200m) away. Regular buses run to Mirandela, Vila Real, Viseu, Porto, and Miranda do Douro. Slightly less frequent services connect to Chaves, Coimbra, Lamego, and Lisbon.

MURDERED WIFE
Among the past inhabitants of Bragança's castle tower was the unfortunate Dona Leonor, wife of Dom Jaime, who was imprisoned here by her husband on suspicion of adultery. Jaime later had his captive murdered in Vila Viçosa, the principal seat of the Bragança dukes (few of the ducal dynasty actually spent much time in Bragança).

CELTIC PIGS
The Trás-os-Montes boasts some 200 or more *porcas*, or *berrões*, granite pigs or boars, some up to 6 feet (2m) in length and almost certainly pagan in origin. Little is known of their intended purpose, although they were probably involved in the fertility cults practiced by local Celtic and Ibero-Celtic tribes. The Celts had numerous deities, and saw cause for worship in all manner of natural objects and phenomena. A boar, in this context, might have been seen as a symbol of strength and power. Most of the *porcas* have been moved over the centuries from their original sites, usually circular enclosures suggesting some sort of temple; many are now installed by roadsides and in village squares. Some have inscriptions, most of which date to the 1st–3rd centuries AD, although the objects themselves are almost certainly older.

and Afonso V. The ramparts offer extensive views, while the keep houses a modest regimental museum, the Museu Militar (tel: 273 322 378. *Open* Fri–Wed 9–noon, 2–5).

South of the fort is the **Igreja de Santa Maria** (1710–1715), noted for its barrel-vaulted *trompe l'oeil* ceiling and painted *Assumption*. Just behind the church lies the unusual **Domus Municipalis**, founded on an irregular pentagonal plan, and probably the oldest town hall in Portugal. It is also one of the few civic buildings in the country to have retained its Romanesque appearance (similar buildings, like many of the country's churches, were usually altered in the 16th and 18th centuries). Near by, just beyond the keep, stands the town's **pelourinho** (**pillory**), a Gothic affair mounted astride a *porca*, one of the region's famous prehistoric granite pigs (see panels, left and on page 78).

OTHER SIGHTS Immediately north of the citadel, on Rua São Francisco, stands the little church of **São Bento▶▶**.

This is Bragança's most appealing church, and features a painted ceiling similar to the one in Santa Maria as well as a rarer *mudéjar* ceiling in the chancel. The latter's neo Moorish design, speckled with patterned wooden inlays, was a favourite among architects during the Manueline period. Some 200 yards (200m) to the west lies **São Vicente**, lauded for its gilded altarpiece and reputedly where Dom Pedro the Cruel and Inês de Castro were secretly married in 1354 (see page 164).

A short walk further west, on Rua do Conselheiro Abilio Beça, brings you to the **Museu do Abade de Baçal▶▶** (tel: 273 331 595. *Open* Tue–Sun 10–5. *Admission: inexpensive*). In the 16th-century Bishop's Palace, its collection includes a range of ecclesiastical artifacts, ethnographic displays, wooden canopies from local churches, and paintings by Abel Salazar and Alberto de Sousa. Its gardens harbor a selection of archaeological fragments, among them a collection of ancient stone *porcas*.

The walls and castle of the old citadel command the heights of Bragança

PRACTICALITIES

The Chaves tourist office lies in the gardens just to the east of the old town center at Rua Terreiro de Cavalaria 1-Dto (tel: 276 340 660). The nearest train station is at Vila Real, some 38 miles (61km) distant. Regular buses run to the town from Braga, Bragança, Vila Real, and Mirandela, the nearest major towns, as well as from Lisbon, Coimbra, Porto, Viseu, Lamego, and Amarante.

Tiled decoration in the Misericórdia

▶▶ Chaves   76B2

Chaves means "keys" in Portuguese, a clue to this sleepy town's strategic role over the centuries. Lying just 7.5 miles (12km) from the Spanish border, it has long been a crucial link in northern Portugal's defensive armor. It first rose to prominence, however, as a result of its thermal waters, whose healing qualities led the Emperor Flavius Vespasianus to found the small colony of Aquae Flaviae here in AD 78. Around 20 years later the settlement received a further boost, when the Emperor Trajan built a 300-foot (90m) bridge across the Tâmega, the river on which the town stands. This provided a vital link in the road joining Braga and Astorga (in present-day Spain), creating a bridging point that encouraged the town's subsequent development. However, both the Moors and Suevi razed the town in later centuries. In 1160, on its recapture from the Moors, a castle was built as a riposte to the nearby Spanish fortress of Verín.

Chaves today occupies a less important role, although its position at the heart of fertile country—an unusual commodity in the Trás-os-Montes—makes it one of the region's more important agricultural centers. It is also the largest town for miles around, providing a good base for excursions, as well as being a peaceful and pretty place in its own right.

TOWN SQUARE Life in Chaves centers on the **Praça de Camões▶▶**, the old town's main square. This is home to most of the key sights and lies close to the former keep, the garden-flanked **Torre de Menagem**, all that survives of the town's 14th-century fortress. Two sturdier 17th-century fortresses remain to the east, but one is closed to the public and the other, the Forte de São Francisco, has been converted into a hotel (tel: 276 333 700). The keep's four floors house the **Museu Militar**, a military museum whose collection moves chronologically through displays on medieval warfare to exhibits relating to World War I and Portugal's wars in Africa (tel: 276 340 500. *Open* Tue–Fri 9–12:30, 2–5:30, Sat–Sun 2–5:30. *Admission:*

inexpensive; includes entry to Flaviense Museum). Steps lead to the ramparts, where dizzying views extend across the town and its surrounding country.

On the square itself, which is watched over by a statue of Dom Afonso, first Duke of Bragança, stands the **Igreja da Misericórdia▶**, whose interior is swathed in *azulejos* depicting New Testament scenes, including episodes from the *Life of Christ*. On the square's southern flank lies the **Igreja Matriz**, a church whose Romanesque origins can still be seen in the ancient main portal. To its rear stands the town's Manueline pillory. On the *praça*'s northern edge is the **Museu da Região Flaviense▶ ▶** (*Open* the same hours as Museu Militar), a moderate collection housed in a former Bragança palace. Its slightly disordered displays are devoted to folk and archaeological treasures, including numerous prehistoric and Roman remains, coins, sculptures, altars, ox-carts, and other ethnographic artifacts.

OTHER SIGHTS Chaves' **spa** (*Open* all year) lies to the west of the old town's tight little huddle, and is set in a pleasant park that reaches down to the river. The water emerges at a steamy 163°F (73°C), making it one of the warmest thermal springs in Europe. As is so often the case with spas, the water doesn't taste terribly good, but, if the claims are to be believed, it's useful in the treatment of gout, rheumatism, liver problems, obesity, hypertension, and digestive ailments.

Following the riverside gardens round to the south, you reach Trajan's Roman bridge, the **Ponte Trajano▶**. It is still a stirring sight, despite having lost various of its arches and parapets over the centuries. You can rent pedalo boats for a closer look, but don't be tempted to swim in the river—it's too polluted for safety. While in town be sure to sample some of Chaves' famous hams and sausages, as well as its *folar*, a pork bread, all of which are renowned across Portugal (*presunto*, a smoked ham, is the best). The region's robust red wine makes the perfect accompaniment to all three specialties.

Chaves was a key bridging point on the ancient road to Spain

CHAVES POTTERY
Chaves is renowned not only for its pork products, but also for its distinctive black pottery. Made for centuries in the surrounding villages, the appealingly naive ware acquires its distinctive luster by being fired in an ash- and earth-covered pit, a process that restricts the amount of oxygen present during firing. Examples can be bought at shops around the town, but a less expensive place to browse is the village of Vilar de Nantes, one of the main centers of production (the village is also known for its basketmaking).

Trás-os-Montes

PRACTICALITIES
Miranda's tourist office is on Largo do Menino Jesus (tel: 273 431 132). A large *feira*, or market, takes place on the first weekday of every month.

DANCING
Miranda is widely renowned for a dance, the *pauliteiros*, performed by the town's menfolk on saints' days and feast days, most notably the feast of St. Barbara (the third Sunday in August). *Paulitos* are sticks, which the men strike, suggesting the event has its origins in an ancient sword dance. Music is provided by bagpipes, cymbals, and drums.

Mogadoura Castle ruins near Miranda do Douro

▶▶ Miranda do Douro 76C1

Miranda glowers at Spain from a promontory above the Douro gorge. Its outskirts are modern, but the five cobbled streets and white houses of the old center are a delight and it has two outstanding sights: a cathedral and a museum. The town dates back to at least Roman times, but the date fixed in its collective memory is 1762, when an explosion caused by besieging Franco-Spanish troops destroyed 200 houses, much of the castle, and killed 400.

Miranda's former **cathedral▶▶▶** (*Open* Wed–Sun 10–12:15, 2–4:45, Tue 2–4:45) and its "city" status arose after 1545, when the Church, fearful of the rising influence of the Bragança dukes, appealed to Pope Paul III to make the town the seat of a bishopric (thus shifting one axis of power from Bragança to Miranda). The appeal was promptly granted, and work began on the cathedral seven years later. In the event, the diocesan capital was transferred to Bragança in 1782, although the cathedral remains a memorial to two centuries of religious renown. Its highlights include a high altarpiece, decorated with reliefs of the *Assumption* and *Episodes from the Life of the Virgin*, several allegorical 16th-century paintings depicting the *Months of the Year*, and a 16th-century chest used as the cathedral safe.

The town museum, the **Museu da Terra de Miranda▶▶▶** (tel: 273 431 164. *Open* Oct–Mar, Mon 2–5:15, Tue–Sat 10–12:15, 2–5:15, Sun 10–12:15; Apr–Sep, Mon 2:30–5:45, Tue–Sat 10–12:45, 2:30–5:45, Sun 10–12:45. *Admission: inexpensive*) is equally captivating, largely because of the wonderful variety and eccentricity of its exhibits. Local costumes include some of the thick woolen capes for which the region is famous (modern copies can be bought in local craft shops). The best displays, however, are those which offer illuminating insights into the region's rural way of life, such as an iron grille used to hang slaughtered pigs and a cork container used to keep water warm.

The region is famous for the strange dialect spoken in its remoter areas. Mirandês, the only such patois in Portugal, is a mix of bastardized Latin, Galician, Spanish, and Hebrew.

►► Parque Natural de Montesinho (Montesinho Nature Park) 76C2

The Montesinho (or Montezinho) Nature Park, created in 1979, lies in Portugal's northeastern extremity, bounded by Spain to the north and Bragança to the south. It is one of the country's largest protected areas, extending for 290 square miles (750sq km) across the Serra do Corôa and Serra do Montesinho, and embracing a region of benign rolling hills (ranging in height from 1,444 feet, or 440m, to 4,875 feet, or 1,486m, to 4,875 feet, or 1,486m, wood-swathed valleys, and vast spreads of fertile agricultural land. The **scenery►►►** is timeless and the area is one of the last bastions of an ancient way of life, one that even in the rugged outback of the Trás-os-Montes is fast disappearing.

Old ways of life die hard in Rio de Onor, a typical Montesinho village

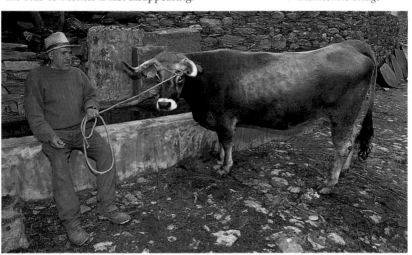

85

VILLAGES Some 90 villages and hamlets lie scattered around the park (with a total population of less than 10,000), any combination of which will reveal a host of alluring pastoral and traditional vignettes. Some settlements, such as Fresulfe or Sernande, bear Germanic names, memorials to the Visigoths who founded them. If a few are slightly spoiled then it is perhaps the fault of returning emigrants, whose newfound wealth is suddenly lavished on modern dwellings which seem at odds with the slate-roofed houses that have stood locals in good stead for centuries.

One of the more famous villages is **Rio de Onor**, its fame due largely to the fact that it was the subject of an anthropological study in the 1950s. It is also known, intriguingly, because its huddle of houses straddles the border between Portugal and Spain. Little distinguishes the two halves of the village—just the name Riohonor de Castilla and a slightly superior road surface on the Spanish side. Life here, as in other local villages, has been communal in the strictest sense since time immemorial, with land, crops, flocks, and grazing all shared or divided according to practical cooperative principles. A communal dialect, Rionorês, a mixture of Spanish and Portuguese, is also spoken locally. Coming here offers a glimpse of life from centuries past (the road to Bragança is barely 20 years old)

PRACTICALITIES
The head office of the Parque Natural de Montesinho is located in Bragança at Apartado 90, Lote 5, Bairro Salvador Nunes Teixeira (tel: 273 381 234. *Open* Apr–Sep, Mon–Fri 9–12:30, 2–5:30). It provides leaflets on the park's flora and fauna, hiking routes, and details of other outdoor activities. It also offers advice on camping, and carries lists of the park's *casas abrigos*, rural accommodations that can be rented nightly or on a weekly basis. Accommodations are otherwise thin on the ground, although in some villages it is usually possible to rent private rooms.

Storm clouds gather above the Montesinho Nature Park

POMBALS

If you drive, bike, or walk around Montesinho Park it won't be long before you come across a *pombal*, or pigeon coop. These distinctive white horseshoe-shaped buildings date from the days when pigeons were bred and kept as food. Most *pombals* are almost identical in size and shape, and they form a beautiful complement to the region's gentle landscape.

but it is just as picturesque as any number of villages in the region. Fresulfe, Santo Cruz, and Monfreita are other hamlets you might aim to squeeze into an itinerary.

FLORA AND FAUNA If you can get off the beaten track—not difficult to do—or manage a little hiking, then you should be rewarded with an insight into the park's noted flora and fauna. A variety of microclimates here buck the climatic trend of the *terra fria*, the region of the Trás-os-Montes known for the harsh extremes of its summer and winter weather. The park's wetlands, woodlands, moorland, and grassy meadows support a wide variety of wild flowers, including cistus, arbutus, violets, orchids, asphodel, clematis, campanulas, wild crocuses, and a number of heathers. Among the rarer fauna are eagles, black storks, and the Iberian wolf, together with smaller mammals such as hares, martens, red and roe deer, otters, and wild boar.

HIKING If you want to walk it's worth calling in on the park's main information office in Bragança (see panel on page 85), which has a handful of pamphlets on local hikes. The Sabor river valley near França, 6 miles (10km) north of Bragança, is particularly pretty and easily accessed. França is a good launching pad for walks generally and is connected (like Rio de Onor) to Bragança by one or two buses daily. You should also be able to rent bikes here, or sign up for pony riding in the hills round about. Inquire at the park office for further details.

►► Vila Real 76A1

Few visitors come to Vila Real for its intrinsic charm, which, truth be told, is rather lacking. Most come instead to visit the **Solar de Mateus►►►**, the beautiful baroque villa immortalized on the labels of Portugal's famous Mateus Rosé wine bottles. It lies some 2.5 miles (4km) east of the town, which, for all the beauty of its setting (it is sunk amid vineyards and backed by misty mountains), is a place that has been spoiled by light industry and extensive suburbs. The villa is therefore best seen while traveling to or from Bragança, or as a day trip from either Amarante or Lamego (see pages 115 and 116–117).

Strictly speaking, the *solar* is a *quinta*, or manor house, rather than a palace. According to Portuguese lore a house can only be called a palace when a member of royalty has spent a night in the building. It was completed around 1745, a time when baroque architecture in Portugal was close to its zenith. The architect is unknown, although most authorities cite Nicolau Nasoni, an Italian who was the greatest influence on the evolution of the baroque in northern Portugal (much of his best work is to be found in Porto). In appearance the palace is as alluring as the wine labels suggest, the contrast of its whitewash, granite, and pinnacled roof forming a beautifully pleasing whole. To the building's left stands a chapel (1750), executed in similar vein. It, too, is attributed to Nasoni, or to José de Figueiredo Seixas, one of his pupils. The pool in front of the palace was added in the 1930s. Thirty-minute guided tours (tel: 259 323 121. *Open* summer, daily 9–1, 2–7; winter, daily 9:30–1, 2–6. *Admission: expensive*) enable you to see the interior, whose furniture, engravings, paintings, and carved ceilings are a perfect foil for the 18th-century exterior. To the front and rear of the palace are some exquisite formal gardens, distinguished by a wonderful tunnel-like avenue of box hedges.

PRACTICALITIES
Vila Real's tourist office is the building with the eye-catching Manueline windows at Avenida Carvalho Araújo 94 (tel: 259 322 819).

You can reach Vila Real by train on a little branch line from Peso da Régua to the south (Peso lies on the Douro–Porto–Pocinho line). The station is located across the river just 500 yards (0.5km) east of the town center.

The main Rodonorte bus terminal is just north of the center on Rua Dom Pedro de Castro. Note that buses for Mateus leave roughly half-hourly from alongside the police station just west of the town hall.

87

Sleeping beauty—the Solar de Mateus near Vila Real

Emigration has been a fact of life in Portugal for centuries, first as a feature of the great voyages of discovery that shaped its far-flung empire, but more recently as a result of the desperate poverty that has wracked this most economically backward of countries.

ABSENT POPULATION

Some 3 million Portuguese, or 30 percent of its 10 million population, are estimated to live and work abroad. Many remit their money home, only returning to Portugal during the summer before leaving again for their "temporary" homes in Europe, Canada, Brazil, Venezuela, and the United States.

HOMEWARD BOUND

Whereas early emigrants to Brazil and North America often settled permanently, the trend of more recent migrants to Western Europe has been to return to Portugal, either on retirement for good or long enough to see family and friends. Year by year many pay another installment on their dream home—the often gaudy *casas de emigrante* that have sprouted in many of the Minho and Trás-os-Montes towns and villages. These exiles have been joined by the so-called *retornados*, the Portuguese emigrants forced by war to flee Portugal's former African colonies. Some 700,000 of these unfortunates, many of them penniless, returned in the 1970s. Another 100,000 may return now that Macau, another Portuguese colony, has reverted to Chinese rule.

Portuguese emigrants bound for the New World in 1926

Discovery "God gave the Portuguese a small country as cradle but all the world as their grave." So wrote Antôntio Vieira, a 17th-century Jesuit priest, encapsulating the peculiar triumph and tragedy of Portugal's long history of emigration. Portugal has been a nation for centuries—far longer than many European countries—and the Portuguese as a people have a strong attachment to the country of their birth. At the same time they have long been driven by dreams of discovery, the fate of many a people whose country looks out to sea. The Portuguese even have a word for this impulse, *partidas*, whose noble connotations once signified the urge to seek wealth and glory in foreign lands. First it drove a handful of explorers, disciples of Henry the Navigator, into voyages of discovery (see pages 226–227), and later it prompted Portuguese emigrants to settle the new lands. Madeira and the Azores were the first to be filled, followed by Africa and more distant lands. Settlers flocked to the colonies not only for the chance of a new life and the promise of land, but also for the opportunity to seize a share of the gold, spices, and other prizes of the empire.

Brazil After Africa, the next great wave of emigration was to Brazil, prompted by the discovery of gold at the end of the 17th century. Thousands were lured west in the first great gold rush of modern times, and the exodus intensified soon after with the discovery of diamonds. At first the drift of emigrants excited little concern as the gold pouring in from South America funded a new wave of palace- and church-building in the home country.

Half-deserted villages are a legacy of Portugal's long history of emigration

As the Portuguese consolidated their presence in Brazil, however, the New World began to attract economic migrants driven not by *partidas* but by poverty. The reasons were many and, taken together, provided powerful incentives for a huge number of Portuguese to abandon their country. The Napoleonic Wars, along with the civil unrest that followed, left Portugal financially crippled, while the Industrial Revolution that gathered pace elsewhere in Europe passed Portugal by.

Patterns of land ownership that had remained entrenched for centuries kept most Portuguese in feudal bonds, while work, even in the burgeoning cities, was hard to come by. Between 1886 and 1926 an estimated 1.3 million people left Portugal for Brazil. Worse was to follow.

Europe When the lure of Brazil subsided, emigrants began to look closer to home. The Portuguese have a little joke that Europe was the continent they discovered last as it was here that they turned next. Poverty continued to be the driving force, reinforced by the desire to escape the conscriptive measures introduced by Portugal's new Republican government. Mozambique and Angola also took more emigrants (100,000 by 1945) as did Argentina, Venezuela, and the United States. Later, as Salazar's dictatorship took hold, conscription (again) and unpopular colonial wars compounded the ever-present urges of hunger and poverty.

The countries of northern Europe remained the exiles' favored destination, particularly after World War II when labor shortages there provided an economic lifeline to the peasants of the Minho, Trás-os-Montes, and the Azores. Around 1.3 million Portuguese emigrated between 1926 and 1966, out of a total population of 7 million. The oil crisis of the mid-1970s, when recession struck Europe, together with the revolution of 1974, stanched the flow of emigrants, although an extraordinary number of Portuguese still live and work abroad: 780,000 in France, 80,000 in Germany, 70,000 in Switzerland, and 35,000 in Britain.

FIGURES
No one can ever know the exact numbers of exiles and immigrants of Portuguese blood now settled abroad. However, Brazil probably has a Portuguese population of well over a million, some 1.2 million US citizens are of Portuguese extraction, South Africa has 650,000 Portuguese, Canada has 400,000, Venezuela has 160,000, and Australia is home to some 50,000.

Fides

Spes

Quis. Audivit
llquam tale

The Minho

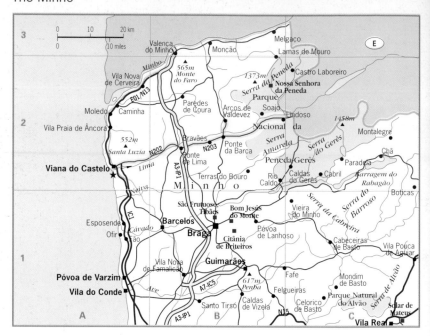

GETTING AROUND

You need your own transportation to get the most out of areas such as the Peneda-Gerês National Park. A car is also useful, although to a lesser extent, to uncover the best of the Lima and Minho valleys. This said, the bus network extends to even the most remote areas, with large towns such as Braga and Guimarães offering a plethora of long-haul and local connections. Trains from Porto run to Braga and Viana do Castelo, with onward connections from the latter along the Minho Valley as far as Valença do Minho.

Pages 90–91: ornate carving in Braga's Cathedral

Opposite: the scenery of the Minho is some of the loveliest in Portugal

THE MINHO Every country has a region that has been more than usually blessed with its share of natural beauty, and in Portugal that region is the Minho. Running from north of Porto to the Spanish border, the area is a bucolic ensemble of gentle river valleys, pastoral vineyards, and rolling woodlands. On the higher granite plateaus, forests and woodlands are interspersed with windy, sun-dappled pastures, and ranged across the landscape lie dozens of villages and thousands of smallholdings, the bedrock of a way of life that has seen little change over the centuries. Oxen still pull plows across the steeply terraced land, and festivals and country fairs continue traditions that date back centuries. To the modern visitor it all looks impossibly quaint, but to generations of locals the realities of a traditional way of life have been reason enough to leave. Like the Trás-os-Montes to the east, the Minho has long been blighted by emigration. The region is picturesque, but, in the words of Henry James, it is the "picturesqueness of large poverty."

TOWNS AND VILLAGES This remains less true in the towns, where light industry and tourism have brought an increasing measure of prosperity. **Braga**, the Minho's capital, bustles with commercial vigor, in stark contrast to its traditional role as Portugal's leading religious center. The town itself is nice enough, but it is the sanctuary at Bom Jesus, with its sublime baroque staircase, that makes a visit here unmissable. Nearby **Guimarães** is equally compelling, not least because it was the cradle of modern Portugal, having been the country's first capital and the birthplace of its first king.

Other towns are smaller, but no less interesting. Many, though, are best seen as part of an extended tour, something that is easily accomplished as the Minho is a small

The Minho

DANCES
The Minho's folk-dances are renowned across Portugal. Most are distinguished by powerful rhythms, and many are accompanied by traditional songs. Two of the most forceful are the *gota* and *vira espanhol*, while the *perim* and *malhão* are designed to show off the traditional costume of dancers to best effect.

region, and ambling between the close-lying towns and villages is simple. This is particulary true of the area's two main rivers, the Minho and the Lima—both timelessly beautiful—along which are dotted villages that can be linked as part of a leisurely drive (see page 97). On the Minho, the more northerly valley, **Valença do Minho** is the main stop, one of several fortress towns that have long guarded Portugal's border with Spain. On the Lima, the prettier of the two rivers, **Ponte de Lima** and **Ponte da Barca** are the main diversions. Neither have much by way of sights, but both manage to capture the rural essence of old-world Portugal.

Enjoying the Minho's sandy coastline

Capela dos Reis, Braga Cathedral

NATURAL ATTRACTIONS Beauty of a more uncompromising nature awaits in the **Parque Nacional da Peneda-Gerês**, Portugal's only national park, an area of high granite hills and mountains ideally suited to hiking and outdoor activities. This is a remote region, however, and is still not properly equipped to deal with large numbers of visitors. Much the same goes for the Minho's coast, although for different reasons. Vast beaches line the region's shoreline, an area dubbed the Costa Verde, or "Green Coast," by the tourist authorities. It is green for a reason, namely the large amounts of rainfall it receives—and even when it's not raining, summer days remain at the mercy of Atlantic depressions. Sea temperatures are cool as a result and the number of resorts few, despite the glorious beaches. This said, lively little **Viana do Castelo** has made the best of it, and is the closest thing in the region to a traditional seaside town.

MARKETS AND FESTIVALS Food and wine, as elsewhere, provide attractions in their own right (see panel), but perhaps the Minho's most tempting peripheral charm is to be found in its plethora of renowned festivals and markets. Virtually every town has a vast weekly market (that at Barcelos is extraordinary), while religious festivals, or *romarias* (held in honor of local patron saints), take place in most towns and villages. All are an excuse for the townspeople to let their hair down, with music, dancing, and traditional costumes usually well to the fore. Some of the more famous include the Festas Gualterianas in Guimarães (first weekend in August); Braga's Festas de São João (June 23–24) and Holy Week festivities (Easter); and, the most famous of them all, Viana do Castelo's spectacular Nossa Senhora da Agonia, held during the weekend closest to August 20.

WINE
The Minho is famous for Vinho Verde, an easygoing and lightly sparkling wine made (officially) nowhere else. Low in alcohol (usually around 9 percent), it is best drunk very chilled, either as an aperitif or with seafood. Most of the wine comes from climbing vines, introduced into the region in the 17th century to make the best use of the Minho's limited agricultural land (other crops and fruit could be grown under the trellised or trailing vines). *Verde* ("green") refers not to the wine's color but to the "youth" of the wine when it is drunk (usually the year after production). Some 60 percent of Vinho Verde is actually red, although it is still usually drunk chilled. Gatão, sweeter than most brands, is one of the best-selling wines, along with Alvarinho.

The weekly market in Barcelos is one of Portugal's largest

INFORMATION

Barcelos's tourist office, which occupies the old town keep, is located between the Campo da Feira and the old center on Largo da Porta Nova (tel: 253 811 882).

BARCELOS COCKS

Wherever you go in Barcelos it's hard to avoid the ubiquitous "Barcelos cock," painted pottery and wooden models of which assault you from every ceramic shop and souvenir stall—it has even been adopted as an emblem by the Portuguese tourist authority. The cock's story is simple, and repeats a tale told (with variations) across the Iberian peninsula. It concerns a Galician pilgrim bound for Santiago de Compostela who found himself unjustly accused of theft on leaving Barcelos. Despite his pleas of innocence, he was found guilty and sentenced to death. Looking at the roast cockerel being prepared for the judge's dinner, he invoked the help of St. James, saying that if he were innocent the dead cock would sit up and crow. The bird promptly performed as required, ensuring the man's release.

►► Barcelos 92B1

Barcelos is worth visiting not so much for the town itself—although it does have its charms—as for its famous weekly **market►►►**. This means timing a visit for Thursday morning, but as accommodations are almost impossible to come by on Wednesday evenings it is probably best to come here for the day (perhaps from Braga or Viana do Castelo). The market is in the Campo da República, or Campo da Feira, a vast open space crammed with row upon row of stalls selling everything from chickens and chainsaws to peas and pottery. More picturesque than the stalls, however, are the rows of women seated before mats or crates laden with the produce of their smallholdings. The market also has a wealth of handicraft stalls.

There is plenty more to see. On the market square stand the **Igreja de Nossa Senhora do Terço►►** (on the northern flank) and the **Templo do Senhor da Cruz** (in the southwestern corner). The former, part of an 18th-century Benedictine abbey, features a glorious spread of *azulejos* on the *Life of St. Benedict*, created in 1713 by António de Oliveira Bernardes, one of the masters of 18th-century tile design (he also worked on the Lóios chapel at Évora; see page 198). The church of Senhor da Cruz, built in 1708, is best known for its gilt and plasterwork, as well as for its Greek-cross plan, which was to influence church design across the region.

A few hundred yards to the southwest, in the pretty cluster of hillside streets making up the old town, the main sights perch above the bucolic banks of the Rio Cávado. The 13th-century **Igreja Matriz**, altered in the 16th and 18th centuries, has a Romanesque doorway and a gold-tinged interior laden with more 18th-century *azulejos* and baroque decoration.

Just to the west lies the **Solar dos Pinheiros**, a captivating 15th-century Gothic townhouse, built around the same time as the town's *pelourinho*, or pillory, just to the south. If the weather is fine, pay a visit to the **Museu Arqueológico** (*Open* daily 10–12, 2–6. *Admission free*), an open-air museum housed in the grounds of the former Paço dos Condes, palace of the Counts of Barcelos (later the Dukes of Bragança).

Drive

Rio Lima

See map on page 92.

A drive from Viana to Lindoso through the towns and countryside of one of Portugal's prettiest river valleys 47 miles (75km).

The Lima may not have the length or sedate majesty of the Tagus, but it lacks for nothing in terms of scenery. The river rises in the central highlands of Spain and flows into the sea at Viana do Castelo (see pages 108–109). There are few sights along its course, but the countryside lining its banks is some of the most pastorally alluring in the country. You could easily drive east all the way from Viana, but the valley's best stretch lies between Ponte de Lima and Lindoso. The latter is a convenient point of access to the northern part of the Peneda-Gerês National Park (see pages 106–107). The route is largely self-evident—you follow the N202 and its continuation, the N203, along the valley's entire course.

From Viana the road follows the river's northern bank, idling across flattish country fringed by wooded hills. The first major town (14 miles, or 23km) is **Ponte de Lima►►►**, a pleasingly somnolent place (except in high summer). Of Roman foundation, it still boasts an evocative Roman bridge, a pretty parish church, the Igreja Matriz, and a tree-lined riverside promenade, the Alameda. At the end of the latter stands the convent of Santo António, whose church houses a modest museum. The streets, as ever, are delightful to wander in, particularly on Mondays, when the town comes alive during its fortnightly market.

Beyond Ponte de Lima the valley changes character as vine-covered hills begin to rise from the river's sinuous curves. Some 8 miles (13km) east of the town be certain to stop off in **Bravães►►►**, which contains the 12th-century Igreja de São Salvador, one of Portugal's finest Romanesque churches. Its main doorways, swathed in carvings, are outstanding, and are complemented in the interior by frescoes of St. Sebastian and the Madonna. **Ponte de Barca►►**, the next town, is almost as delightful as Ponte de Lima (once you have passed through its suburbs, which, as in many Portuguese villages and towns, provide an ugly introduction to the historical center). A modest 3-mile (5km) diversion to the north takes you to the equally appealing village of **Arcos de Valdevez►►**.

The magnificent Romanesque doorway leading to São Salvador in Bravães

Painted, patterned, and enameled tiles as a decorative art form are not unique to Portugal, but in no other country in Europe will you come across azulejos used so prolifically or so beautifully as an adornment to churches, shops, and homes—and even bus depots and train stations.

A CONTINUING TRADITION

Portugal's penchant for *azulejos* has not dimmed over the years. Tiles are still used as a form of contemporary decoration, one of the most notable examples being the painted *azulejos* created between 1987 and 1990 to decorate several of Lisbon's new Metro stations.

98

*Top: tile-decorated house in the Baixa, Lisbon
Below: the tiled ticket hall in Porto's train station*

Roots To the untutored eye one tile may look much like another, except for the colors. However, Portugal's *azulejo* tradition evolved through several clearly distinguishable phases, across several centuries. The first European tiles appeared in Spain, where they were used as decoration in Andalucia, a region that had long been in thrall to the Moors. Portugal's tiles also have their origins in Moorish architecture, the Portuguese word *azulejo* probably being a corruption of the Arabic *azraq* ("azure") or *zalayja* (meaning a smooth stone or polished piece of terracotta). They arrived in Portugal in the 15th century courtesy of Dom Manuel I, who was so impressed with the tiles in the Alhambra (in Granada) that he vowed to use them in his own royal place at Sintra.

These earliest tiles, or *alicatados*, were simple, single-color designs, usually cut into pieces to form geometric patterns. Early designs were hampered by the inability of craftsmen to mix tin-glazed colours, a problem resolved by using strips of metal foil, ridges of clay, or rivulets of linseed oil to separate different-colored enamels prior to firing. Further refinements were pioneered in the 16th

century, when majolica, an Italian method of production, was introduced. This involved coating the clay in a layer of white enamel which was then colored directly, thus increasing the number of decorative and painted possibilities. Flemish influences later superseded those of Spain, producing increasingly naturalistic and narrative designs.

Heyday The tile's evolution took a step backwards during Portugal's subjugation to Spain (1580–1640), a period of relative austerity. Financial restraints meant churches were decorated with cheaper monochrome tiles, although at the same time the arrival of Spanish craftsmen introduced a new vitality of design to the more reactionary Portuguese. Over the same period a new form of decoration was introduced, the so-called *de tapete*, or "carpet," in which 4, 16, or 36 blocks of blue and green tiles were arranged to resemble carpets or tapestries. With the restoration of the Portuguese monarchy in the second half of the 17th century, *azulejo* design received a further boost. The more traditional colors—blues and yellows—were complemented by green and purple (created with copper- and manganese-based glazes), while the narrative scope of panels was extended to include mythological scenes or episodes from daily life. Blue and white designs also became popular, thanks largely to the arrival in Europe of Ming Dynasty porcelain from China.

Simplicity Further innovation and decorative daring accompanied the arrival of João V, whose reign (1706–1750) coincided with the flood of newly discovered gold from Brazil. The resulting wealth allowed ever more complicated designs to be contemplated, tiles being used to describe vast pictorial scenes, while their borders became a riot of tiled tassels, cherubs, and other decorative motifs. Simpler designs were also popular, notably tiles that displayed a single motif, a style that owed much to Dutch tiles of the period. The emphasis on simplicity was encouraged in the aftermath of the 1755 earthquake, when the massive scale of rebuilding called for vast numbers of cheap tiles. Simpler motifs also predominated after the opening in 1767 of the Fábrica Real de Cerâmica, a huge factory that could produce tiles in large numbers.

At the beginning of the 19th century people began to cover entire church and house fronts in tiles, a habit copied from Brazil, where it had been found that tile facades were the best way to keep out rain and humidity. In time, the habit spread to all manner of private and civic buildings, notably shops, markets, and train stations.

HIGHLIGHTS
For the best overview of Portugal's *azulejo* tradition you should visit the Museu Nacional do Azulejo in Lisbon (see page 56). Other outstanding displays can be seen at the Palácio Nacional de Sintra (see page 67), the church of Lóios in Évora (see page 198), the Misericórdia in Viana do Castelo (see page 109), and Porto's train station (see photograph opposite and page 124).

99

Pictorial scenes began to appear on tiles in the 18th century

PRACTICALITIES

Braga's tourist office is at Avenida da Liberdade 1 (tel: 253 262 550), just off Praça da República, the town's central main square. The bus station (tel: 253 616 080) lies about five minutes' walk west of the square at Central de Camionagem. Regular daily services run to a wide range of local and national destinations, notably Porto.

The train station is further afield at Largo da Estação, 15 minutes' walk to the south of the main square. Services run to Nine, where you change for trains to Porto, Barcelos, and Viana do Castelo.

Note that Braga is also the home of the headquarters of the Peneda-Gerês National Park (see pages 106–107); the office is 20 minutes' walk west of the center in Avenida António Macedo (tel: 253 203 480. Open Mon–Fri).

FOUNTAINS

Bom Jesus's staircase begins with the Fountain of the Five Wounds, whose water issues from five spouts representing the Wounds of Christ and the five bezants of the Portuguese coat of arms. Each of the following five levels contains a fountain designed to symbolize one of the five senses. Thus water pours from eyes, ears, nose, and mouth, while touch is symbolized by a figure pouring water. This symbolic scheme suggests that pilgrims must overcome the earthly temptation of the senses before attaining the cardinal virtues—faith, hope, and charity—which are symbolized by the figures of the Fountain of the Three Virtues. Beyond this, the staircase balustrade is lined with statues of Old Testament figures.

►► Braga 92B1

The Minho's capital is one of the most religiously fixated towns in Portugal. The Church has been a dominant force in Braga for centuries (the town was once the seat of the primate of all Spain), and today Braga hosts some of the most important (if somber) of the country's Holy Week celebrations. It also lies close to the shrine of Bom Jesus, one of the masterpieces of European baroque.

Two millennia ago, Bracara was an important Roman colony, having been made capital of the newly conquered territory of Gallaecia in 27 BC (the present-day Minho and Galicia). No fewer than five Roman roads converged on the town, making it the focus of trade for a hinterland that extended many hundreds of miles. In AD 409 it was conquered by the Suevi, who made it their capital. In 585 it was sacked by the Visigoths, who absorbed it into their kingdom, and then around 703 it passed to the Moors. Today, Braga's traditional conservatism is giving way to a new commercial vigor, a change that has seen it become the largest town in Portugal north of Porto. Development has resulted in new roads and ugly suburbs, but the compact old center remains just as charming as ever.

OLD TOWN For all Braga's churches, only one, the **Sé (Cathedral)**►►►, really merits an extended visit (*Open* daily 8–6). Begun around 1070, it now comprises a confusing medley of architectural styles, and only the south door and the main portal arch survive from the original Romanesque building. The latter, sheltered beneath an arched Gothic porch, features fascinating Burgundian-influenced carvings depicting scenes from the *Chanson de Roland* and the *Roman de Renard*. The interior, a baroque conversion, boasts impressive ribbed vaulting and some tremendous carved and gilded woodwork.

To view its highlights, however, you must buy a moderately priced ticket for the **Museu de Arte Sacra** (*Open* winter, 8:30–5:30; summer, 8:30–6:30), which houses an impressive and varied collection of church treasures that is slightly spoiled by dismal presentation and wretched labeling. More worthwhile is the **Capela dos Reis** (off the cloisters), which contains the tombs of Teresa and Henry of Burgundy, the cathedral's founders and parents of Afonso Henriques, Portugal's first king. Alongside them lies the mummified body of Archbishop Lourenço Vicente, hero of the Battle of Aljubarrota.

Other sights include the former **Paço Episcopal (Archbishop's Palace)**►►, the vast building located opposite the cathedral (now the public library), and the lovely **Palácio dos Biscainhos** (tel: 253 217 645. *Open* Tue–Sun 9–12:30, 2–5:30. *Admission: inexpensive*), the best of the many eye-catching period buildings around town. It houses a modest museum crammed with furniture, carpets, tiles, and silverware, and there are also some peaceful gardens to the rear.

BOM JESUS You'll probably see the stunning baroque staircase at **Bom Jesus**►►► depicted in tourist literature long before you see it in reality. One of the best-known and most photogenic sights in northern Portugal, it lies in lovely wooded country just 3 miles (5km) east of Braga. Begun by the local archbishop in 1723, it was completed some 60 years later, while the neoclassical sanctuary at its summit dates from 1837. Surprisingly, given the staircase's splendor, there was no overwhelming reason—no miracle or sacred shrine (as at Fátima)—for its construction. This hasn't prevented it from becoming one of the country's most popular points of pilgrimage, although many people come for the beauty of the gray granite and whitewashed surrounds rather than as an act of faith. The woods hereabouts are also popular for walks and picnics, particularly at weekends.

You can drive or catch a water-powered **funicular** to the sanctuary, but it is far better to climb the staircase itself. This lets you enjoy its baroque folly at close hand, as well as the lovely **views** that unfold as you ascend. For believers, the climb represents a spiritual journey, a notion underlined by the symbolic arrangement of the stairway's landings, chapels, and fountains. A path winds up from the car park at the foot, a Holy Way lined with chapels and the Stations of the Cross. Beyond it lie the **Stairway of the Five Senses** and **Stairway of the Three Virtues**, both part of a unified schematic plan (see panel opposite). To enjoy the site at its best, aim to visit during the week, when things are considerably quieter.

SÃO FRUTUOSO AND TIBÃES
The chapel of São Frutuoso, located 2 miles (3.5km) northwest of Braga, is one of Portugal's oldest Christian buildings. Built by the Visigoths in the 7th century, it was later appropriated by the Moors and incorporated into the neighboring church in the 18th century. A short way beyond the road to the chapel lies Tibães, once Portugal's greatest Benedictine abbey but now an evocative ruin.

Beautiful views reward the climb to the top of the staircase at Bom Jesus

101

The ruins of the ancient Citânia de Briteiros, a Celtic stronghold 2,000 years ago

▶▶ Citânia de Briteiros 92B1

The Citânia de Briteiros is among Portugal's most complex and enticing archaeological sites. Perched on a 1,106-foot (337m) hilltop, it consists of a hill settlement, or *citânia*, which dates back to the days before the Roman invasion. Such hill forts were typical of the Castro culture that prevailed in northern Portugal in the neolithic era, and later were adopted and refined by the Iron Age Celtic tribes which entered the Iberian peninsula around 600 or 500 BC. Some 27 *citânias* have been discovered on the Minho coast, along with another 16 in the region between Braga and Guimarães. The Citânia de Briteiros, one of the best preserved, probably dates from 300 BC and may well have been one of the last Celtic strongholds before capitulation to the Romans around 26–19 BC.

Excavations, however, suggest that the fort continued to be inhabited until at least AD 300, undergoing little change—unlike Conimbriga (see page 148)—at the hands of its Roman conquerors.

The site (*Open* Tue–Sun 9–12:30, 2–5:30. *Admission: inexpensive*) was excavated in 1875 by Dr. Martins Sarmento, an archaeologist from nearby Guimarães. Most of the finds are now in the Guimarães museum, named after Sarmento (see panel on page 104), but plenty remains at the site to make it worth a visit (a plan is available at the entrance to help you understand the settlement). You can distinguish the low granite walls of some 150 huts, two of which Sarmento reconstructed to provide a vivid picture of how they might have appeared (their verisimilitude is now disputed). Also still clear are the various streets and paths that threaded through the settlement, together with two sets of outer walls (there were originally three or four) and traces of the original drainage and water systems. Away from the main settlement to the southeast lies the site's most contentious structure, often referred to as a funerary chamber but now believed to have been a cistern or bathhouse.

GETTING THERE
It is an easy enough drive to Citânia de Briteiros from Braga or Guimarães (it lies roughly equidistant between the two). Buses from Guimarães to Caldas da Taipas and Póvoa do Lanhoso pass the excavations. From Braga you need to take a bus to Caldas da Taipas and change there for the local bus that passes the site.

▶▶ Guimarães 92B1

Guimarães is almost the cradle of modern Portugal, having been its first capital and the birthplace of its first king, Afonso Henriques. Today, it is a large and bustling city, pocked with industrial outskirts (linen is a local specialty) but graced with one of the country's more beguiling and dignified old centers. Wandering through the attractive cobbled streets is a pleasure in itself, a pastime that leads you through a labyrinth of little lanes between tiny squares and past innumerable grand old houses. There is also a fine church in the town, two interesting museums, and, if you want to stay, a pair of magnificent *pousadas*—one in town and the other in nearby Penha (see panel on page 105).

HISTORY Guimarães began life in the 10th century as little more than a small earth and wood fortress, a huddle of houses, and a monastery built by the Countess Mumadona, a local noblewoman. Its rise to prominence began in 1095, when Henry of Burgundy strengthened the fortress and used it to house his new wife, Princess Teresa, illegitimate daughter of Alfonso VI, king of Léon and Castile. Alfonso had given his daughter to Henry partly as thanks for the latter's help against the Moors. With her came a dowry that included the principality of Portucale, part of the kingdom of Castile that would form the kernel of modern-day Portugal.

In about 1110 Henry and Teresa had a son, Afonso Henriques, who would become the new country's first king (see page 30). In 1128, at the Battle of São Mamede, Afonso supplanted his mother, who had acted as regent on Henry's death. He then attacked the Moors, refusing at the same time to acknowledge Alfonso VII as the new king of Castile. Instead, Afonso swore allegiance to the papacy, which belatedly recognized his dynastic claims in 1179. Guimarães remained his capital until 1143, when he moved his court to Coimbra.

COLEGIADA Guimarães's most important church, **Nossa Senhora da Oliveira** (**Our Lady of the Olive Tree**), lies in the central Largo da Oliveira and forms part of a complex of monastic buildings known as the **Colegiada▶▶**. It occupies the site of the monastery founded by the Countess Mumadona in the 10th century. Its name, however, dates from the 14th century, when an olive tree from the nearby shrine of São Torquato was replanted in front of the monastery to provide oil for the lamps of the conventual church. Traumatized by its uprooting, the tree not unnaturally died. It remained lifeless until September 8, 1342, when a cross placed on it caused the tree miraculously to sprout new foliage. The strange Gothic canopy and stone cross in front of the church celebrate the event.

Numerous buildings have come and gone on the site of the Colegiada since its foundation. Much of the present complex dates from around 1340, notably the Gothic pediment of the main portal and the bulk of the collegiate church. Within the monastery lies a set of earlier Romanesque cloisters, built in the 13th century and altered a century later as part of the extensions ordered by João I. As in the great abbey at Batalha, the new building work was carried out to honor a royal pledge in the wake of

PRACTICALITIES
Guimarães's main tourist office is just south of Largo do Toural at Avenida Resistençia ao Fascismo (tel: 253 412 450. *Open* Mon–Fri); the other is in Praça de Santiago just north of the Colegiada (tel: 253 518 790. *Open* Mon–Fri). The train station (tel: 253 412 351) is ten minutes' walk south of the center. There are regular trains to Porto. The bus station (tel: 253 516 229) is 15 minutes' walk to the west. Frequent express buses link to Porto and Lisbon. Local buses run regularly to Braga and Almarante.

103

SÃO FRANCISCO
This 15th-century church (remodeled in the 17th century) is worth visiting for the beautiful 18th-century *azulejos* in the chancel, its stately 16th-century Renaissance cloisters, and the ornate coffered ceiling of the sacristy. Find it beyond the gardens on the southern flanks of the old town.

Gilt and glitter in São Francisco

MUSEU DE MARTINS SARMENTO

This fine museum lies on the western fringe of the old town, partly contained within the 14th-century Gothic cloisters of the church of São Domingos (tel: 253 415 969. *Open* Tue–Sun 9:30–noon, 2–5. *Admission: inexpensive*). It takes its name from the 19th-century archaeologist responsible for many of the excavations at the neighboring Celto-Iberian forts at Sabroso and Citânia de Briteiros (see page 102). Most of its exhibits come from these two sites. Highlights include the famous *Colossus of Pedralva*, a huge granite figure dating from around 1000 BC; like similar statues from Trás-os-Montes, it may have figured in primitive fertility rites. More striking still is the Pedra Formoso, once believed to be a sacrificial altar but now thought to have formed part of the entrance to a funerary chamber.

104

João's victory against Castile at the Battle of Aljubarrota in 1385 (see pages 168–169).

Most of the surviving conventual buildings are now part of the superlative **Museu de Alberto Sampaio**▶ ▶ ▶ (tel: 253 412 465. *Open* Tue–Sun 10–12:30, 2–5:30. *Admission: inexpensive*), a wide-ranging museum named after a local sociologist. Its highlight is a sumptuous 14th-century triptych (three-paneled painting), given to Guimarães by João I, although stories vary as to how he came by it. Some say its silver gilt was made from the king's melted-down measuring weights, while others claim it was captured at the Battle of Aljubarrota (see pages 168–169), having formed part of a traveling chapel carried by Juan I, João's defeated Castilian adversary. Other treasures include the tunic reputedly worn by João during the battle, a large Manueline cross, and a wealth of outstanding ecclesiastical silver.

TO THE CASTLE On leaving the convent, turn right out of Largo da Oliveira to pick up **Rua de Santa Maria**▶ ▶ ▶, an ancient thoroughfare linking the monastery with the castle that glowers over the old town to the north. This beautiful street is lined with fine old buildings, the loveliest of which is the former convent of Santa Clara, now the local **Câmara Municipal** (**Town Hall**).

As you climb towards the castle you pass the **Paço dos Duques** (**Ducal Palace**)▶ ▶, built at the beginning of the

The castle at Guimarães, cradle of a nation

15th century by Dom Afonso I, illegitimate eldest son of João I (tel: 253 412 273. *Open* daily 9:30–5. *Admission: inexpensive*). Afonso became the first Duke of Bragança, and in time the building became one of the Braganças' principal ducal residences. It was constructed along Burgundian lines, partly because Afonso's architect was French, and partly because the duke had developed a cosmopolitan taste for foreign architecture during his service as a European diplomat. Today, the building suffers from a drastic restoration that took place in 1933, when it was remodeled on Salazar's orders to provide an official state residence. Inside, however, the various state rooms remain worth a look, principally for their redoubtable fireplaces and beautiful carved oak ceilings. There are also some outstanding tapestries, a bristling collection of armor and weapons, and a wide range of carpets, furniture, porcelain, and paintings.

Beyond the palace lies the church of **São Miguel**, a 12th-century Romanesque building which contains a font that reputedly was used to baptize the infant Afonso Henriques. Immediately above the church stands the **Castelo**►► (*Open* daily 9:30–5. *Admission: inexpensive*), begun by Mumadona and enlarged by Henry of Burgundy. Today, despite the dramatic appearance of its many towers, the castle rather lacks atmosphere, partly as a result of the fact that it was stripped for building stone in the 19th century.

PENHA
The best excursion from Guimarães is to the gentle slopes of Penha (2,024 feet, or 617m), 3 miles (5km) southeast of the town. It is one of the highest points of the Serra de Santa Caterina, offering wideranging views, and shelters the former monastery of Santa Marinha da Costa, founded in 1154 by Dona Mafalda, wife of Afonso Henriques. The wonderful medieval building is now a *pousada* (see page 255), but the fascinating chapel and beautiful gardens are open to all. If you stay, eat, or order a drink at the bar here, you'll catch a glimpse of more of the complex. Take a bus for Roque from the main tourist office in Guimarães; leave it at Costa, from where the monastery is a short walk.

INFORMATION
The tourist office in Gerês (tel: 253 391 133) is at the top end of town on the main street, Avenida Manuel Francisco da Costa. The main park information center (tel: 253 390 110) is a little farther up the same street beyond the spa. Both offices have information on hiking, but note that the readily available maps of the region are not suitable for detailed route finding.

ORGANIZED TOURS
Several companies in Braga offer organized walking, camping, and pony-riding tours into the Peneda-Gerês National Park. Inquire at the town's tourist office (see panel on page 100) for further details.

106

An ancient espigueiros, *or granary, near Soajo*

►►► Parque Nacional da Peneda-Gerês   92B2

If the Minho is the most beautiful area of Portugal—as many claim—then presumably it follows that the region's most beautiful enclave, the Peneda-Gerês National Park, is particularly outstanding. Devotees of other areas would probably disagree, but few parts of the country can match the scenery, flora, or fauna of this lovely park, nor its hiking and range of other outdoor activities.

Peneda-Gerês, currently Portugal's only national park, divides into two: the southerly region around the Serra do Gerês range; and the more northerly—and much wilder—area around the Serra da Peneda. The main center in the south is **Caldas do Gerês** (known simply as Gerês), one of the few places in the park with a plentiful supply of accommodations and a range of services. Elsewhere rooms are in short supply, so be sure to check with the various park centers and tourist offices before you set off (see panel).

Buses link certain villages in both the north and the south of the park, but to get the best out of the region you really need a car. Roads between the park's two sections are not terribly good, so the best plan of attack is to tour first one and then the other. In the south, you should start from Gerês, explore the country around the village, and then take the minor road east towards Montalegre. You can then return to Gerês or Braga on the N103. In the north, you can approach the park from Ponte da Barca to the west or Melgaço to the north. If you want to link up from Gerês and the south, the only road access is a short cut through Spanish territory to Lamas de Mouro. From here a road runs south, giving access to Soajo and Lindoso, two of the park's more interesting villages.

THE SOUTH Gerês, easily reached from Braga, is a spa town set in a wooded gorge, its pleasant pace of life disturbed only during summer weekends when huge numbers of people come here before heading off into the park. This is a good place to stay—if only because there are more accommodations here than in the rest of the park put together; it is also a useful source of information.

The most popular excursion from town is to the **Mira-duoro do Gerês**, a viewpoint that overlooks the Caniçada reservoir, one of several artificial lakes in the area. To see the reservoir at first hand, head for **Rio Caldo** (which has plenty of accommodations) and then loop north to São Bento (another good viewpoint and pilgrimage destination) before returning to Gerês by way of Campo de Gerês. Another coherent itinerary involves the road southeast to Ermide, from where you can head east to Montalegre (which has accommodations) via the tiny villages of Pincães, Cabril, and Paradela.

THE NORTH If you want to experience a taste of wilderness, head straight for the northern part of the park, which is quieter and less commercialized than the southern region owing to its relative inaccessibility. Most people make for **Soajo**, a remote village now increasingly dotted with new houses built by returning emigrants. It is widely renowned for its evocative crop of *espigueiros*, or grain stores. Some 20 or more of these curious granite constructions—resembling small houses topped with a cross—are

located just to the northwest of the village. They stand on a stony terrace, whose naturally windblown site made it ideal for winnowing grain. Once threshed, the grain was stored in the *espigueiros*, which were raised and roofed in slates to offer protection from rats.

More *espigueiros*, together with an equally traditional way of life, can be found at **Lindoso** (lindo means "beautiful"), reached along a steep road southeast from Soajo that affords grand views of the Lima Valley. By contrast, heading north to Lamas de Mouro provides a trip through a broader slice of the park. En route you pass the superbly situated **Nossa Senhora da Peneda**, a noted point of pilgrimage, while from Lamas you can make an excursion east to **Castro Laboreiro**, a remote village (again marred by modern houses) known for its hardy sheepdogs.

HIKING Walking is one of the pleasures of the Peneda-Gerês National Park. Unfortunately, most of the available maps are not terribly good and there are relatively few marked trails. However, there is a useful guide in English with recommended walks (see "Further reading" on page 251), and the park authorities are in the process of marking out the so-called Trilho de Longo Curso, a long-distance trail that will eventually traverse the park. At present two sections of the path are marked and documented in park pamphlets: from Cabril to Paradela and from Soajo to Lamas de Mouro; yellow markers and an acorn logo indicate the trail.

Woodland and water meet in the Peneda-Gerês National Park

LUCKY DIP
During the sorting of grain and corn in the shadow of the *espigueiros*, any man lucky enough to come across a rare red corncob may, according to tradition, claim a kiss from the woman of his choice.

The Minho

▶ **Valença do Minho**   92B3

Valença do Minho, more commonly known simply as Valença, sits on the southern bank of the Minho looking across to Spain. Its position has long made it a key bastion in Portugal's northern defenses, hence the superb double **fortress** that embraces the picturesque warren of streets making up the **old town▶▶**. The town's site proved virtually impregnable over the centuries, withstanding numerous Spanish and French attacks. These days its charm has left it virtually defenseless against the Spanish tourists who surge across the river to stock up on ceramics and cheap linen. However, if you are able to stay overnight you will find the town recovers its poise once the trippers have gone. As an added incentive, the town's *pousada* is one of the best in the region. Only the big weekly market (held on Wednesdays) is of interest in the modern town. The cobbled streets of the old town, by contrast, are well worthwhile, as are walks around the ramparts and down by the river. Views from the castle walls, in particular, are well worth the climb.

The town also serves as a useful base if you want to explore the Minho Valley to the east and west. One of the best excursions is to **Monte do Faro▶▶**, a 1,860-foot (565m) mountain some 4 miles (7km) from the town. Here, the panorama from the summit (you can drive all but the last little stretch) extends across the Minho to the Atlantic and mountains of Galicia. To the west you might visit the somnolent little riverside town of **Caminha▶**, known for its parish church, the Igreja Matriz, which boasts one of the country's most impressive wooden ceilings. En route you could drop in on **Vila Nova de Cerveira▶▶**, a town that retains its charm despite the crowds of day-tripping Spaniards. Perhaps the most rewarding part of the Minho Valley, however, lies east of Valença and can be enjoyed by driving along the river to the little fortress towns of **Monção▶▶** and **Melgaço▶**.

▶▶ **Viana do Castelo**   92A2

The Minho's tourist authorities, chasing visitors' gold, gamely try to promote their coastline as the Costa Verde ("Green Coast"), quietly neglecting to point out that while the beaches are stunning—huge and virtually undeveloped—the weather can often be appalling. This said, if you are blessed with sunshine then Viana do Castelo, the nearest thing to a resort on this section of the Atlantic coast, is an appealing prospect. Prosperous and likeable, the town is attractively poised on the Lima estuary with the tree-covered hill of Santa Luzia and its basilica framing it to the rear. It also hosts one of northern Portugal's premier festivals, a jamboree dedicated to Nossa Senhora da Agonia (held on the nearest weekend to August 20).

Wealth came to the area in the 16th century, when local fisherman began to net Newfoundland's Grand Banks. Merchants had long traded from the port, which became the most important in northern Portugal, shipping cod, wine, and textiles to England, and farther afield to Russia and Scandinavia. Proceeds from this trade went to finance the building of the Renaissance and Manueline houses that scatter the old center. To see the best of them, wander up and down **Rua de São Pedro** and **Rua Cândido dos Reis**.

More fine buildings gather around the main square, Praça da República, notably the 16th-century Paços do Concelho (town hall) and the Igreja Matriz (parish church). The latter has a pair of Romanesque towers, although the town's grandest sight is the superb Renaissance **Misericórdia▶▶**. The church alongside this house has some captivating *azulejos*, while still better ceramics can be found in the interesting **Museu Municipal▶▶** (tel: 258 820 678. *Open* Tue–Sun 9–12:30, 2–5:15. *Admission: inexpensive*), housed in an 18th-century palace on Rua Manuel Espregueira. Tiles cover its upstairs rooms, which also contain an outstanding collection of glazed earthenware, while downstairs rooms are devoted to furniture, ivories, and other precious artifacts.

The fine local beach, **Praia do Cabedelo▶▶**, situated across the estuary, can be reached by ferry from the foot of Avenida dos Combatentes, the town's principal street.

PRACTICALITIES
Viana do Castelo's tourist office (tel: 258 822 620) lies 200 yards (200m) southwest of the central Praça da República just off Praça da Erva. The train station (tel: 258 821 315) is just to the north of the old town at the northern end of the main Avenida dos Combatentes.

The Basilica of Santa Luzia, Viana do Castelo

109

Porto and the Douro

111

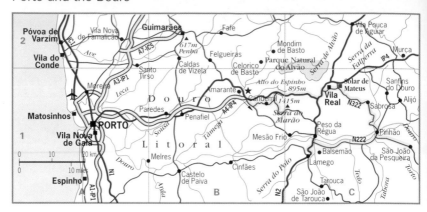

Pages 110–111: old houses in Porto crowd down to the docks on the River Douro

BOAT TRIPS
Once the Douro was a relatively wild and turbulent river, its path to the sea interrupted by waterfalls, whirlpools, and some 200 rapids. These days its fury has been tamed by eight major dams. Trips up the river remain possible, however, thanks to a series of locks, and many people choose to take a cruise as a means of sightseeing. These vary greatly in length and price. The shortest merely ply up and down the river in Porto's immediate environs, offering views of the city's famous bridges and a glimpse of some of the more local waterfront villages. Others spread over one or two days, venturing further up the river and offering a full package of food and accommodations. See the panel on page 126 for further details or consult the Porto tourist office (see panel on page 120).

PORTO Portugal's second city needs little introduction. For centuries its name has been synonymous with port, a wine produced along the banks of the Douro, the beautiful river that twists its way to the city through some of the country's loveliest scenery. Port still travels to Porto, or Oporto ("the Port"), although these days it gets there by road or rail, the traditional old boats once used now largely consigned to history. Much of the wine is also still stored in the city, decanted into barrels in the "lodges" that line the Douro's southern banks. Trips to these lodges provide the main incentive for a visit here, for Porto has a reputation as an industrial city with little for tourists. However, while sights are relatively thin on the ground, there is actually more to see than popular wisdom would suggest, not least the wonderful Museu do Soares dos

Porto's atmospheric waterfront district, the Ribeira, is lined with cafés and restaurants

Reis and the sumptuously decorated Igreja de São Francisco. And, as ever in Portugal, the modern suburbs conceal a tiny and delightful historic center.

THE DOURO The "River of Gold" is an appealing waterway that has its source in Spain but which enjoys its finest moments in Portugal. Put your mind to it and you should

Terraced slopes above the River Douro

The shrine of Nossa Senhora dos Remédios at Lamego

uncover some of the country's loveliest scenery while exploring its meandering course. Steeply terraced vine-covered hillsides plunge to the valley in its upper reaches, while lower down the deeply cut terrain gives way to gentler but no less pretty countryside.

Although driving the river's entire length is rewarding, it is also relatively time-consuming. You should allow a day, for example, to follow the valley's twists and turns from Porto to Pinhão, a little town known for its high-quality port. As an alternative, you might take the faster road to **Amarante**, a bucolic little town on the Tâmega river, and then cut south to explore the upper (and more spectacular) part of the Douro. You should also make a point of visiting **Lamego**, a baroque town known for Nossa Senhora dos Remédios, an important point of pilgrimage. And if you are driving, give some thought to your onward destinations, for itineraries from the upper Douro lead to Viseu, Vila Real, and the more remote corners of the Trás-os-Montes.

▶▶ Amarante 112B1

Amarante is unattractive on the outskirts, but remains a delightful town at its heart. Old balconied houses amble down to the willow-lined river, while the rest of the town rises in graceful tiers to meet the green-tinged hills to the rear. Founded around 360 BC as "Turdetanos," the town changed its name in honor of Amarantus, one of its later Roman governors (although other sources suggest the name comes from Ante Moranum, meaning "In Front of the Serra do Marão"). Much of the town's history, as well as its main sights, centers on the figure of São Gonçalo, a 13th-century hermit saint who spent much of his time in the town. Legend claims that he built a bridge here in 1220 (to reach his hermitage), a structure that survived until 1763, when it was replaced by the present triple-arched baroque span.

SÃO GONÇALO On the northern side of the bridge, off Praça da República, stands the church and monastery of **São Gonçalo▶▶**, the town's principal sight. Begun in 1540 under Dom João III, it was completed (some four kings later) in 1620. The loggia to the left of the side doorway, a fine Italianate Renaissance work, contains statues of the kings in question (João III, Sebastião, Henrique, and Felipe I). The doorway itself is surmounted by a statue of Gonçalo (died 1259), whose tomb lies in the ornately embellished interior to the left of the main altar. The saint's matchmaking powers (see panel) are the reason for the tomb's worn appearance, for tradition suggests that those hoping to get married need only touch Gonçalo's effigy for their wish to come true. Unfortunately, the statue was built in a soft limestone not designed for repeated caressing.

One of the monastery's two cloisters houses a small **museum** (*Open* Tue–Sun 10–12:30, 2–5. *Admission free*), devoted mainly to Amadeo de Sousa-Cardoso (died 1918), a local artist whose Cubist-inspired paintings achieved international renown. Elsewhere in the town the pretty streets provide their own rewards, particularly those by the river (notably Rua 31 Janeiro). The church of São Pedro (275 yards, or 250m, west of the main square on Rua São Pedro) has some lovely bands of decorative *azulejos* and a rich coffered wood ceiling.

PRACTICALITIES
The tourist office (tel: 255 432 259) forms part of the Câmara Municipal, which occupies one of the two former cloisters of São Gonçalo.

Amarante's train station lies on Rua João Pinto Ribeiro, just under 0.5 miles (1km) northwest of Praça da República, the town's main square.

The bus station is closer in, but lies in the town's opposite (southeastern) corner on Avenida 1 de Maio (across one of the two bridges over the Tâmega).

115

LOVE AND FERTILITY
Amarante is closely associated with marriage and fertility—there are even those who would like to claim its name derives from the word *amar*, meaning "love." The town's saint, São Gonçalo, is also closely associated with courtship, having gained a reputation as a matchmaker. As a result he is considered locally the patron saint of marriage, as his tomb in the parish church bears witness. Over the years, however, he has probably been absorbed into an ancient local fertility cult whose origins predate Christianity by centuries. Nonetheless the saint's festival (held in the first weekend of June) still provides the focus for the town's amatory traditions. During the festival, for example, it is the custom for unmarried young men to offer phallus-shaped cakes (*bolos*) to the town's young women.

The tomb of São Gonçalo, a local patron saint of marriage

PAIN
Some pilgrims to Lamego's famous sanctuary still ascend many of its 700 steps on their knees. They do not, however, scourge themselves in the manner of earlier pilgrims, at least not—as was once the custom—with leather whips tipped with balls of wax embedded with glass splinters.

Lamego and its 12th-century castle

▶▶ Lamego   112C1

Lamego is a pretty and prosperous town set in hilly countryside alongside the River Balsemão, a tributary of the Douro. The vines and fruit trees that swathe the hillsides are the source of the town's prosperity, whose wealth and well-being are manifest in the tidy streets and the fine patrician houses clustered in the old center. Above the rooftops rise two hills, one crowned with the ruins of a 12th-century castle, the other with the wonderful baroque sanctuary of Nossa Senhora dos Rémedios, one of the country's most important sites of pilgrimage.

The town's historical importance stems from its role as a gateway to the mountainous lands to the north, and from its position on a trade route between eastern and western Portugal. It was a bishopric as early as the days of the Suevi, and in 1143 hosted Portugal's first Cortes, or parliament. This group of nobles, clergymen, and townspeople met to recognize Afonso Henriques as the country's first monarch, and also fixed the law of succession by which no foreigner could become king.

In the 16th century the town acquired further wealth through its role as a producer of velvet, satin, and taffeta, although its principal export has always been wine. In the 18th century Pombal built one of the region's first major roads to move wine from Lamego to Porto, and today a quarter of local production still goes to the city to be made into port.

THE TOWN Try to resist climbing to the castle and sanctuary immediately and spend a little time in the town center instead. It is dominated by the **Sé (Cathedral)**▶▶, begun in the 12th century and remodeled in the 16th and 18th centuries. The alterations left only the base of the campanile as a monument to the building's Romanesque origins. The extravagantly decorated triple portal (1508–1515) catches the eye, as do the carved choir, the organ, and the interior's vault frescoes, the latter the work of Nicolau Nasoni, better known for his architectural projects in Porto. The cathedral's highlight, however, is the silver altar frontal (1758–1768) in the Capela do Sacramento, crafted by one of Nasoni's anonymous contemporaries.

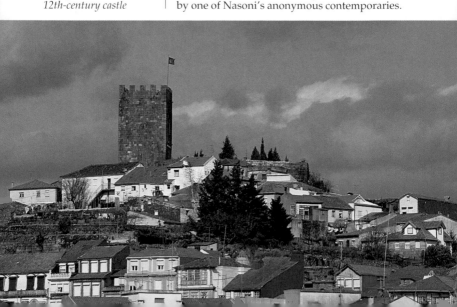

An ornate fountain enlivens one of Lamego's squares

BALSEMÃO
This little hamlet, located just 2 miles (3km) north-east of Lamego, contains the deceptively plain-fronted Capelo de São Pedro (Chapel of St Peter), one of Portugal's few remaining early Christian monuments. Probably begun in the 7th century (the facade is 17th-century), it was built either by the Suevi or Visigoths. Later it accumulated a variety of medieval embellishments, some commissioned by Dom Afonso Pires, Bishop of Porto (died 1362), whose sarcophagus tomb dominates the cramped interior.

117

Immediately across Largo do Camões, the town's main square, lies the **Museu de Lamego▶▶▶** (tel· 254 612 008. *Open* Tue–Sun 10–12:30, 2–5. *Admission: inexpensive*). This is one of Portugal's most intriguing provincial museums and contains a wealth of fascinating artifacts, the most treasured of which are five painted panels by Vasco Fernandes, or Grão-Vasco. This is all that remains of a 20-piece retable commissioned for the Sé by Bishop Dom João de Madureira in 1506 (the remaining panels were lost during restoration work on the cathedral in the 18th century). The Flemish-influenced panels depict the *Creation, Annunciation, Visitation, Presentation in the Temple*, and *Circumcision* (the central figure in the last is a portrait of Dom João). Other exhibits include six outstanding 16th-century Brussels tapestries, many decorated *azulejos*, liturgical silverware, unusual statues depicting a pregnant Madonna, and several dismantled and beautifully decorated baroque chapels.

OUR LADY OF THE REMEDIES The sanctuary of **Nossa Senhora dos Remédios▶▶▶** (*Open* daily 9–7) draws thousands from across Portugal with the promise of miraculous interventions and remedial healing (see panel). The main pilgrimage here is held on September 8, but celebrations take place over a couple of weeks either side of this date. The sanctuary is approached by a glorious 700-step double staircase, a baroque confection lavishly decorated with chapels, fountains, urns, statues, and colored tiles that was modeled on the stair at Bom Jesus near Braga (see page 100). At its summit sits the so-called "Court of Kings," flanked by otiose arches and pillars, and a belvedere with views over Lamego and the surrounding countryside. For casual visitors, however, the church itself is something of an anticlimax, chill and plain after the decorative pyrotechnics of the approach.

SÃO JOÃO DE TAROUCA
A small village, about 20 minutes' drive (or bus trip) from Lamego, São João de Tarouca contains a 12th-century abbey church that once made up part of Portugal's first Cistercian abbey (1124). Inevitably, much of the interior was remodeled in the 18th century, when 4,700 colorful *azulejos* were added to the chancel and north transept. However, the vast granite tomb (1354) of Dom Pedro, Count of Barcelos, survives. Pedro, the illegitimate son of Dom Dinis, became an important medieval writer. Note, too, the vast 14th-century granite Madonna and the intriguing choir stalls.

Wine has been made in the Porto region for centuries, but "port" gained renown comparatively recently. It is one of Portugal's glories, a unique wine that owes its special character to the peculiar way it is made and the exceptional conditions under which its grapes are grown.

Vines growing high above the Douro

118

RED AND WHITE
There are two basic types of port, which vary according to the grape used and the length of time they are allowed to mature. Red, or *tinto*, is the best known and most common port; it is usually young, distinctive, and highly fruity. "Blended" ports are reds, the blend comprising different vintages from different years and the quality depending on the aging of the various wines used. White, or *branco*, is made from white grapes and is usually dry; it makes a delicious aperitif if served chilled.

LATE-BOTTLED PORT (LBV)
This is a port that is not quite up to vintage standard but is still deemed good enough to mature in the bottle rather than in the cask. Typically, it is bottled after about four to six years.

History Wines from the Douro were exported to Britain as early as the 14th century, but it wasn't until the beginning of the 18th century that "port" wine began to be taken seriously. Between 1679 and 1685, and again during the Spanish Wars of Succession (1702–1714), Britain prohibited the import of French wines, initially as a retaliatory measure against France, which had banned the import of English cloth. British merchants quickly moved to fill the gap by importing Portuguese wine. In 1703 the trade received a further boost when the Metheun Treaty lowered duty on Portuguese wine imports to a third of those on French wines. In return, Britain received preferential treatment for textile imports into Portugal.

So great was demand for Portuguese wine that British entrepreneurs began establishing their own Portuguese estates, or *quintas*. These led in turn to an influx of British shippers—Croft, Warre, Sandeman, Dow, Graham, and others—to Porto. By 1756 the British shippers enjoyed a monopoly on trade, enabling them to keep down the prices paid to growers as well as passing off all manner of inferior wine as port in order to meet demand. This led the Marquês de Pombal to form the Companhia Geral da Agricultura dos Vinhos do Alto Douro, a trade association that created a state monopoly to fix prices and demarcate the area in which port grapes could be grown. Although the laws were later relaxed, the demarcated area has remained little changed to this day.

Harvest Grapes from the specially demarcated regions—covering a total of some 25,000 growers—are picked between mid-September and mid-October: the precise time varies according to the amount of sun, temperature, and rainfall in any year. Sun is, of course, crucial, as is temperature—summer temperatures in the region can hit 109°F (43°C), but winter temperatures can drop to 12°F (-11°C). Powdery local soils also play their part, for they consist of unusual yellow schist, boulders of which help retain the heat of the daytime sun.

After picking, the grapes are pressed, not, as in the past, under foot, but mechanically. Some producers now claim feet were better as they didn't crush the seeds (which release unwanted tannin into the mix), while apologists for mechanization claim it makes no difference to the final taste. After pressing, grape sugars react with natural yeast from the skins (which also add color) and fermentation begins to produce alcohol. Barely has fermentation begun, however, than the juice, or "must," is run off into vats (usually after two days) and Douro grape brandy added (one part brandy to four parts must). This leaves about half the grape sugar intact within the wine, and it is this that gives port its special character.

Production The brandy rich brew is then stored in the lodge, or *armazém*, of the wine estates that dot the Douro countryside. Over the winter the region's icy temperatures help clear the wine, removing some of the cloudiness that accompanies fermentation. In March the wine is moved to the lodges of the shippers and producers in Vila Nova de Gaia, a southern suburb of Porto (see page 127). In the past, much of the port was moved on *barcos rabelos*, traditional square-sailed and flat-bottomed boats specially adapted for the purpose. Each carried in excess of 60 "pipes" of port, a pipe being equivalent to around 141 gallons (532 liters). Today, it's all done by tanker or train. Until as recently as 1987, port could only be called port if it had matured at Vila Nova, but congestion in the lodges now means that it can be matured elsewhere on the Douro. The wine is stored in casks or steel vats before being decanted, depending on quality (see panels), for further maturation in bottles or wooden "pipes."

VINTAGE PORT

The best port—vintage port—is wine which has been selected from specially named vintage years. It spends just two to four years in the cask before being bottled and then left to age for at least a further ten years. Since 1974 a port must have been bottled in Portugal to be labeled a vintage. Crucially, port that ages in the bottle matures by reduction, turning a deep-red color. Port that ages in the cask, by contrast, matures through oxidation, and turns a lighter amber color. So, the longer the cask maturation, the lighter the color.

RUBY AND TAWNY

Ruby, or *tinto-aloirado*, is slightly older than red port, hence its different color, and will often be blended from a variety of more aged vintages. Tawny, or *aloirado*, is made from port which has aged longer in the cask (usually at least seven years), a process that imparts its distinctive golden-brown, or "tawny," color.

Boats carrying port— now a rare sight

Porto and the Douro

INFORMATION

Porto's main tourist office (tel: 22 205 2740) is at Rua do Clube Fenianos 25, off Praça General Humberto Delgado at the top of Avenida dos Aliados, Porto's main boulevard. There are smaller offices in Praça de Dom João I (tel: 22 205 7514) and across the river in Vila Nova de Gaia (tel: 22 370 3735). The airport also has a small information counter (tel: 22 941 2534).

ARRIVING BY AIR

Porto is the transport hub for northern Portugal, and the easiest way to get to the city is by plane. Various international flights serve the city and there are daily flights from Lisbon. The airport (tel: 22 948 2141), Francisco de Sá Carneiro (or Pedras Rubras), lies about 8 miles (13km) north of the city center; taxis connect to downtown or you can use the half-hourly 56 shuttle bus, which drops passengers off at Jardim da Cordoaria by the university building. The bus ride takes around 40 minutes, although it is wise to allow an hour during busy periods. Better still is the new Aerobus, which leaves every half hour and drops passengers at Avenidas dos Aliados and main hotels.

►►► Porto   112A1

Portugal's second city makes a rumbustious counterpart to Lisbon. Bustling, busy, and no-nonsense in atmosphere, it has far fewer sights and far less obvious charm than the capital despite a magnificent site—perched on the northern banks of the Douro—that would be the envy of almost any city in the world. Porto is where much of Portugal's wealth is generated, although the dismal prospect of its factories and suburbs—the source of this wealth—is confounded by a wonderful little old quarter and an atmospheric waterfront. A cathedral, a pair of churches, and a couple of museums are the only sightseeing beacons, but most visitors come to the city for one thing—port.

HISTORY Porto first rose to prominence under the Romans, when the River Douro—long a division between north and south—formed a major obstacle on the important road route between Lisbon and Braga. Two settlements grew up on opposite banks of the river: Cale, the older of the two, on the south bank; and Portus, meaning "Harbor," on the north bank. By the 8th century the area between the Minho and the Douro marked the limit of permanent Moorish settlement, and in time the region took its name, Portucale, from the town at the Douro's mouth. In 1095 the area was part of the dowry included in the marriage of Dona Tareja (Teresa), daughter of the king of Léon and Castile, to Henry of Burgundy. Henry subsequently moved the region's capital to Braga but retained the old name of Portucale as a label for the province. Soon after, the area became a stronghold from which the reconquest of "Portugal" began (under Henry's son, Afonso Henriques), eventually lending its name to the entire country (see pages 30–31).

Pedro IV in Porto's Praça da Liberdade

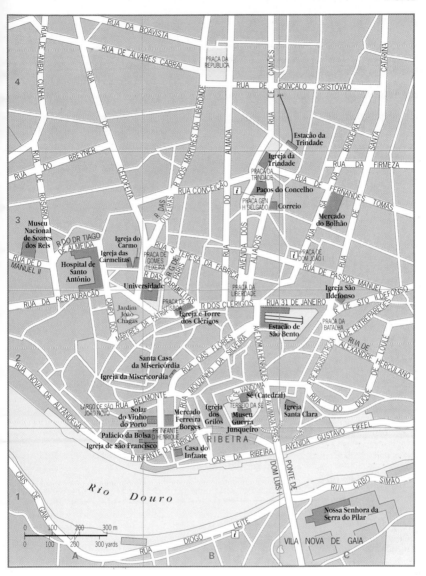

Porto featured in Portugal's royal annals again in 1387, when it played host to the marriage of João I and Philippa of Lancaster. One of the sons of this marriage, Henry the Navigator, was born and learned his maritime trade in the city. At the age of just 19 Henry was entrusted with 20 galleys built in Porto, part of the force that made the famous attack on the Moorish stronghold of Ceuta in 1415. This attack, incidentally, is said to have given Porto's citizens their famous nickname of *tripeiros*, or "tripe eaters" (see panel on page 126).

During the Middle Ages Porto's harbor developed apace, the city forging long-lived trading relations with northern Europe and England in particular. The English presence in the area began as early as 1147, when a group

HARD WORKING

A famous Porto proverb suggests that "Coimbra studies, Braga prays, Lisbon shows off, and Porto works."

ARRIVING BY TRAIN

Porto has three main train stations. Trains from the Douro Valley and the north arrive at the central Estação de São Bento (tel: 22 200 2722). Narrow gauge trains from the north, however, notably from Guimarães and the resort of Póvoa de Varzim, use Estação da Trindade (tel: 22 200 5224), north of the city center behind the Trindade church. Trains from Lisbon and the south usually terminate at the Estação de Campanhã (tel: 22 536 4141), several miles east of the center. Change here for the five-minute ride to the São Bento station.

ARRIVING BY BUS

There are several bus terminals. However, the most important companies, including buses to Lisbon, mostly share a bus station in Rua das Carmelitas near the Torre dos Clérigos. Otherwise, companies from southern destinations generally use the depot at Rua Alexandre Herculano 366; those from northern destinations stop at Praça Filipa de Lencastre or Praça General Humberto Delgado.

ARRIVING BY CAR

Porto and Lisbon are connected by a fast road—driving time is about three hours. Porto is also the focus of many main routes in northern Portugal, notably to Braga and Amarante. Avoid the city center, where traffic is heavy and parking impossible. If you are renting a car in Porto, pick it up only as you leave the city.

Opposite: Porto's old Ribeira district

of crusaders docked at the harbor and were persuaded to divert their martial endeavors to the Moorish invaders in Portugal. They were, according to one chronicler, little more than "plunderers, drunkards and rapists, men not seasoned with the honey of piety." A more decorous breed of Englishman arrived in the form of merchants in the 13th century, when the recovery of Seville from the Moors reopened the Mediterranean to trade. Mercantile treaties over the years cemented the Anglo-Portuguese alliance, notably the Commonwealth Treaty of 1654 and, more particularly, the Metheun Treaty of 1703. Among other things, the latter lowered the duty on the import of Portuguese wines into Britain in return for concessions on British textiles, thereby giving an important boost to Porto's nascent wine industry.

ORIENTATION Porto is a rambling and initially confusing city, raggedly spread over the hills and bluffs on the northern bank of the River Douro. For the most part, however, you can ignore the anonymous suburbs that stretch along the river in a 4-mile (6km) sprawl to the sea. The center of the city, in so far as it has one, is made up of two large squares, Praça General Humberto Delgado and Praça da Liberdade, these linked together by the broad Avenida dos Aliados. To the east of this boulevard is a lively grid of streets, of which the most important are Rua de Passos Manuel and Rua de Santa Catarina. This area contains the old Bolhão market and many of the city's best stores. To the west of the boulevard are still more shopping streets, together with several grander thoroughfares that house the hospital, university, law courts, and Museu Nacional de Soares dos Reis, the principal museum in Porto.

South of Avenida dos Aliados lies another nodal point, São Bento, Porto's grand old train station. South again is the warren of streets and alleys that makes up old Porto, one of the best areas of the city (along with the shopping streets) in which to wander at random. Farther south still lies the Ribeira, formerly a waterfront working district but now teeming with bars and restaurants that form the main focus of Porto's colorful nightlife. From here there is access to the Ponte Dom Luís I, the famous two-tiered bridge that carries cars and pedestrians to the suburb of Vila Nova de Gaia. The latter is home to some 60 or so port wine lodges, many of which open their doors—and their bottles—to visitors.

CENTER Avenida dos Aliados and its adjacent squares are filled with banks, offices, and, at the northern end, the Town Hall. These are not places to linger, but since they provide a home to the tourist office (see panel on page 120) they make as good a point as any to begin a tour of the city. During the day, locals and visitors cram the bustling shopping streets to the east, whose highlight is the wonderful old **Mercado Bolhão▶▶** (*Open Mon–Fri 7–5, Sat 7–1*). This two-story, half-open municipal market is crammed with fruit, meat, cheese, bread, and fish stands, with a cacophony of noise and a riot of color providing constant accompaniments. Close by, at Rua de Santa Catarina 112, stands the famous **Café Majestic**, one of the most alluring of the city's old-fashioned art deco cafés. A similar monument to early 20th-century

Moving port in the old-fashioned way

GETTING AROUND
Porto is small enough to explore on foot, although the city's many different levels involve a lot of puffing up and down hills. Tickets for the buses (or the one streetcar route) can be bought at newsstands and tobacconists. One-, four-, and seven-day passes are available. The route taken by the city's streetcar, the 18, is well worth traveling for its own sake. Taxis are plentiful but can be difficult to hail on the street; they can be picked up at ranks or ordered by phone (tel: 02 528 061). Make sure the meter is turned on when you set off.

elegance can be found at the **Estação de São Bento►**, Porto's stately 1896 train station, whose entrance hall is decorated with pretty tiles (1905–1930) depicting historical scenes and the rural traditions of northern Portugal.

Before heading for the old city to the south, it is worth wandering a couple of hundred yards to the west to take in the **Igreja dos Clérigos** (*Open* Mon–Sat 10–noon, 2–5, Sun 10–1, 8–8:30) and **Torre dos Clérigos►►** (tel: 22 200 1729) , which lie off Praça de Lisboa. The latter, a 246-foot (75m) tower, is one of Porto's landmarks and offers a view over the city that should help you get your bearings (*Open* daily 10–noon, 2–5. *Admission: inexpensive*). The *igreja*, or church (1732–1749), the first in Portugal built on an oval plan, was designed by Nicolau Nasoni (1691–1773), an architect much influenced by the Italian baroque. Nasoni played a key role in the introduction of the baroque into northern Portugal, an ornate style (notice the church's garlands, scrolls, and decorative festoons) in marked contrast to the more restrained baroque style created at the same time in Pombaline Lisbon.

North of the church, incidentally, lies part of the Cordoaria district, which is becoming increasingly well known for its clusters of art galleries (some of the best congregate on Rua Galeria de Paris). The grid of streets north and south of the Praça de Lisboa is also a good place to look for little workers' restaurants, ideal places to sit down and enjoy an inexpensive lunch.

If the old city looks too daunting at this point you can continue west from here (a longish walk) to the **Museu Nacional de Soares dos Reis►►**, Porto's most important museum (tel: 22 339 3770. *Open* Tue 2–6, Wed–Sun 10–12:30, 2–6. *Admission: moderate*). Its collection consists largely of Portuguese paintings and sculpture from the 19th and 20th centuries, and takes its name from the Portuguese sculptor Soares dos Reis (1847–1889), whose works are liberally represented. The most stimulating of the paintings are the Impressionistic works of Henrique Pousão, who died tragically young in 1884 aged 24, along with the more naturalistic canvases of Silva

Porto (1850–1893). Elsewhere, by way of contrast, there are paintings from earlier centuries, together with displays of decorative and applied arts from Portugal and abroad.

OLD PORTO Walking south from the Clérigos church and tower, preferably along the Rua dos Flores (lined with old shops and 18th-century houses), will take you to the **Igreja da Misericórdia▶**, an impressive 16th-century church. Restored by Nasoni in the 18th century, it's a little too overbearing for its modest surroundings, although the reason to come here is not so much the church itself as the adjacent **Santa Casa da Misericórdia▶▶** (tel: 22 200-8371. *Open* Mon–Fri 9–12:30, 2–5:30. *Admission free*). This contains the *Fons Vitae*, one of the city's greatest paintings. It was probably commissioned by Dom Manuel I around 1520, just before his death, and shows the king, his wife, and eight children gathered around a bowl collecting the blood of the crucified Christ. Of unknown authorship, the work shows a distinct Flemish influence—Holbein is among those cited as the painter. In fact, it was probably the work of an indigenous painter schooled in northern European habits.

Porto's **Solar do Vinho do Porto (Port Wine Institute)▶▶** provides a comfortable setting in which to choose from a vast range of ports to drink by the glass (tel: 22 609 4749. *Open* Mon–Fri 10 AM–11:45 PM, Sat 11 AM–10:45 PM). It is housed on the first floor of the Quinta da Macieirinha at Rua Entre Quintas 220, to the west of the city center close to the Jardim do Palácio de Cristal.

Just 100 yards (100m) to the south, off Praça do Infante D. Henrique, lies the **Igreja de São Francisco▶▶▶** (*Open* Apr–Oct, Mon–Sat 9:30–6; Nov–Apr, Mon–Sat 9:30–4:30), Porto's most striking church (the entrance is on Rua de São Francisco). Its Gothic origins, still manifest in the exterior, are completely submerged in the interior by one of Portugal's most amazing decorative displays. Gilt, stucco, and all manner of baroque and rococo exuberance cover the altars, walls, and vaults. This costly veneer, added between 1726 and 1746, was at odds with every Franciscan ideal of poverty, but perfectly in tune with the orgy of excess prompted by the influx of Brazilian gold into Portugal in the 18th century.

Another temple to money and materialism is Porto's **Palácio da Bolsa (Stock Exchange)▶**, immediately next door to São Francisco (tel: 22 339 9000. *Open* guided tours Nov–Mar, daily 9–12:30, 2–5:30; Apr–Oct, daily 9–12:30, 2–6:30. *Admission: moderate*). Built in 1834, its massive and grandiloquent neoclassical facade was clearly designed to suggest solidity and financial probity. Similar considerations prevail in the interior, where size and scale are paramount, the building's bluster nowhere more apparent than in the vulgar "Arab" main hall, a 19th-century rehash of the Alhambra in Granada.

Incidentally, Henry the Navigator was reputedly born in the nearby **Casa do Infante** (the town's customs house for five centuries), a rather unexciting building located in Rua da Alfândega off the southern side of Praça do Infante D. Henrique.

CATHEDRAL Wending your way to the top of old Porto, you reach the flagstoned **Terreiro da Sé**, an esplanade

EMERGENCIES
● Police: 22 200 6821 or 22 339 4140.
● Hospital: Hospital de Santo António, Rua Prof. Vicente José de Carvalho (tel: 22 207 7500).

POST AND PHONES
Porto's main post office (tel: 22 340 0200) is situated near the tourist office in Praça General Humberto Delgado. You can also make international phone calls from here.

No hard sell in Porto's backstreet stores

MARKETS
Porto's vivacious daily market, the Mercado Bolhão (*Open* Mon–Fri 7–5, Sat 7–1), is located in Rua de Sá da Bandeira just behind the main post office. Flea markets are often held by the cathedral (the Sé), on Alameda das Fontaínhas and along Calçada de Vandoma; they are usually busiest on Saturdays.

Porto and the Douro

RIVER TRIPS
For short 50-minute boat trips on the Douro contact Turisdouro (tel: 22 370 8429) or Rota do Douro (tel: 22 375 9042). Boats leave roughly hourly Monday to Saturday (May–October) from the quay just south of the tourist office in Vila Nova de Gaia. Companies that run longer one- and two-day cruises include Endouro Turismo on Rua da Reboleira 49 (tel: 22 208 4161) and Ferreira & Rayford Turismo on Rua Sousa Aroso 352, Sala 30, in Matosinhos (tel: 22 339 3950). The latter runs trips up to the Spanish border.

TRIPE EATERS
Porto's citizens are known among their fellow Portuguese as *tripeiros*, or "tripe eaters." The name reputedly dates from 1415, when the city's entire stock of fresh meat was salted and given over to the naval expedition setting out to capture the Moorish stronghold of Ceuta. So generous were the city's inhabitants that they kept only tripe and other offal for themselves. *Tripas* is still a local culinary specialty.

with views over the city which is home to Porto's gaunt Sé, or cathedral. Also here are a stone tower and the former Bishop's Palace (1772), the latter (now offices) designed by Nasoni. The **Sé▶▶** (*Open* Mon–Sat 9–12:30, 2:30–5:30, Sun 2:30–5:30. *Admission free, cloisters inexpensive*) was founded in the 12th century by Dona Teresa, mother of Afonso Henriques, and like similar cathedrals at Braga, Coimbra, and Lisbon began life as part fortress, part church. This, and the granite from which it is built, account in part for the cathedral's blunt Romanesque appearance, which is only partly softened by the predictable internal reworkings executed in the 18th century. Inside, the highlight is a superb altarpiece (1632–1678), located in the north transept to the left of the high altar. The opposite transept gives access to a set of cloisters (begun in 1385), from where a striking Nasoni-designed staircase leads to the terrace and chapter house. Windows here offer fine views over the cathedral and old streets below, while the cloisters are decorated with 18th-century tiles depicting the *Life of the Virgin* and Ovid's *Metamorphoses*.

The cathedral esplanade, flanked by narrow streets and stepped alleys, makes a good point to begin exploring the old town's more hidden and largely ungentrified corners. Head south, perhaps by way of the flea market on Calçada de Vandoma, and you will reach the waterfront **Ribeira▶▶▶**, Porto's most atmospheric quarter. Dotted with bars and restaurants, this is a district that only really

comes alive in the evening. However, during the day it is still pretty, especially if you make for the Cais da Ribeira, the waterfront's main street, home to a weekday market and overlooked by old houses. The vast Ponte Dom Luís I (1886), most famous of the five bridges that cross the Douro (two old, three modern), is an impressive two-tiered affair, cleverly designed so that it serves two levels of the old city.

VILA NOVA DE GAIA Porto may have comparatively few big sights, but in the numerous **port lodges►►►** scattered across Vila Nova de Gaia, the suburb across the Dom Luís I bridge, it has an attraction that makes a trip to the city more than worthwhile. The lodges, of which there are around 60, proclaim themselves in vast neon signs. However, this modern detail is at odds with their long history, which for many dates back to the beginning of the 18th century and the earliest days of British involvement in the city's wine trade (see page 118). Today, most of the companies belong to multinationals, although the family names of many—and their family-run images—are still carefully cultivated. Many offer free tours and tastings—to join current tours stroll along the waterfront west of the bridge and follow the signs. Note that many lodges are open only from Monday to Friday, and that details and opening times vary from year to year; you can ask for current opening times at the Vila Nova tourist office, located 200 yards (175m) west of the bridge by the Sandeman lodge.

PORT APLENTY
The Sandeman port wine lodge alone stores up to 53 million gallons (200 million liters) of port at any one time.

Past meets present on Porto's appealing waterfront

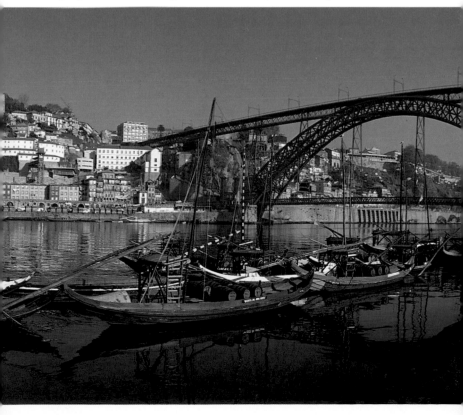

Drive

Vale do Douro

See map on page 112.

A drive from Amarante to Lamego through the heart of Portugal's prime wine producing areas.

The Douro, which rises in Spain, is one of the most important rivers on the Iberian peninsula. However, only the last 134 miles (215km) of its course lies in Portugal, where it threads through some of the country's most beautiful wine country before reaching the sea at Porto. This drive starts at Amarante, looping down to follow the river for part of its course, and ends at Lamego, a town which, like Amarante, is worth seeing for its own sake. The chances are, however, that you will be approaching the drive from Porto. If so, you can either take the A4 highway to Amarante, or, if you have more time, follow the Douro upstream on minor roads virtually all the way from Porto to Lamego. If you decide on the latter, be sure to take the southern bank, which is prettier (N108/N222).You can then follow the drive in reverse—from Lamego to Amarante.

Amarante is a delightful town nestled on the banks of the Tâmega river, but its outskirts have been ruined by a riot of modern building. Once you've seen the town, take the N15, which climbs before reaching the Ovelha Valley. Leave the main road, following the valley eastwards towards

Left: port and other wines are made from the huge vineyards that swathe the slopes of the Vale do Douro

the village of Candemil. The scenery here is green and pleasant, its pine and chestnut woods interspersed with bucolic farming land. Some 2.5 miles (4km) after Candemil, having traversed a craggy valley, you might make a short diversion to Pico do Marão (4,642 feet, or 1,415m), the highest point of the **Serra do Marão**, a wild area of granite hills and mountains. The view from here is superb.

Returning to the main road after your diversion, head north through more dramatic scenery to pick up the N15, which crests the Alto do Espinho pass (2,936 feet, or 895m) before dropping to the Corgo Valley and Vila Real (see page 87). If you wish to vary your itinerary, note that just before **Vila Real** the N2 strikes off south for Pêso da Régua, another scenic route. Otherwise, take the N322 east from Vila Real, pausing to visit the lovely **Solar de Mateus** (see page 87), the building immortalized on millions of Mateus Rosé wine bottles. Beyond Sabrosa you enter the heart of the region's wine country and the road (N323) passes vast hillsides completely covered in terraces of vines. The work of centuries, these terraces exploit every last patch of land on the steep slopes, leaving room only for dusty tracks and small whitewashed *quintas.*

The road finally meets the Douro at **Pinhão**, probably the region's most important center of high quality port wine production. Wine was once shipped down the river from here in *barcos rabelos*, traditional square-sailed and flat-bottomed boats, a few of which can still be seen (the wine is now sent exclusively by road or rail). If you have time you can make an 11-mile (18km) detour on a winding road to the east to the village of São João da Pesqueira; this offers a look at the even more steeply terraced vineyards of the Torto Valley. Otherwise, continue along the Douro by taking the N222 west from Pinhão, a road that follows the river's southern bank for half an hour before reaching the junction for Peso da Régua

(this is situated on the river's northern bank; to reach it, follow the N2 north from its junction with the N222).

Peso de Régua, the self-proclaimed capital of the Upper Douro, has relinquished its title as the main center of quality wine production to Pinhão. However, it still forms a vital administrative center as well as a road and rail hub through which most port passes on its way to the coast. As in other minor towns on the drive, there is little to see here in terms of actual sights, although the tourist office at Rua Da Ferreirinha 505 (tel: 054 22 846) has details of local wine lodges open to the public. From Régua, as the town is usually known, return south on the N2 to Lamego, admiring the fine views along the way.

Selling grapes at Peso de Régua, the heart of port production in the upper Douro Valley

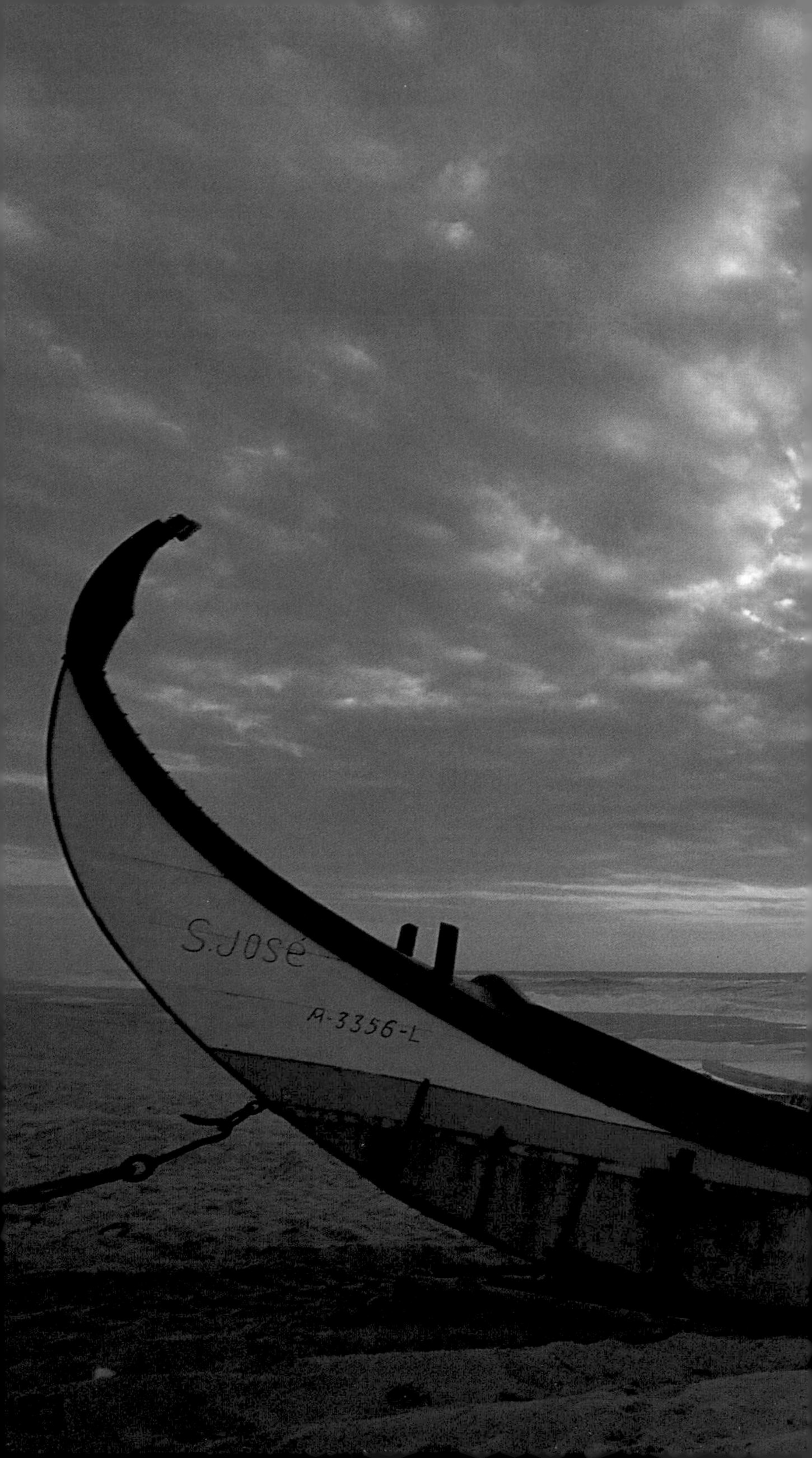
S.JOSÉ
A-3356-L

The Beiras

131

The Beiras

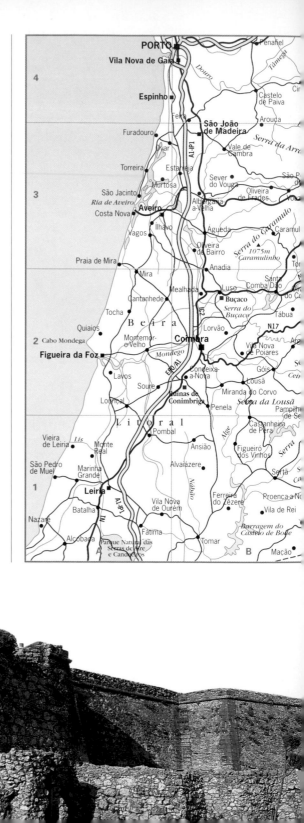

*Pages 130–131:
a traditional fishing boat
drawn up on the beach at
Praia de Mira*

*Below: the fortress and
lighthouse at Figueira
da Foz*

132

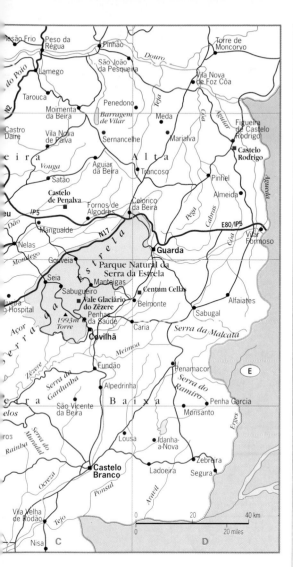

DÃO WINES
These well-known wines come from the southwest of the Beira Alta, the second most productive wine area in the country. They take their name from the Dão, a minor tributary of the River Mondego, and are produced in the triangle roughly marked out by Viseu, Guarda, and Coimbra. Most Dão is red (superior to the white), and at its rounded and full-bodied best can be some of the most consistently good wine in the country. Much of it is blended and matured outside the region, and by law must be matured in the cask for at least 18 months.

THE BEIRAS The three provinces that make up the Beiras form the Portuguese heartland, offering between them some of the least explored and yet most highly evocative towns and landscapes in the country. Occupying the land between the Douro to the north and the Tagus to the south, they divide into the Beira Litoral, a low-lying coastal region; the northerly Beira Alta (Upper Beira), Portugal's most mountainous region; and the southerly Beira Baixa (Lower Beira), where the region's mountains gradually fade into the limitless plains of the Alentejo.

THE BEIRA LITORAL This province is less suited to random exploration than its neighbors, the main sights being concentrated primarily in **Coimbra**, ranked third after Lisbon and Porto in the country's triumvirate of historical cities. The city boasts many fascinating monuments and lovely

Roman mosaics at Conimbriga, one of Portugal's best-preserved ancient monuments

medieval corners, together with Portugal's oldest university, an institution whose student population brings more than the usual vigor to its bars, restaurants, and nightlife. Coimbra also makes a useful base for exploring nearby attractions, notably **Conimbriga**, Portugal's finest Roman ruins, as well as the superb forest enclave at **Buçaco**. The so-called Costa de Prata, or "Silver Coast," is also close at hand, offering a relatively undeveloped line of pine-backed beaches culminating in **Figueira da Foz**, one of the region's best resorts. Just inland from the coast lies **Aveiro**, partly industrial but located at the heart of an area of lagoons, salt flats, and traditional ways of life.

THE BEIRA ALTA Old world traditions also infuse the Beira Alta, whose mountain redoubts contain some of the country's least spoiled villages and landscapes. The **Serra da Estrela** stands out among the latter, a majestic granite range that features mainland Portugal's highest peak, Torre (which just fails to top the 6,600-foot, or 2,000m, mark). The *serra's* grass-topped peaks provide pasture for sheep, giving way lower down to thickly wooded slopes and the arable-farmed valleys below. The valleys, notably the Mondego and Zêzere, have long been the communications corridors and contain the bulk of the area's population. The whole mountain enclave is a region with a proud and independent heritage, having formed the heart of old Lusitania, whose inhabitants doggedly held out against Roman domination (see page 26).

Public transportation to much of this upland fastness is patchy, and to get the most out of the region you really need a car. Almost any route through the mountains should bring you into contact with memorable villages and landscapes. Among the larger settlements worth making for are dark and brooding **Guarda**, a quintessential mountain town, and **Viseu**, a more benign upland spot set among the rambling hills of Dão wine country.

THE BEIRA BAIXA Captivating towns and impressive landscapes are thinner on the ground in the Beira Baixa, where the high mountains of the north, the Serra da Gardunha, ripple away to airy plains in the south. As in the Alentejo—which it resembles—the scenery here takes time to get under your skin. When it does, however, the vast swathes of olive and cork, the almond trees, and the pastoral whitewashed villages can leave impressions as abiding as any in the country. Again, random exploration is a good way to uncover the region's subtle charm. If time is short, however, the dazzling hill village of **Monsanto** is the one unmissable sight, while the local capital, Castelo Branco, a quietly provincial spot, makes the obvious base.

GETTING AROUND The Beiras' main centers are reasonably accessible. Coimbra lies just off the main A1 highway, and is connected by decent roads to Aveiro, Viseu, Guarda, and Castelo Branco. Trains connect to Coimbra from Lisbon and Porto, as well as to Viseu, Castelo Branco, Guarda, and Covilhã (for the Serra da Estrela). There are also trains from Coimbra to Figueira da Foz and Aveiro. Coimbra is the major hub for bus services throughout the region, while Viseu and Guarda lie at the heart of a more patchy mountain bus network.

Opposite: marble and gilt adorn the interior of Coimbra's magnificent 18th-century university library

PRACTICALITIES

Aveiro's tourist office is at Rua João Mendonça 8 (tel: 234 423 680).

The train station (tel: 234 381 632) is at Largo Estação at the top of the main street in the northeastern corner of town. There are frequent trains from Porto (30 minutes), Coimbra (1 hour), and Lisbon (5 hours).

The bus terminal is near the station, but there are more long haul connections from Águeda (12 miles, or 20km, away), which is linked by regular buses from Aveiro's train station.

BOATS

Aveiro's lagoon is renowned for its *moliceiros*, traditional flat-bottomed boats used to collect seaweed and eels (a local specialty) in the shallow lagoon of the Ria de Aveiro, whose average depth is just 6 feet (2m). The boats have a sail and can also be propelled, gondola-like, with a long single oar. Long-pronged rakes (*ancinhos*) used to drag in the seaweed are hung around the boats' distinctive curving prows, which are famous for their simple but beautifully painted decoration. Inevitably, the numbers of these boats are declining as mass-produced artificial fertilizers replace those traditionally made from seaweed. A little museum, the Museu do Mar (in Ilhavo, 3 miles, or 5km, south of Aveiro), has a collection of boats and maritime artifacts (closed through 2000 for renovation; tel: 234 329 608 for details).

Aveiro is flanked by the peaceful waters of a large lagoon

▶▶ Aveiro

132A3

Busy Aveiro is a place to visit not so much for its monuments as for the beaches to the north and south. None quite matches the beaches of the Algarve, but most have the advantage of relative peace and quiet, especially if you walk for a few minutes from the more crowded stretches of sand. Many back on to the Ria de Aveiro, an ethereal lagoon surrounded by villages, pine forests, and herb-scented dunes, and known for its traditional painted boats, or *moliceiros* (see panel). Unfortunately the number of these boats is rapidly declining. In the past they were mainly used to collect seaweed (*moliço*), which is used for manufacturing fertilizer, one of the town's two traditional industries—the other is salt production (pyramids of salt dot the town's outskirts). These twin concerns have recently been joined by a roster of more modern industries, developments that have turned the Aveiro region into one of the country's leading industrial areas after Lisbon and Porto.

CANALS The town's industrial sector inevitably results in some fairly grim outskirts, but things pick up once you reach the old center, which is dissected by attractively bustling canals and low-slung bridges. During much of the Middle Ages Aveiro's coastal position ensured its primacy as a port and there was no need for waterways. However, a colossal storm in 1575 altered the course of the River Vouga and closed the mouth of the lagoon. Thereafter the harbor began to silt up, plunging the town into an economic tailspin. The decline was only reversed in 1808, when a channel was forced through to the sea, many of the town's walls being sacrificed in the process to provide stone for the breakwaters.

Aveiro's main sight is the **Convento de Jesus▶▶▶**, on Rua Santa Joana (tel: 234 423 297. *Open* Tue–Sun 10:30–5:30. *Admission: inexpensive*). Founded in 1458, it owes its fame to the arrival seven years later of the Infanta Joana, daughter of Dom Afonso V (see panel opposite). Various additions were made to the building over the

years, notably a superlative baroque collection of carved and gilded wood in the church interior. This is at its best in the chancel, whose bewilderingly rich decoration is complemented by tiles depicting episodes from the life of Joana. The princess's beautiful rose-colored tomb in the lower chancel (*coro baixo*) was commissioned in 1699 by Dom Pedro II. The tomb was designed by royal architect João Antunes and took 12 years to complete, much of this time being spent creating the work's delicate Florentine marble inlay. Leave a moment or two to look at the cloisters, one of whose chapels contains the diverting *Tomb of João de Albuquerque*.

The convent also houses Aveiro's **museum** (the same hours), whose interesting collection features Coimbra sculpture, ceramics, vestments, baroque statuary, ivory work, and a variety of religious artifacts. Its highlights are several naive Portuguese paintings, principally a portrait of Joana, *St. John the Evangelist*, and the *Senhora da Madressilva* (*Madonna of the Honeysuckle*).

BEACHES Aveiro has no beach of its own, but plenty of sand can be found just half an hour to the north or south. On the whole there is less development to the south—and almost none between Praia de Mira and Figueira da Foz—but rather more as you head north towards Espinho. To the south, **Praia de Mira►►** is probably the best bet, but for something closer to Aveiro head for **Costa Nova** (1.2 miles, or 2km). To the north, the nearest beach is 20 minutes' walk from São Jacinto, a vibrant but not particularly pretty little port; it does, however, have the additional attraction of a ***reserva natural***, a nature and bird reserve that protects some of the best dune habitats in Europe. Contact Aveiro's tourist office (see panel opposite) or the reserve's visitor center (tel: 234 331 282) for more details; two hour guided tours of the reserve are available.

If you can live without beaches but want to see more of the lagoon, then sign up with one of the interesting day-long boat tours available in Aveiro. Again, details are available from the tourist office.

137

The traditional boats of the Aveiro lagoon are renowned for their beautifully painted prows

Portuguese cooking is based on hundreds of years of trying, with poverty and limited culinary resources being the key to a robust but often mouthwatering cuisine. The natural bounty of land and sea inspires fine soups and main courses, while the demands of the famous Portuguese sweet tooth ensure a wide range of tempting cakes, desserts, and pastries.

Sardines and other fish are staples of Portuguese cuisine

138

MENUS
The menu is known as the *lista* or *ementa*. The *ementa turistica* is not a tourist menu but the menu of the day. It is usually extremely good value, at least in less ambitious restaurants. The *prato do dia* is the dish of the day, while eating à la carte is *à lista*. Food in Portuguese restaurants is still some of the least expensive in Western Europe, but watch out for extras such as wine and service and cover charges.

DRINKS
Tap water across Portugal is usually perfectly safe to drink, but mineral water (*água mineral*) is available everywhere. Tea (*chá*, pronounced "shah") is popular and is usually drunk plain; be sure to drop into at least one of the country's pretty tea-houses (*casas de chá*). Most Portuguese take their coffee in short espresso-like shots known as *uma bica* or *um café*; if you prefer your coffee long and milky, order *um galão* or *uma meia de leite*. Aside from the many local wines, there are some national brands of beer (*cerveja*): in the south the most common brand is Sagres, while in the north it is the red-labeled Super Rock.

Soups Portuguese food is nothing if not wholesome. Its hearty and filling qualities reveal themselves immediately in the meal's first course, which across most of Portugal consists of often excellent soups (*sopa*). One of the most common is *caldo verde*, or "green broth," a northern dish based on potato, sliced Galician cabbage, olive oil, and generous hunks of ordinary or blood sausage (*tora*). Another is *sopa à alentejana*, one of the many bread-based soups (*açorda*) served across the country. These appear in a myriad of guises, one of the best being *sopa de coentros*, a garlic, bread, and cilantro concoction topped with a poached egg. Seafood broth (*sopa de mariscos*) and fish soups (*sopa de peixe*) are ubiquitous near the coast, while in southern areas around the Algarve you may find refreshingly chilled *gaspacho*. Other soups to look out for include *grão* (chickpea), *legumes* (vegetable), *feijão verde* (green bean), *coelho* (rabbit), and *canja de galinha* (chicken, rice, and egg).

Seafood Fish and seafood are Portuguese staples, culinary treats that are often tastier and more inventive than the country's meat dishes (see below). The smell of grilled sardines (*sardinhas assadas*) might almost be called the national perfume, while salted cod (*bacalhau*) is the undoubted national dish, a fish so ubiquitous there are said to be 365 ways of cooking it—one for every day of the year. Undisguised it can be bland, and even with all the trimmings it is still hard to see quite why it so excites Portuguese passions. Far more appetizing is *caldeirada*, a bouillabaisse-like stew that runs a close second to *bacalhau* in national popularity. Other common fish include *lenguado* (sole), *pescada* (hake), *robalo* (bass), and *atum*

(tuna), while among seafood delicacies (*mariscos*) you can expect lots of (often expensive) *mexilhões* (mussels), *lagosta* (crayfish), *santola* or more commonly *caranguejo* (crab), and *amêijoas* (clams), and exotica such as *eiros* (eels), *polvo* (octopus), and *lampreias* (lamprey).

Meat With one or two mouthwatering exceptions, meat in Portugal tends to be confined to rather unexciting roasts and grills. On the whole, pork (*porco*) is the best bet, either as part of a robust stew such as *cozido à portuguesa* (often served on Sunday) or the famous *porco alentejano* (fried strips of marinated pork in a sauce of baby clams). Roast suckling pig (*leitão assado*) is also tempting, as are the various smoked fillets (*paio*), sausages (*salsicha*), and succulent mountain hams (*presunto*) often served as appetizers (*acepipes varia-dos*). Barbecued chicken (*frango no espeto*) is not to be missed, nor, if you get the chance, is game such as quail (*codorniz*) and partridge (*perdiz*). Reliable standbys include calves' livers (*iscas*) and *bife à portuguesas* (beef steak with a mustard sauce topped with a fried egg). Dishes requiring a stronger stomach include those based on tripe (*tripas*), one of Porto's great specialities.

Desserts Portugal owes many of its outstanding pastries to the work of nuns, who over the centuries concocted decadently delicious cakes which they sold as a means of supplementing their incomes. Teashops, cafés, and bars invariably stock a tasty selection of pies and other titbits—*pasteis de nata* (custard tarts) are some of the best. In restaurants, by contrast, puddings often start and finish with the extremely common *arroz doce*, a type of rice pudding laced with cinnamon, or the equally widespread *pudim flan*, a close cousin of *crème caramel*. Fruit or ice cream are favorite standbys; choose the excellent local fruit when it is in season—figs, plums, peaches, and cherries are particularly good. Cheese (*queijo*) is also widely served, some of the best being sheep or goat's cheeses such as *queijo da serra* ("mountain cheese"), de Castel Branco, or de Azeitão. Ignore the dull Gouda-like Flamengo in favor of soft cheeses such as *cabreiro*, *rabaçal*, or *quejinhos*.

139

RESTAURANTS
A small neighborhood restaurant may be called a *tasca*, while a *casa de pasto* is a type of local inn that serves inexpensive, table d'hôte, three-course meals, usually at lunchtime only. More infor-mal still is a *cervejaria*, or "beer house," which will serve beer and snacks. Some cafés and bars serve light meals: look out for a sign outside advertis-ing *comidas* (meals). A *marisqueria* specializes in seafood (from *mariscos*, meaning shellfish). Note that Portugal's meal times are considerably earlier than those of Spain: lunch runs from around 12:30 to 2:30, and dinner from around 7:30 to 10:30. In rural areas and smaller restaurants you will find it difficult to get served after about 10 PM.

Cheese cakes, an Alentejan specialty

PRACTICALITIES

Buçaco can easily be seen on a day trip from Coimbra (17 miles, or 27km). Alternatively, you could stay near by at the elegant little spa town of Luso (2 miles, or 3km), which is linked to Coimbra by buses and trains. You will want to explore the woods on foot, but note that you can drive to the hotel and the little Museu Militar (devoted to the Peninsular Wars), as well as to the *obelisco* (obelisk), the Cruz Alta, and other viewpoints.

Paths lead from the Hotel Palace do Buçaco to the woods

TREES

The monastic care lavished on the woods at Buçaco over 1,500 years has resulted in an arboretum of quite incredible range. It is estimated that there are around 700 varieties of trees here, including some 400 indigenous species such as oaks and mastics, and around 300 exotic varieties, among them sequoias, eucalypts, ginkgos, thujas, Himalayan pines, Chile pines, and amazing Mexican cedars.

▶▶▶ Buçaco   *132B2*

Buçaco is one of the loveliest and most famous woods in Portugal, a tiny wall-enclosed oasis of peace and magic offering gentle walks, distant views, secret grottoes, mossy pools, hidden glades, and thousands upon thousands of ancient trees. It covers just 260 acres (105 hectares) on the slopes of the Serra do Buçaco, upon whose ridges the Duke of Wellington won one of the most decisive battles of the Peninsular Wars. At the heart of the woods lies a ruined Carmelite monastery (there are other monastic ruins dotted throughout the forest), together with the extraordinary Hotel Palace do Buçaco, a luxury hotel fashioned from a late 19th-century royal hunting lodge. Designed by an Italian, both the exterior and interior of this famous Portuguese establishment represent outlandish pastiches of Manueline Renaissance style.

WOODS There has been a monastic presence at Buçaco since the 6th century, when Benedictine monks built the first monastery here. Between the 11th and 17th centuries

the region fell under the protection of Coimbra Cathedral, whose priests had inherited it. Nonetheless, Buçaco continued to have a monastic presence, the monks living there kept free from temptations of the flesh by a papal decree of 1622 in which Gregory XV forbade women from entering the woods on pain of excommunication. In 1628 the area received a fresh monastic lease of life with the arrival of Carmelite monks, who built a new monastery and encircled the ancient woodlands with a perimeter wall. They also continued the good husbandry of almost a millennium by planting numerous trees, many of them exotic species brought back by Portuguese explorers in Africa and the New World (see panel). In 1643 the monks obtained another papal decree, this time from Urban VIII, which threatened excommunication to anyone who damaged the forest's trees.

BATTLE The Battle of Buçaco, one of the major battles of the Peninsular Wars, took place on the ridge just above Buçaco, a redoubt that Wellington, its main protagonist, described as "that damned long hill." By 1810 Napoleon's generals and the French had already made two attempts to invade Portugal. In May of that year they embarked on a third. Some 65,000 troops duly set off from Valladolid to

Viseu under the command of Marshal Masséna. Their first target was Coimbra, a stepping stone to Lisbon.

Wellington, meanwhile, needing to buy time to complete a defensive arc around the capital (see panel), set about defending the main road to Coimbra. Masséna, finding his way blocked, decided to approach the city by marching across the Buçaco hills. Wellington then moved his troops onto a ridge above the forest, keeping most of his 52,000 soldiers—about half of whom were British—hidden from view below its crest. Despite Wellington's position on the strategically superior high ground, and against advice, Masséna decided to attack up the ridge's steep slopes. He lost 5,000 men in a series of doomed charges, while Wellington, for his part, was able to withdraw at leisure towards Lisbon.

WALKS Glorious little paths crisscross Buçaco's woodlands, slipping past flower-strewn glades, waterfalls, fern-fringed pools, and ten tiny hermitages that were once used as retreats by the area's 17th-century monks. At the same time you are free to wander off the tracks—a particularly good idea during summer weekends, when the woods can become too crowded for their own good.

The Hotel Palace do Buçaco makes as good a place as any to begin exploring; it also sells maps and is open to nonresidents for meals, snacks, and drinks. Be sure to take in the ruins of the old Carmelite monastery immediately to the south. One of the area's best strolls takes you west to the **Cruz Alta**, a phenomenal viewpoint (1,788 feet, or 545m), while a walk to the north runs past the **Fonte Fria**, a spring that cascades down 144 steps into a flower-ringed pool. From here, the path then continues past a little lake to the **Vale dos Fetos**, an avenue of ferns, pines, and ancient sequoias. You then turn south to the **Portas de Coimbra**, another fine viewpoint, and return to the hotel. Neither walk should take more than an hour or so.

WELLINGTON'S LINES
Despite his pummeling at Buçaco, Marshal Masséna still expected to be able to march on Lisbon. However, the battle had bought Wellington time to complete three defensive lines around the capital (the work took a year, and proceeded in almost total secrecy). As Masséna crested a ridge at Torres Vedras on October 9, 1810, he was therefore flabbergasted to see a landscape bristling with fortifications—126 vast masonry forts, 247 guns, a militia of 29,000, and, drawn up to the rear, Wellington's 60,000-strong army. Masséna fired a few desultory shots, but knew he could never breach this barrier. On November 15 the French army left Portugal, never to return.

The Hotel Palace do Buçaco was built as a hunting lodge for the Portuguese monarchy

ARRIVING

Coimbra is connected by regular trains to Lisbon's Santa Apolónia station, Aveiro, Figueira da Foz, Guarda, and Porto. The town has three train stations: Coimbra A (tel: 239 834 998) is west of the city center, but most through trains (Lisbon–Porto) stop only at Coimbra B (tel: as Coimbra A), 1.5 miles (3km) to the north. From here frequent local trains run to Coimbra A (no further ticket is required). Coimbra Parque handles trains on the lovely rural line to Lousã.

The city is connected by bus to other centers: the bus terminal (tel: 239 827 081) is in Avenida Fernão de Magalhães, about 0.5 miles (1km) northwest of the city center.

Drivers should be aware that most of the old center is closed to traffic; perimeter parking lots are well signposted.

►►► Coimbra   132B2

Coimbra is one of Portugal's greatest cities, renowned for its university, its beauty, and its checkered historical past. Coimbra's period of ascendancy lasted a little over a century, from 1143, when it became capital of Portucale under Afonso Henriques, the country's first king, to 1255, when Afonso III moved the royal seat to Lisbon. Today, it has the air of a provincial town, albeit a lively one, the students of its prestigious university having generated a plethora of bars, cafés, nightlife, and inexpensive eating places. These alone would make it a pleasant place to spend some time, even without its brooding Romanesque cathedral and distinguished university buildings. Modern development has slightly dulled the city's medieval allure, but there is considerable charm still in the old center, a tangle of alleys winding around a steep hill topped with the cathedral and university. The best place to start your exploration is at the tourist office (see panel opposite), part of the bustling commercial district at the foot of the hill. From here you can walk up Rua Ferreira Borges into the old quarter through the Arco de Almedina.

CATHEDRAL Coimbra's imposing **Sé Velha►►►** (tel: 239 825 273. *Open* 10–6. Closed Fri and Sun) is among the most impressive Romanesque buildings in Portugal. It was commissioned by Afonso Henriques at a time (around 1162) when Coimbra was the fledgling capital. The city then lay close to the border of Moorish and Christian territory, hence the building's fortress-like appearance, a characteristic shared with other Portuguese cathedrals of similar vintage. The date of foundation makes it Portugal's oldest cathedral, although its name, Sé Velha ("Old Cathedral") merely serves to distinguish it from Coimbra's Sé Nova ("New Cathedral"), an uninteresting affair located near by that was built by the Jesuits in the 17th century.

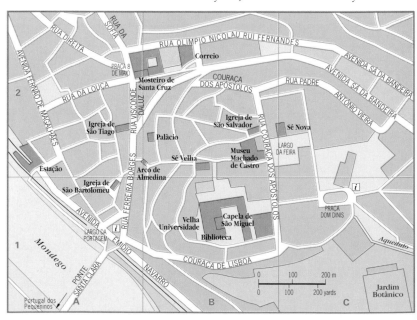

INFORMATION
Coimbra's main tourist office (tel: 239 833 019) is on Largo da Portagem, about 175 yards (150m) south of the Porta de Almedina, the gateway that provides the best approach to the old upper city. There are also offices in Praça Dom Dinis (tel: 239 832 591) and in Praça da República (tel: 239 833 202).

143

Legend has it that the older cathedral replaced a mosque on the site, a distinct possibility given that the city's first governor, Dom Sesnando, was reputedly a Moor who converted to Christianity. Its form, despite its predecessor, is entirely Christian, and owes much to the design of French Romanesque churches. These in turn were largely modeled on the vast church at Cluny and other prototypes in the Auvergne (the cathedral's architects, masters Bernard and Robert, were Frenchmen of Auvergne extraction). The masters' work has remained largely unblemished by the passage of time, unlike the majority of Portuguese churches where successive architectural epochs have invariably left their mark. Ironically, the exterior's major addition, a Renaissance porch (1530) on the north side, one of Portugal's earliest Renaissance creations, has fared worse over the years than the building's earlier fabric.

Inside, the Romanesque is also triumphant, various later additions—notably a plethora of 16th-century *azulejos*—having been swept away. The result is a beautifully plain church, its simplicity relieved only by occasional works of art, of which the most notable is the Gothic high **altarpiece**, or retable. A masterpiece of carved and gilded wood, it was created by two Flemish masters, Olivier de Gand (Ghent) and Jean d'Ypres, and depicts scenes of the *Nativity* and *Resurrection*. Below are represented the four *Evangelists* and the *Assumption of the Virgin* surrounded by four saints. The chapel to the right of the chancel contains a Renaissance work by Tomé Velho, a pupil of Jean de Rouen, leading light of Coimbra's famous school of

SCHOOL OF SCULPTURE
Coimbra's particular appeal to sculptors was the local *pedra de Ançã*, a limestone that proved more workable than the granite of Porto and the marble of Lisbon and the Alentejo. As easy to carve as wood, the stone weathers to a lovely honey color, but also has the unfortunate tendency over the years to become weak and friable. The city's reputation for learning, together with its strong humanist tradition, also attracted artists, as did the wealth that poured into Portugal at the beginning of the 16th century. Around 1520 a group of French sculptors joined forces with João and Diogo de Castilho to form what would become known as the Coimbran School, a movement whose sophisticated Italianate forms were eventually diffused throughout Portugal.

BOTANICAL GARDEN
Coimbra's little Jardim
Botânico (ten minutes'
walk southeast of the
old center) was founded in
the 18th century in strict
adherence to reforms laid
down by the feared
Marquês de Pombal.
Although now a little tatty,
the garden makes a pleas-
ant escape from the city,
and is lined with exotic
plants and trees from
around the world.

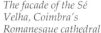

144

*The facade of the Sé
Velha, Coimbra's
Romanesque cathedral*

sculpture (see panel on page 143). Rouen himself carved
the Manueline-influenced font (1520) just in front of the
chapel. A door in the south aisle leads to the simple cloisters, whose chapterhouse contains the tomb of Dom
Sesnando, Coimbra's first Christian governor (died 1091).

MUSEUM Around 50 yards (50m) east of the cathedral, on
Largo Dr. José Rodrigues, lies the **Museu Machado de
Castro**▶▶▶, named in honor of an 18th-century sculptor
who was born in Coimbra (tel: 239 823 727. *Open* Tue–Sun
9:30–12:30, 2–5:15. *Admission: moderate, free Sun mornings*).
Not surprisingly, the museum is weighted towards sculpture, and contains some of Portugal's most important
Gothic and early Renaissance carvings. The collection is
housed in the former episcopal palace, a predominantly
16th-century building that has considerable appeal in its
own right. The loggia on its west side is particularly noteworthy, offering a captivating view over the cathedral
and the rooftops below.

Among the highlights in the museum's left wing are
works by Master Pêro, a pioneer of Gothic sculpture in
Coimbra, in particular his *Nossa Senhora do Ó* (ca1330) and
a fetching *Madonna and Child*. Most people's favorite
piece, however, is a tiny mace-clutching medieval knight
on horseback, an anonymous work whose depiction of a
secular subject was unusual in Gothic art.

The most arresting works of subsequent centuries are
those of Nicolau Chanterène, a French sculptor who
worked in Coimbra between 1518 and 1528, and one of the
greatest of all 16th-century artists who moved to Portugal.
His sojourn in the city followed his work at Belém (see
pages 60–61), but predated his more mature carving in
Évora (see pages 195–199) and Óbidos (see pages 176–177).
His best work here is the *Virgem Anunciada* (his Coimbran
masterpiece is to be found in the
monastery church of
Santa Cruz; see

page 146). Look out, too, for Jean de Rouen's *Entombment*, one of several pieces by this prolific sculptor, as well as works by Houdart, who succeeded Chanterène as leader of the Coimbran School.

Other floors of the museum contain further valuable artifacts, among them a welter of paintings, ceramics, and porcelain, as well as an outstanding collection of gold and silverware. Among the paintings, look for works by Vicente Gil and Josefa de Óbidos, the latter one of the few female Renaissance painters to have achieved widespread eminence (see pages 176–177).

Also leave time to wander into the **Cryptoporticus**, a two-story honeycomb of galleries that underpins the palace. Built by the Romans, it may have served as a granary but more probably acted as the foundations for the site of Coimbra's Roman forum.

UNIVERSITY Coimbra's venerable university, **Velha Universidade▶ ▶** (on Largo Dom Dinis), is Portugal's oldest and most prestigious seat of learning (tel: 239 859 800. *Open* daily 9:30–12. *Admission: moderate*). A symbol of national pride, it has seen many of the country's most eminent men and women pass through its portals, among them Luís de Camões (Portugal's great epic poet), Santo António (better known as St. Anthony of Padua), and even António Salazar, the country's infamous dictator (who also taught here for a period). Given Coimbra's pride in its institution, it is ironic that the university was founded in Lisbon (in 1288). The fruit of a collaboration between Dom Dinis and a trio of churchmen, it was created largely on the wishes of the latter, the Church having appealed to Pope Nicholas IV to approve the venture (the Church tended to bankroll such institutions as students often became clerics).

During the next century the university began to accept lay students, moving its seat back and forth between Lisbon and Coimbra in the process. Although its status is now unquestioned, standards then were often slipshod, a state of affairs that prompted the appointment in 1534 of André de Resende. On the king's orders this firebrand chastised the assembled worthies with the words "when nearly the whole of Europe is being reborn…we ought to feel truly ashamed of our gross ignorance and slothfulness." Three years later the university was permanently installed in Coimbra, occupying a royal palace donated by João III. Some two centuries later the university saw more changes, this time instigated by the Marquês de Pombal (see page 38). He not only demolished the city's castle (to make way for new faculty buildings), but also added natural sciences to the curriculum and abolished the sale of doctorates and other corrupt practices.

Today, the university still dominates the old city, although its ancient buildings are now mingled with various concrete apartments, the unfortunate result of a "modernization" process initiated by Salazar. The buildings which you should make a point of seeing center on the **Patio das Escolas**, a courtyard overlooked by a clock tower (1733) that was once used to summon students to lectures; its nickname is *A Cabra*, meaning the "Goat." A stairway to the right leads to a ticket booth, where you

The ornate ceiling of the University's Capela de São Miguel

145

STUDENT PRANKS
Many of Coimbra's 20,000 students indulge in a variety of typical traditions, some of which date back over 400 years. Most take place in a week of madness in May known as the Queima das Fitas. Some students wear black capes whose hems are edged with cuts—the more cuts, the more frequently they have been disappointed in love—and many sport colored ribbons, each color denoting a different faculty. Sometimes the narrow ribbons worn by students in their first years of study are ceremoniously burned and then replaced with wider ribbons before their fifth and final year. Most students arrange themselves in so-called "republics," groups of 10 to 20 who share rambling apartments and living expenses.

CAFÉS AND BARS
Coimbra's best cafés and traditional coffeehouses can be found along Rua Ferreira Borges and its northern continuation, Rua Visconde da Luz. Both lie to the west and just below Coimbra's hill. More atmospheric cafés and restaurants can be found in the warren of rather down-at-heel streets around Rua das Azeiteiras in the Baixa district just to the west.

PORTUGAL DOS PEQUENINOS
This attraction, "Portugal for the Little Ones," is ideal for anyone traveling with children (*Open* Apr–Sep, daily 9–7; Oct–Mar, daily 9–5:30. *Admission: moderate*). It is located about 200 yards (200m) across the bridge by the tourist office, and consists of scale models of famous Portuguese monuments and rather historically (and architecturally) dubious "traditional" houses typical of Portugal's former colonies (the attraction dates from the 1950s, when Portugal still had colonies). The models are all large enough for kids to clamber in, and there is also a small children's museum.

Opposite: the entrance to Coimbra's 900-year-old university

buy one ticket for the Sala dos Capelos and another for the famous library and main university building.

The **Sala dos Capelos**, once the throne and assembly room of the royal palace, is now used for formal ceremonies such as the conferring of degrees. It takes its name from the cap (*capelos*) awarded to graduating students. Its main points of artistic interest are the grandiose Manueline wood ceiling and the stern-faced portraits of Portugal's kings ranged around the walls. Rather more appealing, however, is the balcony that runs around the exterior walls, offering broad views over the city.

Back in the courtyard, the central door leads to the **Capela de São Miguel**, intricately decorated with frescoes, 17th-century tiles, twisted pillars, and a quite extraordinary organ. The decor here, however, is as nothing compared to that in the **Library** (entered off the left of the courtyard), three interconnected rooms built between 1717 and 1723 during the reign of João V. Gilded and marbled wood occupies every nook and cranny, sometimes offset by multicolored Chinese lacquerwork and richly inlaid furniture. Venerable leather-bound books, some 30,000 in all, stand in vast floor-to-ceiling shelves.

MONASTERY The **Mosteiro de Santa Cruz►►** stands at the foot of Coimbra's hill (in Rua Visconde da Luz), making it a convenient last sightseeing stop (tel: 239 822 941. *Open* Mon–Sat 9–noon, 2–5:30, Sun 4–6. *Admission free, cloister inexpensive*). Most of the structure was built along Manueline lines in the 16th century, largely replacing a Romanesque convent begun during the reign of Afonso Henriques. Its founding fathers were two clerics, Telo and João Peculiar, who built a small priory in 1131 to house 12 Augustinian monks. Its first prior was São Teotónio, Afonso Henriques' confessor.

Santa Cruz's attractions are almost all bound up with Coimbra's group of eminent 16th-century sculptors (see panel on page 143), many of whom executed pieces of work for the monastery. The first of these is the church's now badly weathered porch, built in 1520 by Nicolau Chanterène and Diogo de Castilha, but spoiled by later 18th-century additions.

The western frontage was designed by Diogo, and decorated with statues by Chanterène and Jean de Rouen. Chanterène makes another, more distinguished, appearance inside the church, where his pulpit is widely regarded as one of Portugal's great sculptural masterpieces. He also carved the tombs of Afonso Henriques and his son, Sancho I, who were disinterred from their graves in front of the old priory in 1520 and reburied in bays flanking the high altar.

Elsewhere, the **sacristy** (1622) contains some impressive furniture and a handful of paintings, the most notable of which is a depiction of *St. Vincent* by García Fernandes. The **cloisters** (1524), archetypal Manueline creations, are by Marco Pires. Their **chapter house**, however, while adorned with predictable intricacy, pales besides the beautiful *coro alto* (**choir**), which you can reach via a staircase from the cloister. The work of French and Flemish craftsmen, its stalls are decorated with castles and galleons designed to recall Portugal's voyages of discovery and imperial conquest.

MUSEUM

Conimbriga's wonderful museum, the Museu Monográfico (tel: 239 941 177. *Open* Tue–Sun 10–1, 2–6), provides an important accompaniment to the excavations, which might otherwise appear simply as piles of rather meaningless rubble. It has few explanations in English, but the various rooms and displays, which are arranged thematically, still bring alive aspects of trade and day-to-day life in the former colony. Larger finds such as statues, busts, mosaics, and funerary monuments are also displayed. Be certain to stop off in the café and picnic area to the rear, which offer a lovely panorama over the surrounding countryside.

Roman splendor at Conimbriga

▶▶ Conimbriga

132B2

Conimbriga is one of the most impressive Roman sites on the Iberian peninsula (*Open* daily 9–1, 2–5/6. *Admission: inexpensive*). Occupying the site of an earlier Celtic Iron Age settlement (800–500 BC), this fortified settlement began life around 200 BC on the old Roman road between Olissipo (Lisbon) and Bracara Augusta (Braga). It reached its peak in the 1st century AD, thanks largely to redevelopment instigated during the reigns of the emperors Augustus and Vespasian. Its name is an amalgam of *briga*, an old Celtic suffix meaning a fortified site, and *conim*, referring to a rocky spur. Its decline began with the Frankish and Alman invasions of AD 260–270, incursions that led to the building of a hastily raised defensive **wall**, one of the site's more startling features. In the event, the wall proved of little use, and in the 6th century the site was abandoned in favor of Aeminium, a better-defended Roman colony that evolved into modern-day Coimbra (see pages 142–147).

Only a fraction of the site has been properly excavated, but what is on display more than merits a visit. After a trip to the museum (see panel), follow the old "Roman Way" up to the former defensive wall, which made use of virtually any building material—houses, columns, bas-reliefs—that came to hand. Much of the residential area beyond the barrier was subsequently abandoned, but there remain the substantial ruins of the **House of the Fountains** (on the right), whose former rooms are marked out by paving stones and bases of columns. Note the wonderful spread of mosaics and the pool at its heart, a rare feature. Beyond the wall stands the **Villa of Cantaber**, one of the largest private Roman houses to have survived. Beyond it to the left lies the site of the forum and the artisans' quarter (not fully excavated), and to the right the remains of a bath complex and aqueduct.

► Figueira da Foz   132A2

Figueira da Foz has been one of the country's most popular beach resorts with Portuguese families since the early 1900s. Initial impressions of the town, however, can be offputting, for a faintly industrial fringe taints the approaches, while the beach front to the west of the town is backed by ranks of modern apartment buildings. The wide and busy **beach**, however, is magnificent, while the grid of pedestrianized streets behind the sea front is a warren of appealing stores, restaurants, and bars. Take Figueira for what it is—an unpretentious but fun modern resort—and there are few more pleasant places for a bit of sun and sea on this part of the coast.

The town's site has been occupied for millennia, thanks to its position on the mouth (*foz*) of the River Mondego. Wellington disembarked his troops here at the outbreak of the Peninsular Wars in August 1808, and it was their subsequent advance south that led to the first battles of his campaign at Vimeiro and Roliça. More recently, a deepwater terminal has allowed the rapid development of the local fishing fleet, one of the reasons for the town's industry and the troublesome pollution that goes with it.

If you want time off from the beach, make for the **Museu Municipal Dr. Santos Rocha** (tel: 233 402 840. *Open* Tue–Sun 9:30–12:30, 2–5:30. *Admission free*) on Rua Calouste Gulbenkian (north of the beach and town center). It features an impressive miscellany of paintings, sculpture, archaeological finds, furniture, and pottery, together with a titillating collection of 19th-century beach photographs. Also worth a look is the **Casa do Paço** (tel: 233 422 159. *Open* Mon–Fri 9:30–12:30, 2–5:30. *Admission free*), situated in Largo P. Vita Guerra 4 (on the waterfront by the marina and municipal gardens). On the site of the former episcopal palace, it is notable for its walls, covered in some 7,000 Delft tiles, part of a cargo from a ship wrecked locally in the 18th century.

The beach at Figueira

PRACTICALITIES

Figueira's train station (tel: 233 428 483) is in the east of the town in Largo Estação, a good 25 minutes' walk from the beach and central grid of streets. Several trains a day connect to Coimbra and Lisbon. The bus station (tel: 233 423 095) lies north of the central grid at Largo Luís de Camões.

In summer reserve hotel rooms in advance. Inquire at the helpful tourist office (tel: 233 422 610), on the beachfront Rua 25 de Abril by the clock tower. Before accepting rooms from touts at the station check they are not located too far from the center (best bets are on Rua Bernardo Lopes and Rua da Liberdade).

WHAT'S IN A NAME?

Figueira da Foz means "Fig Tree at the Mouth of the River," although nobody seems to know how the name came about.

The Beiras

Elegant, galleried town-houses in Guarda

The top of Guarda's age-old pillory

150

▶ **Guarda** 133D3

Guarda is cold, bleak, and almost incessantly windswept—and no wonder, for at 3,465 feet (1,056m) above sea level it is the highest town in Portugal (its inhabitants also like to claim that it is Europe's highest *city*). Its site, an obvious one for any defending force, has probably been inhabited since prehistoric times and reputedly served as a military base for Julius Caesar. Later it became a Visigoth fortress, and later still a Moorish citadel. It was retaken by Afonso Henriques, although the present town was only "founded" in 1199 by Sancho I. Its name, *guarda*, is an obvious reference to the defensive role forced upon it by its proximity to the Spanish border, and as late as 1811 the Duke of Wellington made use of its strategic possibilities during the Peninsular Wars.

Today, Guarda's height and its bitter winters, not to mention the modern quarters below the old town, give the place a dour look. At the same time, its restaurants and accommodations make it a good base, while a large student population brings a touch of life and color to its streets and cafés. For information, visit the town's tourist office in the main Praça Velha (tel: 271 212 115). For information on the Serra da Estrela Nature Park (for which Guarda is convenient) you need to visit the park visitor center at Seia (see page 153).

The town has little that could be called essential sightseeing. The chief exception is the gaunt **Sé** (**Cathedral**), just off Praça Velha, whose long period of gestation (1390–1540) resulted in an amalgam of decorative and architectural styles. Gothic grapples with Manueline inside and out, although the Renaissance provides the main highlight: a vast altarpiece, or *retábulo*. This is the work of Jean de Rouen, a leading master of the Coimbran School. Sample, too, the baroque finery of the **Misericórdia** just to the west, as well as the mildly diverting **Museu da Guarda** (tel: 271 213 460. *Open Tue–Sun 10–12:30, 2–5:30. Admission free on Sun and holidays; otherwise inexpensive*) immediately to the south.

▶▶▶ Monsanto   *133D1*

Monsanto (the "Sacred Mount") is one of the Beiras' quintessential hill villages. Perched at 2,487 feet (758m) astride desolate granite slopes, its houses a jumble of weathered stone, its tiny streets often carved from the living rock, it can barely have altered in appearance for centuries. Buses ferry tourists in to gawp at this living fossil, but with no accommodations their fleeting presence is unlikely to change the village. The Lusitanians and Romans both built forts here, although that the present castle ruins—sited on a granite crag and half-lost amidst a jumble of boulders—dates from the days of Dom Dinis. Views from its keep are extraordinary, stretching on clear days to Castelo Branco (30 miles, or 48km) and the wooded slopes of the Serra da Estrela.

Castelo Branco, the capital of the Beira Baixa, is where most people stay locally (although note that a small *pousada* has opened 4 miles, or 7km, from Monsanto). The town itself is largely modern, but none the worse for that as its broad streets are vibrant and prosperous, and its squares and parks tidy and flower-decked. Money comes from trade in cork, honey, cheese, and olive oil, the latter among some of the finest in Portugal. The town is also known the length and breadth of the country for its beautiful bedspreads, or *colchas*, traditionally embroidered by young girls as part of their trousseau. Sieges over the years (Castelo lies just 11 miles, or 18km, from the Spanish border) have put paid to most of its older monuments. The most vicious attack came in 1807, when Napoleonic troops razed much of the district before marching on Lisbon. The ruins of a Templar tower lie above the town, but in the absence of the local museum (closed for long-term restoration) the only thing of note to see is the **Jardim do Antigo Paço Episcopal** (*Open* daily 9–dusk. *Admission: inexpensive*), a 17th-century topiaried garden laid out in the grounds of the former bishop's palace.

151

The former church of São Miguel, within Monsanto's fortress walls

The granite ridges of the Serra da Estrela contain some of Portugal's highest peaks

►►► Serra da Estrela

The towering mountains of the Serra da Estrela, some 35 miles (60km) long by 20 miles (30km) wide, edge across into neighboring Spain. This vast granite range contains some of Portugal's highest peaks and forms the western-most of the great *serras* that rear up across the Iberian peninsula. The upper reaches of the high plateaus are a jumble of bare rocks and perfumed grasses, while the lower slopes are swathed in a rich tapestry of forests. Only the lowest valley bottoms are cultivated, often with rye and wheat. Two of the country's mightiest rivers, the Mondego and Zêzere, have their sources in the mountains.

Many traditional ways of life prevail in the region, but change has recently arrived in the shape of winter tourism (Portugal's only major ski resort is found locally) and through the active promotion of local villages as summer hiking and recreational centers. To this end, much of the region has been declared a *parque natural*, while all land over 3,937 feet (1,200m) has been protected since 1990. This is a beautiful region to explore (park information centers in several villages offer guidance), but it is not one that can easily be seen without your own transportation.

REGIONAL BASE Traditionally, the main base for the region has been **Covilhã►** (to the south), owing mainly to its size and facilities, both unusual in an area this moun-tainous and remote. Although promoted as an outdoor center, Covilhã owes its prosperity to its wool industry, an activity that has led to the development of factories on the plain below the town. The abundance of local sheep pro-vided the industry's initial spur, and the yarn spun here now serves the needs of two thirds of Portugal's textile trade. Sheep also yield the town's other famous product, *queijo da serra*, a pungent cheese made from ewe's milk. Little in the town merits a look, but it is a useful place to stay and the tourist office on Avenida Frei Heitor Pinto (tel: 275 319 560) is the main branch for the region.

EXPLORING The obvious trips from Covilhã are northwest on the N339 to Penhas da Saúde, a small resort in a glacial valley, and beyond that to the summit of **Torre►►**, mainland Portugal's highest peak (6,538 feet, or 1,993m). The ascent, which can be made by car, offers superb views, but because of a restaurant and shopping area the summit hardly offers a wilderness experience.

From below Torre the N339 continues northwest via lovely countryside to **Sabugeiro►►**, one of Portugal's highest villages, which preserves much of the old *serra* way of life. The larger, but not very interesting town of **Seia** has accommodations and the Serra da Estrela region information center at Praça da República 28 (tel: 238 310 440). There is also a tourist office (tel: 238 312 272).

From Seia a mountain road strikes northeast to link with the N232 between Gouveia and **Manteigas►►**. The latter, which is reached on a dramatic road, is perhaps a better base for hiking and exploration than Covilhã. It contains the park's main information center (tel: 275 980 060), in Rua 1 de Maio, with a tourist office near by (tel: 275 981 129). There is a choice of accommodations, with a scenically situated *pousada* a few miles to the west. The park office has details of walks, the trail to Poço do Inferno ("Hell's Well") making a neat circular hike—see below.

From Manteigas, the N338 leads south back to the N339, largely along the scenic **Vale Glaciário do Zêzere**, a perfect U-shaped glacial valley (and one of Europe's deepest).

BELMONTE
This interesting and pleasant little town, perched at 2,000 feet (600m) on a hilly spur, lies 12 miles (19km) northeast of Covilhã just to the east of the *parque natural*. It was the birthplace of Pedro Álvares Cabral, discoverer of Brazil, who was born in the eye-catching 13th-century castle that rises above the town. Next to the castle is the pretty church of São Tiago, home to Cabral's tomb and a miscellany of Romanesque frescoes and carvings. You should also hunt for the fascinating Centrum Cellas, situated 1.2 miles (2km) north of the town off the road to Guarda. Possibly part of a 2nd-century AD Roman villa, it is a blunt, three-storyed granite building studded with windows, and probably owes its survival to its usefulness as a watchtower in the Middle Ages. Belmonte's tourist office is on Rua 1 de Maio (tel: 075 911 488).

153

Walk

Serra da Estrela: Poço do Inferno

The Serra da Estrela stands out for hikers as one of Portugal's few areas of outstanding natural beauty for which high-quality walking maps are available.

The park authorities, in conjunction with the IGC, produce an excellent 1:25,000 sheet, the *Parque Natural da Serra da Estrela*, available locally or from specialist map stores in your own country, before you go. With this as your guide, you should be able to follow part or all of the various trails (labeled T1, T2, and so on).

One of the most popular day walks is to the waterfall known as the **Poço do Inferno** ("Hell's Well"), a circular walk of around five to six hours. It begins from Manteigas, home of the park headquarters, and has yellow waymarks.

Start by the gas station and tourist office, and from there head downhill and over the bridge before picking up the marked trail (T32) southeast through the woods to the falls. A surfaced track returns you to Caldas de Manteigas, just above Manteigas.

You can also approach the falls on track T3 from just above Nave, a village 6 miles (10km) south of Manteigas.

PRACTICALITIES

Viseu's tourist office lies on Avenida Calouste Gulbenkian (tel: 232 420 950), just south of Praça da República (or the Rossio), the town's vibrant main square. The local railroad closed recently, but its route is shadowed by buses; services regularly link to Lisbon, Coimbra, and Guarda. The bus station is close to the town center on Avenida António José de Almeida. The nearest train station is now at Nelas, about 16 miles (25km) south; shuttle buses connect it with Viseu.

Viseu's Museu de Grão-Vasco

154

The capital of the Beira Alta, a sedate and pleasing agricultural town with a long and distinguished history, surveys the rambling wooded hills of the Dão wine country from its 1,640-foot (500m) plateau. The Romans built a camp here, close to which Viriatus, leader of the Lusitanian rebels who harassed the Romans, is said to have fought his last battle (see page 26); the ruins of the camp can be seen on the northern edge of town at Cava de Viriato.

Viseu's star turn is the **Museu de Grão-Vasco▶▶▶** (tel: 232 432 453. *Open* Mon–Sat 10:30–12:30, 2–5:30. *Admission: inexpensive*), devoted among other things to Vasco Fernandes (or Grão Vasco, meaning "Great Vasco"), one of Portugal's finest 16th-century painters (see panel), born in Viseu. The museum, which lies alongside the cathedral in Praça da Sé, ranges over three floors, each full of dazzling *azulejos*, sculptures, ceramics, and 19th- and 20th-century paintings. Its highlights are the works of Vasco and other Portuguese "primitives," and in particular Vasco's famous painting of *St. Peter Enthroned* (a late work), together with a *Calvary* and the cathedral's former altarpiece, a 14-panel work depicting scenes from the *Life of Christ*, probably by Vasco and pupils.

THE VISEU SCHOOL

In the 16th century Viseu was home to an important school of painting. Its two leading exponents were Gaspar Vaz (died ca1568) and Vasco Fernandes (ca1480–ca1543). Vaz learned his trade in Lisbon but, like Vasco, was greatly influenced by the work of Flemish masters, notably Van Eyck. In time, both forged styles of their own, maturing into two of Portugal's finest painters.

The full flavor of old Viseu is revealed in its jumble of streets, little changed since their medieval heyday, and in its sublime cathedral square, the **Praça** (or **Adro**) da **Sé▶▶▶**. In the latter your eye is drawn to the white facade of the Misericórdia (whose interior disappoints), and to the doughty granite bulk of the Sé, whose Romanesque towers frame a 17th-century frontage. The cathedral's interior is delightful, in particular the vaulting (1513), a Manueline showpiece of twisted rope-like stone.

The 18th-century gilded baroque altarpiece is also outstanding, as is the choir, reached by a staircase off the north transept. The cloister, one of the more sedate examples in Portugal, is also appealing. Its second-tier chapterhouse contains a small **museum**, noteworthy for its 12th-century Gospel and a pair of 13th-century Limoges reliquary chests.

►► Vouzela   *132B3*

Portugal is full of sleepy corners where life appears barely to be moving, and if you are in the mood for this sort of easygoing atmosphere you could do worse than follow a meandering route along the Vouga river. The best way to approach the area is on the minor N16 road from Viseu (see opposite). Thereafter, there are plenty of pretty places to stretch your legs and take photographs, although the only spot that really merits an overnight stop is Vouzela, the epitome of the self-contained and quietly prosperous Portuguese town.

The town offers few sights save a Romanesque bridge and 13th-century parish church, but the riverside setting and cluster of old granite houses are a picture of old-world perfection. If you want more background, visit the tourist office (tel: 232 771 515) on the modest main square. Upstairs there is a small and eclectic **museum** (*Admission free*) devoted to local folk artifacts, textiles, paintings, and archaeological remains.

When you tire of lazing around Vouzela, make for **São Pedro do Sul►**, 2.5 miles (4km) to the northeast, one of the oldest and prettiest spas in the whole of Portugal. Today, much of the wood-surrounded complex is modern, but its healing waters have been sampled since at least Roman times, and were a firm favorite among several generations of Portuguese royalty.

If the river valley palls, it is but a short drive south into the heart of the **Serra do Caramulo►**, a redoubt of granite mountains rising to 3,527 feet (1,075m). The highest point, Caramulinho, lies close to the village of **Caramulo►►**, the most important of the tiny hamlets that dot the area (see panel). This is a good base for hiking, but is better known for its wonderful little **museum** (*Open daily 10–1, 2–5. Admission: inexpensive*), whose collection includes superb Tournai tapestries, furniture, silverware, works by Dali and Picasso (who presented them to the museum), and a painting by the British artist Graham Sutherland, given to Portugal by Queen Elizabeth II as a mark of the friendship between the two countries.

CARAMULO

As well as works of art, Caramulo's museum also contains some 60 vintage cars, among them an 1899 Peugeot, a 1909 Fiat, a 1902 Oldsmobile, and a 1911 Rolls-Royce. There are also a handful of veteran bicycles and motorcycles. For more information on the village, visit the tourist office (tel: 232 861 437) on Estrada Principal do Caramulo. The best place to stay locally is the Pousada de São Jerónimo (tel: 232 861 291), set high on a nearby mountain ridge.

The Igreja da Misericórdia at Vouzela

Estremadura and the Ribatejo

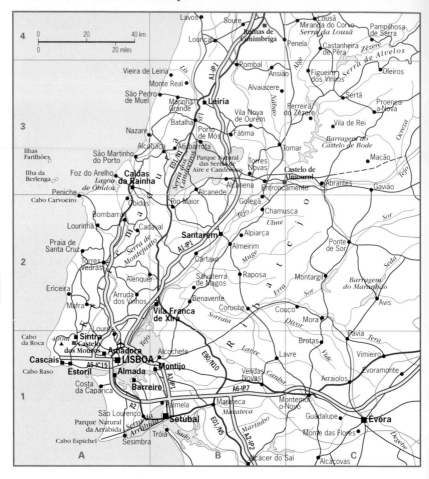

ESTREMADURA AND THE RIBATEJO Estremadura takes its name from the Latin *extrema Durii*, meaning "farthest from the Douro," as it referred to the southernmost area of land recovered from the Moors during the era of the Reconquista (see page 30). Today, the region of Estremadura embraces a broad stretch of Portugal's Atlantic coast, extending roughly from midway down the country to Setúbal in the south. Within its compass lies Lisbon, together with towns and monuments that have witnessed some of the most stirring historical events in the country's history. Slightly to the east of Estremadura lies the Ribatejo, literally the "Banks of the Tagus," an alluvial plain whose monotonous grasslands, grazed by horses and black bulls, form the heart of Portuguese bullfighting country.

LANDSCAPE Inland, the countryside consists of a series of undulating hills and plains interspersed with woods of pine, eucalyptus, and deciduous oaks. Small villages and isolated farmsteads lie scattered across its remoter corners, each the focus of intensely cultivated fields of wheat, maize, vines, olives, and fruit. Local farmers send their

Pages 156–157: the 14th-century walls of Óbidos

produce to Lisbon, an ever-growing metropolis that exerts a powerful pull across the region, drawing in people, services, and transportation. But while the countryside is pretty in its way, and enhanced in places by higher limestone ridges, it has to be said Estremadura and the Ribatejo, on the whole, rather lack the scenic drama and character of other northern regions.

TEMPTING TRIO Dullness, however, is not a charge that can be laid against the area's towns and monuments, which are some of the most captivating in the country. Pride of place goes to the abbey church at **Batalha**, built to commemorate a vital 14th-century victory against the Spanish. Some of the country's most famous kings and princes, together with Portugal's Unknown Soldier, are buried here, surrounded by soaring Gothic architecture and some of the finest decorative carving in Europe.

FISH BOUNTY
The River Tagus was once so fecund that it was said to be comprised of two parts water to one part fish.

Gothic masterpiece: part of the great monastery church at Batalha

The soaring interior of the Mosteiro de Santa Maria at Alcobaça, one of seven Unesco World Heritage Sites in Portugal

Fátima is a point of pilgrimage for millions of Roman Catholics

A close second comes the abbey at **Alcobaça**, also built to commemorate a victory in war, this time against the Moors. Marginally less impressive than Batalha, it none the less features two sublime carved tombs, monuments to Portugal's most romantic historical figures. At **Tomar** stands yet another outstanding building, the Convento de Cristo, raised around a convent-fortress built by the Knights Templars and home to the country's finest example of Manueline architecture. Near by, at Almourol, stands another majestic Templar castle, easily seen on a day trip from Tomar (see panel on page 182).

RELIGIOUS SHRINE At the heart of the triangle formed by Alcobaça, Batalha, and Tomar lies a sight of completely different stamp. **Fátima** is one of the most important religious shrines in the Roman Catholic world, a once tiny village that was transformed by six visions of the Virgin afforded to three young children in 1917. Millions of pilgrims flock to the site every year, many making some of the journey on foot, and even—once they reach the church's massive esplanade—on their knees in the

manner of medieval penitents. Roads around the shrine are invariably busy, crowded as if with refugees fleeing war or some natural disaster. For many the shrine will mean little, and even for the curious it is not, given the potential crowds, a trip to be undertaken lightly. It is safe to say, however, that you will probably never have seen anything like it anywhere else.

ALTERNATIVES Portugal's Atlantic coast will never enjoy quite the same popularity as the Algarve, if only because the water is colder and the sea often dangerous. Where the bays are sheltered, however, and the currents weak, resorts have managed to prosper, and if you fancy sun and sea as a respite from abbeys and religion then you should visit busy little **Nazaré**. Sadly, it is not as quaint as it must once have been, but it is flanked by smaller coastal centers should its crowds prove too much. In complete contrast is the walled town of **Óbidos**, a contender for the title of Portugal's prettiest town and a good base for day trips to the rugged Ilha da Berlenga, an island and bird sanctuary known for its dramatic coastal scenery.

SANTARÉM AND SETUBAL

The Ribatejo's capital is Santarém, perched on the west bank of the River Tagus and overlooking the pasturelands where most of Portugal's bulls are bred. The town was once a Moorish stronghold but is now notable only as a major bullfighting center. The prosperous port of Setúbal, likewise, has nothing to interest the visitor other than the Igreja de Jesus, by the architect of Belém's Jerónimos monastery, and its museum. Set at the mouth of the River Sado, it is a center of the salt industry.

PRACTICALITIES

Alcobaça's tourist office stands opposite the abbey on the main Praça 25 de Abril (tel: 262 582 377)

Buses connect the town roughly every hour to Batalha, Nazaré, and Leiria; there are also three daily express buses to Lisbon. The bus station is about five minutes' walk from the center.

FUN AND FOOD

Seasoned English traveler William Beckford visited the monks at Alcobaça in 1794. Writing of his visit he marveled at the decadence of the place, noting of the kitchen, in particular, that it was "the most distinguished temple of gluttony in all Europe." The abbey's three Grand Priors, he reported, had approached him "hand in hand, all three together," and then, with obvious relish, suggested they go "to the kitchen…to the kitchen… ." Obeying their injunction he found "pastry in vast abundance, which a numerous tribe of lay brothers and their attendants were rolling out and puffing up into a hundred different shapes, singing all the while as blithely as larks in a corn field." The Lord Abbot, wrote Beckford, then observed that "God's bounties are great, it is fit we should enjoy them," a phrase with echoes of the famous pronouncement of Clement VII, the Medici pope, who said on becoming pontiff: "God has given us the papacy, let us enjoy it."

Opposite: the facade of the Mosteiro de Santa Maria at Alcobaça

▶▶▶ Alcobaça   *158B3*

Alcobaça, an otherwise insignificant town, is home to the **Mosteiro de Santa Maria▶▶▶**, one of Portugal's seven Unesco World Heritage Sites and among its greatest abbeys. A masterpiece of Gothic architecture, it is best seen in conjunction with Batalha (see pages 168–171), although most people visit Alcobaça first as Batalha, if anything, is even more impressive (tel: 262 583 469. *Open* Apr–Sep, daily 9–7; Oct–Mar, daily 9–5. *Admission: Apr–Sep moderate, Oct–Mar inexpensive*).

Alcobaça's abbey was reputedly founded in fulfillment of a vow made by Afonso Henriques, Portugal's first king (see pages 30–31). In 1147, so the story goes, Afonso promised to found a monastery dedicated to St. Bernard of Clairvaux (who inspired many crusaders to take up arms) should he succeed in capturing the town of Santarém from the Moors. The town was duly captured, and six years later, in 1153, the king donated land to the Cistercians for the building of an abbey (land which required clearing or reclamation was often awarded to monastic orders). Building work began in 1178, and was modeled on its French sister abbey at Clairval, the first stone being laid a year prior to Portugal's official recognition as a "Christian kingdom" by Pope Alexander III. The nascent abbey, however, was destroyed by the Moors. Work started afresh at the beginning of the 13th century and was completed in 1253.

ABBEY LIFE Alcobaça has been empty since 1834, the year Portugal's monastic orders were abolished. In its day, however, it was the most powerful abbey in the country, with jurisdiction over three ports and 13 towns. After the king, its abbot was one of the most influential men in the kingdom, official "visitor" to the country's Benedictine abbeys and, for many years, the superior of the great Order of Christ, successor to the Knights Templars in Portugal (see pages 180–182). At its height the foundation is said to have sheltered 999 monks, although this figure dropped to just eight following the Black Death. These incumbents not only greatly improved agriculture in the region—it is still one of Portugal's most productive farming areas—but also founded the country's first public school (in 1269) and provided much of the money and scholarly material used by Dom Dinis to found Lisbon university (later moved to Coimbra; see page 145).

ABBEY CHURCH Santa Maria's church is the largest in Portugal, and its interior one of the earliest examples of Gothic architecture in the country. Modeled on the famous Cistercian church at Clairval (1115) in Burgundy in France, its plans may have been drawn up under the first abbot, Ranulph, who was personally dispatched to Alcobaça by St. Bernard. The chances are that he would have been saddened to see what has become of his original **facade**, now bloated to some 720 feet (220m) in length, a disappointingly bland frontage that does little to prepare you for the splendor within. Much of the facade suffered a baroque restoration in the 17th and 18th centuries, only the rose window and main portal (with its statues of saints Bernard and Benedict) having survived from the original. Inside, however, Ranulph would

Pavement tomb in Santa Maria's former refectory

164

have found things more or less as he left them. Sympathetic restoration has removed the accumulation of centuries to return the soaring interior to the beautifully austere appearance of the original. Such simplicity, incidentally, was characteristic of the Cistercians, who traditionally eschewed statuary and elaborate decoration. The nave captivates by virtue of its simplicity and powerful verticality, but the church's main treasures, the beautiful **tombs of Dom Pedro and Inês de Castro▶▶**, are to be found in the north and south transepts. The story of these two lovers is one of the most famous and romantic in Portugal, and has provided the inspiration for any number of plays and poems.

MURDER Dom Pedro was the son of Afonso IV, king of Portugal. Inês, the daughter of a Galician noble, was a lady-in-waiting to the Infanta Constanza of Castile, to whom Dom Pedro was married. On the death of Constanza in 1345, Pedro fell in love with Inês, who moved to the Mosteiro de Santa Clara-a-Velha at Coimbra. Inês's Spanish connections, however, links of which Portuguese kings were ever fearful, allowed a group of leading nobles to turn Afonso IV against his son's lover. The king banned Pedro's proposed marriage to Inês, fearful of its possible implications for the succession, unaware that the marriage had already taken place in secret at Bragança. In 1355 Afonso sanctioned Inês's murder, which duly took place on January 7 that year.

Two years later Pedro inherited the throne from his father. He immediately set about exacting revenge. Two of the three murderers were brought to him at Santarém, where he is said to have torn out their hearts and then eaten them. In 1361 he had Inês's body exhumed, dressed the decayed corpse in a crown and purple robe, and then forced the country's leading nobles to acknowledge her as "queen" by kissing her decomposing hand.

TOMBS Today the tombs face each other, foot to foot, across the transepts, a fulfillment of Pedro's last wishes. His hope, romantic to the last, was that on the Day of Judgment the two lovers would rise and immediately set eyes on one another. The tombs are inscribed with the words *Até ao Fim do Mundo* ("Until the End of the World"). Inês's tomb is in the north transept, supported by six angels and faced with panels depicting the *Crucifixion*, *Scenes from the Life of Christ*, and the *Last Judgment*. In the latter, a superbly graphic relief, the dead, risen from their tombs, stand before God while the damned are hurled into hell's maw. Among the figures supporting the tomb (which have the bodies of dogs and faces of men) is one reputed to depict Pedro Coelho, one of Inês's murderers. Inês's nose, incidentally, was broken off by French troops, who ransacked the church in 1810.

Panels on Pedro's tomb portray scenes from the *Life of St. Bartholomew*, the king's patron saint, and, in the upper frieze, scenes from the lives of the two star-crossed lovers. The rose at its head may symbolize the wheel of fortune or represent further episodes from the pair's lives. Before you leave the church, be sure to note the **Manueline doors** (ca1520) that lead from the rear of the ambulatory beyond the transepts.

ABBEY BUILDINGS To the left of the church you enter the **Claustro do Silencio** (**Cloisters of Silence**), whose lower register was begun in 1308 during the reign of Dom Dinis, making it the oldest Cistercian cloister in Portugal (and a prototype of those to be seen in Porto, Évora, Lisbon, and Coimbra); the upper level, with its Manueline embellishments, was added in the 16th century.

Moving counterclockwise around the cloister, you come first to the former chapterhouse and then to the monks' dormitory, a huge Gothic hall over 200 feet (60m) long (often closed). Next door are Alcobaça's famous **kitchens** (see panel on page 162), into which a stream, diverted from the River Alcôa, flowed to provide water and a ready supply of fresh fish. Alongside lies the refectory, preceded outside by a 14th-century *lavabo* reserved for monkish ablutions. Finally comes the smaller **Sala dos Reis** (**Kings' Hall**), which contains statues of most of Portugal's kings up to José I (died 1777). Also here is a redoubtable bronze cauldron captured from the Spanish in 1385 at Aljubarrota: it was reputedly used to cook up the soldiers' soup before the battle (see pages 168–169). The room's tiles depict episodes from the story of the abbey's foundation.

OVERVIEW
Much of Alcobaça's abbey is closed to the public, including at least four cloisters and seven dormitories. However, if you walk just five minutes to the ruins of the town's former castle, you can enjoy a view over the whole complex.

The monastery is still an oasis of calm and tranquillity

165

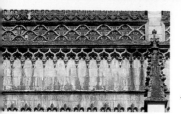

Architecture in Portugal spans over 3,000 years, from the ancient hill forts of the Minho to Lisbon's postmodern Torres das Amoreiras. Much of it was shaped by outsiders—Moors and French monks in particular—but in the great flowering of the Manueline period the country produced a style that was peculiarly Portuguese.

166

GOTHIC ARCHITECTURE
The Gothic arrived in Portugal in the late 12th century, mostly by way of France, and found its earliest expression in the Cistercian abbey at Alcobaça (1178), a model for similar monasteries at Coimbra, Lisbon, and Évora. Although initially slow to take hold, the style came into its own with the church building of the Franciscan and Dominican orders during the reign of Afonso III (1248–1279), reaching its zenith in the mature Gothic masterpiece at Batalha (see pages 168–171). Older churches and monasteries often acquired new Gothic cloisters, while even castles developed modest touches of Gothic decoration.

Manueline trickery in the cloisters at Batalha

Early days Portugal's earliest architectural monuments are the megaliths of the Alto Alentejo, a series of mysterious dolmens (especially prevalent around Évora; see panel on page 197) that date from between 4000 and 2000 BC. A thousand years later came the hill forts of the Iron Age (800–200 BC), of which the best preserved is the Citânia de Briteiros (see page 102). Some of these forts, notably Conimbriga (near Coimbra; see page 148), were later absorbed by the Romans, whose architectural legacy includes temples and aqueducts (such as at Évora), residential villas, and a wide range of stone bridges (at Leiria, Chaves, and elsewhere).

Of the later so-called "barbarian" architecture, little remains save a handful of Visigothic chapels such as those at Beja (see page 191) and Balsemão near Lamego (see panel on page 117). Nor does Portugal boast much in the way of Moorish buildings, although the Moors' architectural influence is obvious in numerous ornamental details and the walls and fortresses of countless towns.

Romanesque Indigenous Portuguese architecture began to find its feet during the 11th century, the era of the Romanesque, a time when Portugal itself was emerging as a nation state. Many Romanesque influences were imported from France, brought by the monks of Cluny and Moissac, or by Burgundian knights drawn south to fight the Moors. To these must be added the influence of the Spanish shrine of Santiago de Compostela. This imparted a Galician flavor to the many Romanesque churches of northern Portugal, where the use of granite added a distinctive local touch to the imported styles. Numerous cathedrals, often designed by French architects, were built during the Romanesque era, a period that also saw the construction or restoration of many castles. As a result, Portuguese cathedrals often repeat, outwardly at least, the military appearance of adjacent fortresses, most notably at Coimbra, Braga, Lisbon, and Porto.

Manueline Portugal's great individual contribution to European architecture was marked by the Manueline period (ca1490–1520), named after Manuel I, the king under whom the style first flourished. Simply put, it marked the country's transition from Gothic (see panel) to Renaissance, and reflected the self-confidence, not to mention the inflow of wealth, that accompanied Portugal's medieval voyages of discovery. Strongly, even excessively florid in style, its effect was most marked in the decorative sphere, where maritime motifs

ECLECTICISM

Architecture in Portugal, already crippled by the 1755 earthquake, received a further blow in 1834 when the dissolution of the religious orders removed an important source of architectural commissions. Thereafter, the country's new buildings embraced a variety of half-hearted styles, many of them throwbacks to earlier glories, notably the neoManueline work of romantically inclined architects at the end of the 19th century.

167

proliferated alongside twisted columns, spiral pillars, and a cornucopia of fantastic details. While the basic plan of buildings often retained a Gothic simplicity, their embellishments—notably in the famous window at Tomar (see page 183)—were flamboyant in the extreme.

Portugal's newfound wealth allowed for numerous innovative commissions, as well as financing the import of skilled craftsmen from Spain, Italy, and the Low Countries. In time these new arrivals brought a more conventional Renaissance influence to bear on Portuguese architecture (although Portugal's acceptance of the Renaissance came later than elsewhere in Europe).

The baroque had a similarly belated birth, mainly because it coincided with the period of Spanish domination. Once into its stride, however, the style triumphed in buildings such as the palace-monastery at Mafra (see page 69), not to mention a host of religious and civic buildings in the north, notably Bom Jesus (see pages 100–101) and the Solar de Mateus near Vila Real (see page 87). In the south, by contrast, the baroque's exuberance was curtailed by the 1755 earthquake, which necessitated a return to a simpler neoclassical style known as "Pombaline." Thereafter, innovation in Portuguese architecture was at a premium (see panels).

MODERN ARCHITECTURE

Portugal's belated entry into the mainstream of European life, and with it the injection of vast amounts of capital, has produced a rash of new building, much of it— for example, Lisbon's mirrored-glass monsters and the Algarve's "Moorish" villa developments—of little or no architectural merit. Exceptions include Lisbon's Gulbenkian complex (see pages 55–56) and the work of the so-called "Oporto School," whose leading exponents include Álvaro Siza Vieira (born 1933), the architect entrusted with restoring Lisbon's fire-damaged Chiado district.

PRACTICALITIES

Batalha's nearest train station is at Valado dos Frados, and is linked to the abbey by bus. Alternatively, there are several buses daily from Nazaré and six expresses from Lisbon. There is little around the abbey save bars, restaurants, and souvenir shops. Limited accommodations are available, including a superb *pousada* (see page 257), but the abbey is best seen on a day trip from Nazaré or Fátima. The village has a small tourist office in Largo Paulo VI (tel: 244 765 180).

Gothic and Manueline architecture at its finest

▶▶▶ Batalha 158B3

Many countries possess a building which not only stands alone as a supreme expression of a nation's art and architecture, but also comes to embody something that touches chords of pride and sentiment in the national character. In Portugal this building is the **Mosteiro de Santa Maria da Vitória▶▶▶**, the country's finest example of Gothic and Manueline architecture, the last resting place of her Unknown Soldier, and a memorial to one of the defining moments in Portuguese history. Its more popular name is the Mosteiro da Batalha—the "Abbey of the Battle" (*Open* May–Sep, daily 9–7; Oct–Apr, daily 9–5. *Admission: moderate*).

ALJUBAROTTA The moment in question was the Battle of Aljubarotta on August 14, 1385, an encounter that secured Portuguese independence from the Spanish for 200 years. It was fought against Juan I, king of Castile, who had a claim to the Portuguese throne through his marriage to Beatriz, the daughter and only heir of Fernando I of Portugal (see page 33). Marriages of convenience between Portuguese royalty and scions of the Castilian royal family had long been commonplace, acting as a buffer between two neighboring states that would otherwise have been at one another's throats. With

Beatriz's unfortunate match, however, and Fernando's inability to produce a son, the policy looked as if it were about to backfire. When Fernando died suddenly, the country's worst fears were realized: Juan, "consort" of the 12-year-old Beatriz, looked set to become Portugal's de facto king.

Or at least this was the worst fear of some Portuguese countrymen (principally the merchants and lower classes), for in a union with Castile many of Portugal's nobles and leading churchmen saw the potential for increased personal power at the expense of the throne. They had an ally in Leonor, Fernando's widow, who had not only taken a Spanish lover while her husband was still alive but also shamelessly promoted the cause of her daughter's foreign husband. Those opposed to Juan and the Castilian clique found their champion in João of Avis, Fernando's illegitimate half brother (bastards littered three of Portugal's royal dynasties, illegitimacy proving no hindrance to advancement). João promptly murdered Leonor's lover, declared himself king, and chased Leonor from the country. The mob rose up in his support.

BATTLE After two years of confusion and Castilian raids, the Portuguese *Cortes*, or parliament, finally acknowledged João as king. This acclamation brought Juan I storming towards Lisbon at the head of a 30,000-strong Castilian army. Hapless Portuguese citizens intercepted en route were either beheaded or left mutilated. After just seven days as king, João I, accompanied by his faithful lieutenant, Nun' Álvares Pereira, confronted the Castilians near Aljubarrota, 2.5 miles (4km) from the present-day site of Batalha. Although outnumbered at least two to one, the Portuguese employed tactics learned from the English during the Hundred Years War, notably the digging of brush-covered trenches; they also boasted a contingent of 500 English archers, lent by England's King Richard II. Looking at the odds, João thought it opportune to strike a bargain with the Virgin Mary, promising to build a sumptuous abbey in return for her assistance. Within an hour the Castilian standard had been captured, and within a week the invaders had been driven from the country. Three years later work began on the abbey.

BUILDING A large proportion of Batalha, including the church, Sala do Capítulo (Chapter House), and Claustro Real (Royal Cloister), was completed in, or just after the reign of João I (1385–1433). Work progressed first under the blind architect Afonso Domingues, then between 1402 and 1438 it was entrusted to an Irishman, Huguet (Ouguête in Portuguese). A Gothic sensibility infuses the majority of the building, mixed with touches of an almost English Perpendicular style, the latter perhaps in homage to Philippa of Lancaster, João's English wife (see panel on page 170). Various additions to this basic plan were made over the centuries (see below), the most notable being the Manueline decoration that constitutes the abbey's chief glory (added at the turn of the 15th century).

CAPELA DO FUNDADOR The square "Chapel of the Founder" lies immediately to the right on entering the abbey's great church. Completed in 1434, a year after

Hero of the battle: Nun' Álvares Pereira

BATTLEFIELD
The site of the Battle of Aljubarrota lies 2.5 miles (4km) south of Batalha. There is little to mark the spot, save a small chapel that was built after the event. Legend has it that in the hour the battle lasted the Portuguese commander, Nun' Álvares Pereira, worked up a considerable thirst. A fresh pitcher of water is still left in the chapel's porch every day as a little memento. The village that gave the battle its name (actually 6 miles, or 10km, from the battle site) was reputedly defended by the local baker, who fought off a contingent of the Castilian army with nothing more than a wooden spoon. She then apparently baked in her bread oven seven of the soldiers she had dispatched.

The interior of the Capela do Fundador, burial place of João I and Philippa of Lancaster

OLD ALLIANCE

After the Battle of Aljubarrota, João I sought friends on the international stage as an insurance policy against further Castilian attack. He found them in an alliance with England and marriage to Philippa of Lancaster, granddaughter of Edward III and sister of the future Henry IV. The alliance was sealed with the Treaty of Windsor (1386), "an inviolate, eternal, solid, perpetual, and true league of friendship." And so it proved, for the alliance has endured to the present day, the longest in modern diplomatic history. Britain's Charles II reconfirmed the country's ties in 1661 by marrying a Portuguese princess, Catherine of Bragança, although the union failed to stop him taking innumerable mistresses. As recently as the Falklands War of 1982, Portugal offered the use of military bases in the Azores to her long-term allies.

João's death, it is dominated by the canopied **tomb of João I and Philippa of Lancaster**, whose carved effigies lie below a beautiful octagonal lantern. Note the Avis and Lancaster blazons on the tomb, and the Order of the Garter worn by João, founded by Philippa's grandfather, Edward III. To the rear stand the graves of the pair's four youngest sons, together with that of the tragic Dom Fernando on the extreme left (see panel opposite). The canopied tomb second from the right is that of Henry the Navigator, prime mover in the voyages of discovery that laid the foundations of the Portuguese empire (see pages 34–35 and 226–227). Dom Duarte, João's eldest son and successor, is buried in the Capelas Imperfeitas (see opposite).

CLAUSTRO REAL The sublime "Royal Cloister" is reached via a door at the top of the church's left (north) aisle. Swathed in some of the most beautiful decorative stonework in Europe, it was built between 1388 and 1402, the Manueline decoration having been added on Manuel I's insistence at the beginning of the 16th century. Moving counterclockwise you come to the **Sala do Capítulo** (**Chapter House**), in which rest Portugal's two Unknown Soldiers: one fell during World War I, while the other was a victim of the country's African wars. The former refectory on the opposite side of the cloister contains a small museum dedicated to the pair.

Above the tombs rises some of Portugal's most daring **vaulting**, an enterprise completed only at the third attempt, and so dangerous that only criminals on death row were said to have been employed during its

MODERN THREAT
The limestone with which much of Batalha is built has weathered over the years to a beautiful golden-brown. More recently, however, it has begun to be blighted by the effects of acid rain. The abbey is also increasingly suffering the adverse effects of the main N1 highway (notably fumes and vibration), which passes distressingly close to the complex. Plans are continually mooted to "move" the road, although none has come close to serious consideration.

171

construction. When the scaffolding was removed its architect reputedly spent a night alone under his creation to silence those who doubted it would stand. Across the Claustro Real a passageway leads to the neighboring **Claustro de Dom Afonso V**, a more sober cloister begun by Dom Duarte and completed in conventional Gothic mode by his successor, Afonso V (1438–1481).

CAPELAS IMPERFEITAS To reach the abbey's last principal component, the "Unfinished Chapels," you need to leave the church and cloister to enter the self-contained complex from a separate entrance at the rear of the church. The chapels were commissioned by João I's eldest son and successor, Dom Duarte, as a mausoleum for himself and subsequent members of the Avis dynasty. Begun in 1434 by Huguet, they remained unfinished and open to the sky.

Today, the chapels house only Duarte and his queen, Leonor of Aragon. Certain additions were made under Manuel I, however, in the shape of a transitional Gothic porch and impossibly ornate **doorway**, the latter one of the supreme expressions of Portuguese Manueline and Renaissance art. Mateus Fernandes, the architect of this and most of the abbey's other Manueline additions, is buried just inside the body of the main church. The remaining tombs were to have occupied the seven hexagonal chambers that radiate from the chapels' octagonal plan, each of which is divided from the next by intricately carved but unfinished pillars. The later Renaissance balcony above was added in 1533 by João III (1521–1557).

DOM FERNANDO
Not all the sons of João I and Philippa of Lancaster lived happy and fulfilled lives. One, Prince Fernando, was captured in Tangiers in 1437 during a badly bungled raid against the Moors. He was then held as a hostage for the return of Ceuta, a Moorish fortress captured by João in 1415. Although Fernando was initially treated quite well, he eventually died of dysentery in 1443 after five terrible years of torture and imprisonment. His body was then hung upside down from the walls of Fez, and his heart was cut out, embalmed, and returned for burial at Batalha. What was left of the body was returned 22 years later. Fernando's brother, Dom Duarte (João's successor), reigned for just five years (1433–1438), his premature death reputedly brought on by contemplation of his brother's tragic life.

The town of Fátima, the so-called "altar of Portugal," is not only the country's religious heart but also one of the most important shrines in the Roman Catholic world. For the millions of pilgrims who come here annually it is a place of mystery and sanctity, scene of six miraculous apparitions of the Virgin in 1917.

Lúcia, Francisco, and Jacinta, the three children of Fátima

PRACTICALITIES
Visits and pilgrimages to Fátima take place all year, but particularly on the 13th of the month, and especially on May 13 and October 13. Over a million pilgrims can be (and often are) fitted into the church and its piazza, so be prepared for extremely large crowds. You can easily come here as a day trip from either Leiria or Tomar, or from Batalha and Lisbon; all are connected by bus to Fátima. (Note that Fátima is often listed as "Cova da Iria" on timetables.) The nearest train station (tel: 249 566 122) is at Estação de Fátima (15 miles, or 25km) on the Lisbon–Porto line. The town's tourist office is in Avenida Dom José Alves Correia da Silva (tel: 249 531 727).

172

Visions Fátima's story is simply told. On May 13, 1917, three children were tending their parents' flocks in a field at Cova da Iria, close to the small village of Fátima. Lúcia dos Santos was ten, her cousins, Francisco and Jacinta, nine and seven. As they idled about their work the sky suddenly grew bright, revealing the figure of the Virgin apparently hovering above a nearby oak tree. All three saw the apparition but only Lúcia, the eldest, was able to communicate. Her memoirs record that she heard the Madonna—a "Lady brighter than the sun"—say "I am from Heaven. I have come to ask you to return here six times, at this same time, on the thirteenth of every month. Then, in October, I will tell you who I am and what I want."

Dilemmas Needless to say the children's story was greeted with skepticism. A month later, however, all three returned to the spot, and were again rewarded with the Virgin's appearance. By the following month interest had picked up, and this time a few thousand people joined the vigil, although only the children saw the apparition and still only Lúcia was able to talk with the Madonna. By then, events at Fátima were national news and exciting polemic in both religious and political circles. With Republican policies at the time rigidly anticlerical, politicians accused the Church of fabricating the miracle in an attempt to bolster support. The Church, for its part, was anxious on two fronts: firstly, not to offend the politicians and generate still harsher legislation; and secondly,

FÁTIMA'S SECRETS

Three key messages were revealed to Lúcia. The first concerned a vision of hell in which "many souls" were damned through "sins of the flesh" and because they "had no one to pray and make sacrifices for them." Significantly, it also included a plea for peace, as in 1917 Europe had been gripped by war for three years. The second message was more specific and, in the light of subsequent events, potentially more controversial. It was delivered as the Bolsheviks were poised to take power in Russia. "If you pay heed to my request," the Virgin asserted, "Russia will be converted and there will be peace. If not, Russia will spread her errors through the world, causing wars and persecution against the Church." The third secret, revealed in 2000, claimed that a white-robed cleric would be shot, a prophecy connected with the attempted assassination of Pope John Paul II in 1981.

Lighting a candle at Fátima

173

to avoid being tempted into sanctioning what might turn out to be a hoax.

Arrest The simplest thing seemed to be to arrest the three children, and this took place on August 13, the date of the Virgin's next scheduled appearance. It was to no avail: the children were interrogated and released, and the fourth vision occurred on the 19th instead. By October, the month set for the last apparition, some 70,000 people had gathered in the little field at Cova da Iria. They were rewarded with the so-called Miracle of the Sun, in which the skies were said to have cleared, the sun turning into a vast swirling ball of dancing light that cast colored beams onto the multitude below. As the beams struck home, countless miracles occurred—the blind could see, the sick were cured, and the lame were made whole. Still only the children, however, could see the Virgin.

Message At this point Lúcia was entrusted with Fátima's famous three prophecies, the last reputedly so terrible that it remained locked in a Vatican drawer until the year 2000 (see panel). Its contents were said to be too distressing to be revealed to anyone but successive popes.

Francisco and Jacinta were to die shortly after the visions, cut down by the flu epidemic that swept through Europe in 1919 and 1920. Lúcia, however, who is still alive, joined a Carmelite convent near Coimbra in 1928. The same year, on May 13, the anniversary of the first apparition, the cornerstone of Fátima's vast church was laid. Its piazza, when completed, covered an area twice that of the square in front of St. Peter's in Rome. In 1929 the Church, all thought of hoaxes forgotten, sanctioned the cult of Nossa Senhora de Fátima. In 1967 Lúcia and 1.5 million pilgrims joined Pope Paul VI at Fátima to celebrate the 50th anniversary of the visions, and Lúcia turned out again in 1982 and 1991 to welcome Pope John Paul II to the shrine. In 1989 Jacinta and Francisco were officially beatified by the Pope, a halfway house to sainthood.

THE ESTORIL COAST

The resorts along the coast between Lisbon and Cascais are served by several trains per hour from Lisbon's Cais do Sodré station. Ease of access means the beaches are crowded.

GETTING TO BERLENGA

Ferries run to Berlenga— weather permitting—from Peniche (Largo da Ribeira) on the mainland: the operator is Viamar and the ride takes an hour. In June and September one ferry runs daily, and in July and August there are three crossings a day. Tickets are limited to 300 per day to prevent overcrowding, so in the height of summer you may have to arrive first thing in the morning to be sure of a place. Other companies on the harbor in Peniche (such as Tur-Pesca; tel: 262 789 960 or 963 73818) run daily fishing, diving, and sightseeing trips to the island.

ATLANTIC COAST BEACHES

Be sure to stick to the prescribed swimming areas on Nazaré's beach: outside these limits the Atlantic is cold and dangerous. If the beach is too crowded (people do have the habit of erecting tents) you might wish to try a couple of resorts to the south. Some 7 miles (12km) away lies São Martinho do Porto, a developed resort with a large and well-sheltered beach (see also panel opposite). About the same distance south again is Foz do Arelho, with another pleasant beach and a lagoon for swimming.

▶ Cascais and Estoril 158A1

The coastal road linking Lisbon and Cascais, 20 miles (30km) west, is strung along with resorts. Before World War I, smart Lisboeteans came to Estoril, as the neo-baroque luxury hotels along the front bear witness, drawn by its mild climate and sandy beaches. The glory has faded and Estoril nowadays is a rather run-of-the-mill resort and commuter base, with a casino and long-established golf club. Just further to the west is the fishing village of Cascais, to where, at the end of the 19th century, the royal court used to decamp for the summer. Set in a lovely bay, it too has now been overtaken by tourism, though there are still fishing boats drawn up on the beach and some of its charm remains.

▶▶ Ilha da Berlenga 158A3

The Ilha da Berlenga is the largest and only accessible island of an archipelago that lies a few miles off Peniche on the Portuguese coast. Just 1 mile (1.5km) long and 0.5 miles (800m) wide, it is a magical place, washed by azure seas (ideal for fishing and diving) and edged with a rugged granite coastline of bays, headlands, marine caves, and deeply indented inlets. In the past it was the home of Jeronymite monks, who in 1513 left their mother house at Belém to administer to sailors and those wrecked at sea. They were eventually forced to leave following attacks by local pirates.

Today, only a handful of fishermen are permitted to live here, the bulk of the island having been turned into a bird reserve. Many thousands of seabirds take advantage of the situation, among them several types of gull, ducks, puffins, and cormorants. Hiking reveals the best of Berlenga, which has some wonderful cliff and sea views, particularly on the west coast: obvious paths crisscross the barren island (whose highest point is 280 feet, or 85m), roughly waymarked with stones. Perhaps the most appealing thing about Berlenga, however, is the boat ride to the island, which provides excellent views of the many seascapes and coastal landforms.

Boats from the mainland dock at the island's only harbor, edged with fishing boats, a handful of humble houses, and a few bars, restaurants, and stores. You can stay here, either at the campsite or in a scattering of rooms, but it is essential to contact the tourist office at Peniche in advance (Rua Alexandre Herculano; tel: 262 789 571). It is also possible to hire boats or take guided boat trips around the island from the harbor. These take in the highlight of the coast, the Furado Grande, a 230-foot-long (70m) marine "tunnel" that culminates in the Cova do Sonho ("Cove of Dreams"), a small creek and bay edged with soaring red granite cliffs.

▶▶ Mafra 158A2

See Lisbon Excursions, page 69.

▶ Nazaré 158A3

Nazaré is one of those unfortunate little places whose charm has been its undoing. Once it must have been one of the most attractive villages on Portugal's Atlantic coast, blessed with a large and beautiful beach, and infused with an old-fashioned way of life that saw exquisitely painted fishing boats hauled from the sea by oxen, and women in traditional costume carrying trays of fish on their heads. Now the beach is often crowded, the boats are corralled in a new marina, and the traditional ways have been submerged by souvenir stands, burgeoning high-rises, and the shabby commercialism of mass tourism.

This said, you may still catch glimpses of traditional costumes (the people of Nazaré claim to be descended from the Phoenicians) and trays of sardines have not completely disappeared from the quaysides. And if you come slightly offseason, the beach and grid of streets making up **Praia** (the lower town) should not be entirely submerged beneath bodies and souvenir stands. **Sítio** (the upper town) also has its attractions, not least of which is the view from its 360-foot (110m) clifftop location (reached via road, path or funicular from Praia). Still better vistas await if you walk the 500 yards (0.5km) or so to the lighthouse west of the town, whose headland overlooks a superb seascape of cliffs and pounding breakers.

In Sítio itself, drop into the **Igreja de Nossa Senhora da Nazaré**, built in memory of a miracle that saved Fuas Roupinho, one of Afonso Henriques' leading lieutenants during the wars against the Moors (see pages 30–31). Roupinho, so the story goes, was hunting a deer which threw itself over a cliff as it tried to escape. Roupinho's horse threatened to follow it over in its excitement, only being prevented from doing so by its rider's impassioned appeal for divine intervention. Our Lady of Nazaré immediately obliged and Roupinho was saved. The story is perhaps more stirring than the church, although the sanctuary's interior has an appealing spread of 18th-century Dutch *azulejos*.

PRACTICALITIES
Nazaré's tourist office (tel: 262 561 194) is in the lower part of town (Praia) near the cable car station on Avenida da República. In São Martinho do Porto (see panel opposite), the office is in Avenida 25 de Abril (tel: 262 989 110). Check with both offices if you want to stay locally during the high season and have not reserved accommodations. The nearest train station is at Valado dos Frades, with regular connections daily from Lisbon. Frequent buses run daily from Valado to Nazaré, which is also served by direct daily express services from Lisbon.

Plenty of room on Nazaré's large beach

PRACTICALITIES
Óbidos is easily reached by road from Lisbon or the north on the old N1, and is linked by train and bus to most points on the coast to the north and south, including Peniche for the Ilha da Berlenga (see page 174). Trains stop at the station at the bottom of Óbidos's hill, but the ticket office has closed (buy tickets on the train). Buses stop beside the Porta da Vila, from which Rua Direita leads through the town to the tourist office (tel: 262 959 231). Accommodations in Óbidos are varied, with plenty of private rooms and a few top-class expensive options. Among the latter is the Pousada do Castelo, one of the country's best *pousadas* (see page 257).

THE WALLS
If you do nothing else in Óbidos, be certain to walk the town's walls, some parts of which date from the time of the Moors, others from restoration work carried out in the 12th, 13th, and 16th centuries. You can walk the entire way round, glancing down over the town's orange-tiled rooftops on one side and the tree-dotted countryside on the other. A sure step is required for some narrow sections since there are no hand rails. Access points proliferate: the best are near the Porta da Vila and the Castelo.

►►► Óbidos   158A2

Óbidos is as pretty a town as you could hope to find, its small historic center perched atop a limestone crag and enclosed by 14th-century castle walls. Scenes of urban or rural bliss greet you at every turn, whether as glimpses of the fairytale countryside—complete with windmills—spread out below the walls, or the brightly bordered whitewashed houses that line its handful of cobbled streets. This kind of picturesque perfection inevitably attracts its fair share of visitors, and the bucolic surroundings are not totally without modern buildings. Tourism pays the wages, however, and keeps things looking remarkably spruce. And, should you stay the night, the town all but empties of outsiders come evening.

HISTORY Óbidos was recaptured from the Moors by Afonso Henriques in 1148, he and his troops having reputedly advanced upon the town disguised as cherry trees. At that time the town was situated on the sea, but the gradual silting up of the harbor has since produced a lagoon (Lagoa da Óbidos) and a fertile coastal plain that has left it some 6 miles (10km) from the coast. In 1282 the town was visited by Dom Dinis, who was so taken with its charm that he presented it as a gift to his queen, Dona Isabel of Aragón. Thereafter the town became the traditional wedding gift of kings to their wives, for which reason it is sometimes known as the "Wedding City." Dinis built the castle, the town's most striking building (now a *pousada*). Its appearance is so evocative that it is frequently used as a setting for films.

TOWN The main entrance to the old town—and one of the best access points to the walls (see panel)—is the **Porta da Vila**, a double gateway whose interior walls are covered in 18th-century *azulejos*. From here the narrow main street, Rua Direita, leads to **Praça de Santa Maria**, the town's main square, which is dominated by a *pelourinho*, or pillory (see panel on page 78), and the **Igreja de Santa Maria►►**. The latter was the stage for the wedding in 1444 of the ten-year-old Afonso V to Isabel, his eight-year-old cousin. Although it is of ancient foundation, most of the building dates from the Renaissance era. The interior is awash with late 17th-century *azulejos*, most of which are decorated with floral motifs. These provide the backdrop to an outstanding Renaissance tomb (1526–1528) in a bay on the church's left aisle. Last resting place of Dom João de Noronha, one-time castellan of Óbidos, the tomb is crowned by a fine carved *Pietà*, possibly the work of Nicolau Chanterène, an influential French Renaissance artist who became the leading sculptor of the so-called Coimbran School; he also decorated the west door of the Mosteiro dos Jerónimos in Belém (see pages 60–61) and carved the pulpit (his masterpiece) in Coimbra's Mosteiro da Santa Cruz (see page 146).

PAINTER The retable, or *retábulo*, to the right of Santa Maria's high altar is decorated with panels (1661) by Josefa de Ayala, or Josefa de Óbidos (1634–1684), not only one of Portugal's finest 17th-century painters, but also that rarest of historical figures, an eminent female artist. Born in Seville, Josefa came to Óbidos in her youth,

spending much of the rest of her life in one of the town's convents. She was initially an etcher and miniaturist, and her work displays an exquisite eye for detail, particularly in the still lifes for which she is best known. More of Josefa's paintings can be seen in a special room in the town's **Museu Municipal**▶▶ in the town hall alongside the church on Praça de Santa Maria (tel: 262 955 010. *Open* daily 10–12:30. *Admission: inexpensive*). Other rooms in the museum contain displays relating to the Peninsular Wars—weapons, maps, and the like—as well as archaeological finds from the Luso-Roman period.

Parts of the fortifications at Óbidos date back to the time of the Moors

ES

AS

Bullfighting in Portugal is neither as common nor, relatively speaking, as brutal as in Spain, although the combination of grace in the face of danger, of glamour entwined with drama, and of skill matched with courage is every bit as attractive to the Portuguese as it is to their Spanish counterparts.

BULLFIGHTS

The bullfighting season in Portugal traditionally starts on Easter Sunday and ends in October. Fights normally take place twice a week, on Thursdays and Sundays. Most are concentrated in the Ribatejo region, the area where many of the bulls are bred. The most famous centers are Santarém (see panel on page 161) and Vila Franca de Xira (an industrial town north of Lisbon), together with the Praça de Touros in Lisbon (see panel on page 73).

Controversial but colorful, bullfighting is a major spectacle

Spared Bullfighting in Portugal, where the encounter between man and beast is known as the *tourada*, differs from the Spanish *corrida* in two important respects. First, much of the fight takes place between a bull and a mounted rider, resulting in some quite breathtaking displays of horsemanship; and second, the bull—while tormented and injured—is not killed outright. Public killing has been banned since 1799, when the Count of Arcos, son of the Marquis of Marialva, was spectacularly gored to death in front of the Portuguese king and his entire court. Instead, the exhausted animal is led away in the company of gently lowing cows and is then humanely slaughtered.

Horseman The *tourada* opens with the public presentation of the three main groups of protagonists (the *cavaleiros*, *toureiros*, and *forcados*), an elaborate ceremony played out to the accompaniment of traditional bullfighting music. The encounter then starts in earnest with the arrival of the first horseman, or *cavaleiro*. He is always splendidly attired in the costume of an 18th-century nobleman: plumed tricorne hat, highly polished kneeboots with silver spurs, and a lavishly embroidered satin, silk, or velvet coat. His job is then to tempt the bull continually until it tires, avoiding its charges, and—when

the opportunity presents itself—to stab it with darts known as *farpas* or *bandarilhas*.

Crowds judge a *cavaleiro* on his display of skill and courage, and in the grace and overall panache he brings to an encounter. He is helped in his task, however, by a group of assistants on foot, the *peões de brega*, or *toureiros*. Armed with pink and yellow capes, these men tempt the bull to charge in the more familiar Spanish manner, tiring it further and leaving it open to more attacks from the *cavaleiro* and his *bandarilhas*. The bull, for its part, can weigh anything up to half a ton, and will probably have been raised on the farms of the Ribatejo, the traditional heart of Portuguese bullfighting. To reduce the danger to horse and human, the bull's horns are covered in a thick leather thong known as an *emboladas*.

Volunteers Once the bull is sufficiently tired it is the turn of the *forcados*, traditionally a group of unpaid volunteers who would once have been armed with nothing but a wooden fork, or *forcado* (hence their name). There are usually eight in a group, each dressed in white hose, scarlet cummerbund, short coat, and breeches of red-brown or beige. This part of the contest (known as the *pega*) provides the *tourada*'s most reckless interlude. A demonstration of bull against defenseless human, it is designed deliberately to provide the crowd with its thrills and spills, and the *forcados* with a confirmation of their virility and an enhanced reputation among their male confreres.

The leader of the *forcados*, distinguished by his green pointed hat, stands at the head of his men, arraigned behind him in single file, and then challenges the bull to charge with the words *"Toiro, eh toiro."* The bull generally obliges, often tossing the leader and his fellow *forcados* aside in a Laurel-and-Hardy-like procession. Otherwise, the task of the *forcados* is suicidally simple. The leader is supposed to meet the oncoming bull, and then thrust himself between its (covered) horns while his colleagues attempt to wrestle the animal to the ground. If the bull escapes, it falls to one unfortunate (the *rabejador*) to grab its tail and hang on for dear life. Once the bull has been immobilized, a group of cows, copper bells around their necks, are sent in to tempt it from the arena.

POPULAR SUPPORT
The fact that the bull is not killed during the Portuguese *tourada* does not mean that the animal doesn't suffer. Bulls receive several thrusts from the horseman's darts, and suffer again when these are pulled out. The vast majority of Portuguese see nothing wrong in bullfighting, and the articulate and vocal minority who do oppose it are invariably shouted down by a powerful lobby in favor. Whatever your feelings on the subject, you should at least try to avoid bullfights in the Algarve, many of which are staged purely for tourists, thus lacking the sense of tradition that gives at least a modicum of "meaning" to this most controversial of activities.

▶▶▶ Sintra *158A1*

See Lisbon Excursions, pages 67–68.

▶▶▶ Tomar *158B3*

Tomar's Convento de Cristo is one of Portugal's highlights, and one of its seven Unesco World Heritage Sites—a place where art and history are spectacularly combined. The monastery's long association with the Knights Templars and their successors, the Knights of Christ, has produced a complex of buildings in which the architectural and artistic styles of several centuries are gathered together. Tomar itself is a beguiling place, with many churches and pleasant corners, and well worth an overnight stay and a couple of days' leisurely sightseeing.

TEMPLARS King Baldwin I of France founded the Order of the Knights Templars in 1118 during the First Crusade. The order was a military force with powerful religious (and mystical) overtones, and its immediate purpose was to ensure that pilgrim routes to the Holy Land remained open and to protect Jerusalem's Holy Sepulcher from Muslim attack. In time, its scope was extended to cover all manner of crusading exploits, in which regard the knights came to play a leading role in driving the Moors from Spain and Portugal. As early as 1162 the order's Grand Master, Gualdim Pais, a companion-at-arms of Portugal's Afonso Henriques, began to build a fortress-church at Tomar, in the border country between the Moorish and Christian domains. This building was to become the order's headquarters in Portugal and provided the germ of the present monastery complex.

By 1249 the Moors had been expelled from Portugal, where the Templars, as elsewhere, were rewarded for their assistance with tracts of land and rights to countless castles and monasteries. Their temporal power subsequently increased to such an extent that they became a threat to monarchs across Europe. Reaction against their ascendancy was begun by King Philippe-le-Bel of France, who confiscated Templar property across his kingdom. This move was then confirmed by the formal suppression of the order in 1314 by Pope Clement V, a pontiff deeply beholden to the French for his appointment.

NEW ORDER The Templars were then hounded from France and Spain, leading many of its members to seek refuge in Portugal, where Dom Dinis complied with Clement's injunction but at the same time adroitly founded a new order, the Knights of Christ (Ordem de Cristo). This proved remarkably similar to its predecessor, not only taking on former Templars as soldiering knights but also assuming control of the Templars' extensive lands and properties. The vital difference, however, was that this time the order was under royal control. Initially the organization had its headquarters at Castro Marim on the Algarve (see panel on page 232), but in 1356 it moved to its new home in Tomar.

The order enjoyed its period of greatest splendor half a century later under Henry the Navigator (see pages 226–227), who served as its "governor" between 1418 and 1460. Henry abjured the title "Grand Master," incidentally, because the post's vows of poverty proved incompatible

PRACTICALITIES

Tomar's tourist office (tel: 249 322 427) is on the western edge of the old town at the top of Avenida Dr. Cândido Madureira.

The bus station (tel: 249 312 730) and train station (tel: 249 312 815) lie virtually alongside one another on the southern side of town in Avenida Combatentes da Grande Guerra (to reach Avenida Dr. Cândido Madureira, cross the park on the other side of the street and continue straight for a few minutes). Several buses link the town daily to Lisbon, together with frequent trains. There are also several trains daily from Porto.

Opposite: several architectural styles meet in the great Convento de Cristo at Tomar, long associated with the Knights Templar

CASTELO DE ALMOUROL
Some 12 miles (20km) south of Tomar is the Templar castle of Almourol, romantically sited on a craggy little island in the middle of the River Tagus. Gualdim Pais, Master of the Order of Templars, built the fairy-tale castle's crenelated walls and ten towers in 1171, on Roman foundations. Access is easiest by car, from the north bank of the river, 1.2 miles (2km) east of Tancos.

Intricately knotted ropes of stone are often a feature of Manueline sculpture

with his worldly concerns. Henry tapped the order's considerable wealth to help fund the voyages of exploration that laid the foundation of Portugal's far-flung empire (his ships sailed with the order's red Cross of Christ emblazoned on their sails). The order's decline began at the end of the 15th century, however, and was confirmed in 1834 when the Knights of Christ were swept away along with the rest of Portugal's religious orders.

MONASTERY The many buildings of Tomar's magnificent **Convento de Cristo**▶▶▶ (tel: 249 313 481. *Open* Tue–Sun 9:30–5. *Admission: inexpensive*) are surrounded by lovely gardens on the walled and wooded hill that dominates the town's western reaches. The entrance is marked by a 12th-century keep (closed to the public), alongside which stands a triangular cistern whose orientation is said to indicate the position of hidden treasure. The inscription here (something of an overstatement) reads that in 1190 "The King of Morocco came with 400,000 horsemen and 500,000 foot soldiers and besieged this castle for six days."

The entrance to the main convent church is via a doorway, laden with appliqué decoration, designed in 1515 by João de Castilho, a Spaniard in the employ of Manuel I, hence its similarity to the Plateresque architecture of Salamanca and other Spanish centers. Two years later Castilho was transferred to Lisbon by the king to embark on his masterpiece at Belém (see page 60). The church was also added to the abbey on Manuel's orders, forming an adjunct to the famous Templars' Rotonda to the right, the ancient heart of the complex.

TEMPLARS' ROTONDA The strange and evocative 12th-century Rotonda (also known as the Charola) was the

Templars' original church, its octagonal design based on that of Jerusalem's Holy Sepulcher. It was here that they attended services, reputedly while still on horseback (a plaque marks the building's former entrance). The ornate nave (1510–1514) through which it is approached was designed by Diogo de Arruda, João de Castilho's predecessor as Manuel's master of works. Its paintings are attributed to Jorge Afonso, Manuel's court painter from 1508, and take Jesus and Jerusalem as their twin themes. Henry the Navigator, who had a palace built within the monastery walls, constructed a chapel off the Rotonda dedicated to Thomas à Becket, together with two cloisters (of which the complex has seven in all). The chapel and cloisters can be reached via a tile-lined corridor leading east from the octagon.

WINDOW Tomar's most famous sight is not the Rotonda, however, but the extraordinary window on the main facade of the chapterhouse, a highly decorative work that is widely acknowledged as the finest piece of Manueline art in Portugal. It is best admired from the terrace of the Claustro de Santa Bárbara, which, with the adjoining **Claustro Principal** (1557–1566), lies west of the Rotonda. It is worth noting, incidentally, the simple classical High Renaissance style of the Claustro Principal, which provides a striking contrast to the building's earlier Manueline work. The cloister was the brainchild of Diogo de Torralva, an admirer of the great Italian architect Andrea Palladio, and forms part of the alterations to the monastery made by João III (1521–1557), who was responsible for many of the complex's more purely monastic additions.

The **window** itself (1510–1513) was probably the work of Diogo de Arruda (see above). Its extraordinary decoration consists of a wonderfully entwined plethora of maritime motifs, which gather around coral-encrusted "masts" and rise from the carved roots of a cork tree at the base (the old man here may be a sea captain or a portrait of the window's creator). Among the details are ropes (all intricately knotted), cables, seaweed, sails, coral, and anchor chains. The whole is topped by the emblems of Manuel (a blazon and armillary sphere) and the Cross of the Order of Christ.

THE TOWN As you return to town from the monastery you might want to drop into **Nossa Senhora da Conceição▶**, a Renaissance chapel attributed to Diogo de Torralva, the architect responsible for the abbey's Claustro Principal.

In Tomar itself, the place to go is **Praça da República**, the town's elegant main square, whose lovely ensemble of townhouses is complemented by the 17th-century town hall and the church of **São João Baptista▶▶**. The latter, rebuilt for Manuel around 1510, is noted for its imposing Manueline belfry—square at the base and octagonal at the top—together with its exuberant portals (on the north and west sides). Inside, the limestone pulpit is also outstanding, its three faces depicting the shield, spear, and cross of Christ. The side aisles contain six paintings (1538–1539) by Gregório Lopes (1490–1550), one of Portugal's leading 16th-century artists. A couple of blocks to the south is the town's former **synagogue**, now a museum (see panel).

The convent's famous Manueline window

THE SYNAGOGUE
Tomar's well-preserved former synagogue, built between 1430 and 1460, was used as a place of worship only until 1497, when Portugal followed the Spanish example by expelling Jews or forcing them to become Cristãos Novos ("New Christians"). The present building was lucky to survive—few Jewish monuments did so far south. Many Jewish exiles chose to head to the north, whose remote mountain enclaves lay further from the Inquisition's persecuting zeal. Today, the Gothic building houses a museum of Hebrew and other inscriptions, named after Abraham Zacuto, a Spanish astronomer who helped build navigational aids for Vasco da Gama. Note the eight inverted jars in the main chamber, inserted to improve the room's acoustics. The museum is located at Rua Joaquim Jacinto 73 (*Open* Thu–Tue 10–1, 2–6. *Admission free*).

The Alentejo

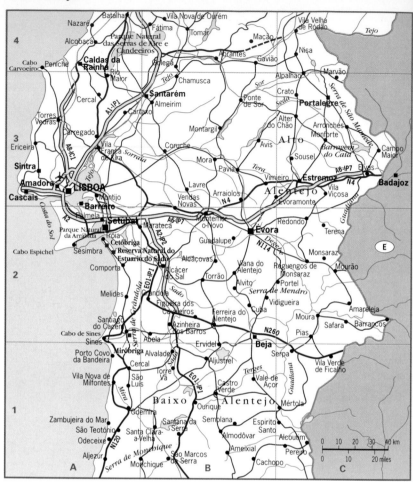

AGRICULTURE

In 1990 some 51 percent of Portugal was classified as agricultural. Around a quarter of all Portuguese workers were farmers, but more than half of these were over 50 years old. A third were illiterate. However, despite this huge agricultural sector, the country still has to import around half of its food.

Pages 184–185: the castle of Marvão and the Alentejan plains

THE ALENTEJO The name Alentejo derives from *Além Tejo*, meaning "Beyond the Tagus." This, Portugal's longest river, flows to the north of the region, eventually entering the sea at Lisbon. The Alentejo is the largest province in the country, occupying almost a third of mainland Portugal, and for the most part consists of vast, sun-drilled plains. At the same time, it supports just 12 percent of the country's population, the lowest of any Portuguese region. Its inhabitants are also some of the poorest in Europe, many having been condemned over the years to work as landless laborers on the vast agricultural estates that dominated the region until 1974 (see below).

To some, the Alentejo's landscapes will appear monotonous—endless plains occasionally buckled by hills covered in the cork and olive trees for which the region is famous. Others, however, will find them possessed of a stark beauty, and dappled with powerful primary colors: the green of spring wheat, the brown of harvested fields, and the blue of overarching skies. Dotted across the red-earthed fields lie towns of whitewashed houses, their windows framed by wisteria, geraniums, and bougainvillea. Age-old villages, full of black-clad women, still boast festivals and rural traditions that remain immune to the advance of the "new" Portugal.

AGRICULTURE Farming has been the Alentejo's savior across the centuries. Although soils are thin and rainfall sparse, wheat and other cereals have been coaxed from the soils over the years, earning the region the title of the "granary" or "breadbasket of Portugal." The Romans were the first to champion agriculture, introducing vast estates termed *latifundia* (in Portuguese, *latifúndios*), a system of feudal land tenure that survived until the 1974 revolution. They also built some 18 dams in the south of the country, the forerunner of an irrigation system which, when combined with the Alentejo's high summer temperatures (these are the highest in Portugal), today produces the region's familiar checkerboard of rippling wheat.

Things changed little under the Moors. In later centuries, city merchants and nobles invested much of their wealth in land, leading to a situation where many of the

POETIC VISION
Fernando Pessoa, a 19-year-old poet, describes the Alentejo as he saw it through a train window on his return from South Africa in 1907: "Nothing with nothing around it/ And a few trees in between/ None of which are very clearly green,/ Where no river or flower pays a visit./ If there be a hell, I've found it,/ For if it ain't here, Where the Devil is it?"

Spring brings a tinge of green to the Alentejo landscape

The Alentejo

A summer haze mists the valleys near Marvão

PORKERS

Pigs often reign supreme in poor agricultural regions, and the Alentejo is no exception. The region's plethora of cork oaks provides enough acorns to keep a whole continent of pigs in clover. Many are little black porkers, most of which end up as hams and sausages or in one of the great Alentejan culinary favorites: *pezinhos de coentrada* (cilantro flavored trotters) or *porco à Alentejana* (marinated pork and cockles in a sauce of oil, onions, and parsley).

large estates were farmed by landless laborers and owned by absentee landlords. With the growth of the Portuguese empire, however, mercantile money found new homes. This led to a crisis of investment in agriculture, a situation that forced Portugal to import grain at the beginning of the 16th century. The introduction of chemical fertilizers at the end of the 19th century brought more land under cultivation, although subsequent attempts at a Soviet-style "Battle for Wheat" under Salazar (notably in 1929 and 1958) met with little success.

LAND REFORMS Come 1974 and the revolution, Alentejo's landless and perennially put-upon laborers provided one of the principal motors of change. By July of 1975 a law was in place that allowed for the expropriation of estates covering more than 1,235 acres (500 hectares) of "dry" land or 123 acres (50 hectares) of irrigated land. Three months later, workers around Beja marched into many of the area's *latifúndios*. Some 2.5 million acres (1 million hectares) were subsequently taken into "common ownership," either through the formation of cooperatives (of which some 900 were created), or by the distribution of cultivation rights to small- or medium-sized farms. By 1976 the figure had risen to 7.5 million acres (3 million hectares).

Within a few years, however, it all began to go wrong. Workers were ill-equipped to deal with a succession of bad harvests, investment from government proved unforthcoming, and membership of the European Union imposed economic imperatives on agriculture that the fledgling

MUSIC

The Alentejo has a musical tradition all of its own, distinct from the impenetrable melancholy and robust rhythms of *fado*. However, its rich vocalizations can sound strange to the untutored ear. The songs are sung unaccompanied, usually by groups of men, or *ceifeiros*. Often they are simple and somewhat austere paeans to death, loss, and unhappiness. Voices take one of three basic parts—*ponto*, *alto*, or *segunda voze*—and one voice leads off, often improvising a phrase that is taken up by the others. Women have their own song, the *saia*, also sung unaccompanied. No one is really sure of their origins, although there is no lack of scholarly debate on the subject.

cooperatives were unable to take on. As a result, the number of cooperatives across Portugal dropped from 1,408 in 1985 to just over 300 in 1988. In the Alentejo, former landowners and foreign speculators began to buy up the old *latifúndios* at depressed prices, so that by 1991 some 1.8 million acres (750,000 hectares) of land had ironically returned to the original owners. Many of these later received vast EU grants to modernize their farms, measures that have done wonders for the balance sheet but little for the former laborers. If anything, it has made things worse, for mechanization has largely done away with many of the old farm jobs.

WHERE TO GO Whether or not you fall in love with the Alentejo's ethereal open spaces, there are a few towns and villages that demand to be included on any Portuguese itinerary. Most of these are in the north, or Alto (Upper) Alentejo, the most notable being **Évora**, a delightful ensemble of monuments from several epochs.

Close behind comes **Elvas**, which possesses some of the most grandiose of the many fortifications that dot the region. Among the villages, **Monsaraz** and **Marvão** stand out, both distinguished by spectacular fortified sites.

You should also visit either of the "marble" towns of **Estremoz** or **Vila Viçosa**, the latter perhaps the more enticing on account of its Ducal Palace, home to many of Portugal's kings and queens. In the south, or Baixo (Lower) Alentejo, the urban attractions are fewer, and **Beja**, with its convent and museum, provides the only real distraction.

Baroque exuberance in the Convento da Conceição at Beja

PRACTICALITIES

Beja's tourist office is located at Rua Capitão João Francisco de Sousa 25 (tel: 284 310 150) to the south of the two linked squares that make up the heart of the town: Largo dos Duques de Beja and Largo de Santa Maria. Transport links are good, with several daily trains to Lisbon and from Évora. There are also train links from the western Algarve. Buses run to and from Évora, Lisbon, Faro, and many other destinations. The train station (tel: 284 325 056) is five minutes' walk to the northeast of the town center, while the bus station (tel: 284 324 044) lies about the same distance to the southeast.

A NUN IN LOVE

In France in 1669 there appeared a translation of several highly wrought love letters, purportedly written by Mariana Alcoforado, a Portuguese nun. Laced with wit, reproach, passion, and despair, they were addressed to her lover, the Count Chamilly, a French cavalry officer. An overnight sensation, the letters quickly became classics of the genre. However, the "originals" have never been found, a fact which when combined with the literary polish of the "translation" has led many scholars to believe they were actually written by Guilleragues, an erstwhile secretary of Louis XIV. The latest Portuguese study, however, claims the letters were indeed penned by Mariana.

►► Beja   186B2

Beja is a pleasant little town at the heart of the Alentejo's southern plains, and makes a satisfying morning's halt if you are bound for Évora or the Algarve. It first enjoyed fame as a Roman colony, glorying in the name Pax Julia, coined following the peace (*pax*) that was signed here in 48 BC between Julius Caesar and the Lusitanians. Half a century later, after the accession of Emperor Augustus, it took the title Pax Augusta. In time, the "Augusta" was dropped and Pax went through a series of corruptions—Paca, Baca, and Baju—before evolving into the present-day "Beja."

Later, the town became first the seat of a Visigothic bishopric and then a Moorish stronghold. However, little now survives of the Moors' four centuries of occupation. In the 15th century Beja was made a duchy, tradition deeming that the second (later the third) son of the Portuguese king should assume the title of Duke of Beja. Today, the town's position, combined with the richest copper mines in Europe (at Neves Corvo), ensures its continuing role as capital of the Lower Alentejo.

CONVENT Beja's principal attraction, the **Antigo Convento da Conceição►►►** (tel: 284 323 351. *Open* Tue–Sun 10–12:30, 2–5:30), holds a special place in Portuguese literature, for it was once home to Mariana Alcoforado, alleged author of the famous *Love Letters of a Portuguese Nun* (see panel). The convent, located in Largo da Conceição, was founded in 1459 by Dom Fernando, father of Manuel I, and was later given to the Franciscan Poor Clares. Architecturally, it provides a perfect example of a building caught in the transition between the Gothic and Manueline styles, its basic form and roofline being predominantly Gothic, and its decoration owing more to the later style.

Its highlights are the cloister, whose walls are covered in *azulejos*, and the sensational **Sala do Capítulo (Chapter House)**, whose every surface is painted in floral motifs or decorated in 16th-century Hispano-Moorish-style tiles (probably made in Seville). The church, teeming with baroque decoration, is also worth a glance, as are its various gilded rococo chapels.

REGIONAL MUSEUM The convent and church buildings also house the **Museu da Rainha Dona Leonor►►** (tel: 284 323 351. *Open* Tue–Sun 10–12:30, 2–5:30. *Admission: inexpensive*), home to a series of Roman and rare Visigothic stonework, several crucifixes, and a collection of flagstones and other archaeological fragments dating back to the Bronze and Iron ages. Among its many paintings, the most important works are a *Descent from the Cross*, an anonymous Portuguese work; *Our Lady of the Milk*, a Flemish work depicting a breastfeeding Madonna; and *São Vicente*, by a follower of the so-called Master of Sardoal. Also look out for the *Escudela de Pero de Faria* (1541), a rare piece of Chinese porcelain, and the reconstruction of the cell window through which Mariana Alcoforado is said to have exchanged sweet nothings with her lover.

Directly opposite the convent and museum, and worth a couple of minutes' exploration, is **Santa Maria**, a small Gothic church whose Moorish foundations are still visible to its rear.

CASTLE Beja's **Castelo** on Largo Dr. Lima Faleiro (*Open Apr–Sep, Tue–Sun 10–1, 2–6; Oct–Mar, Tue–Sun 9–noon, 1–4. Note that it may close earlier in the winter. Admission: inexpensive*) was built by Dom Dinis and adds a picturesque touch to the northern edge of the old town. Until the 18th century its fortifications bristled with over 40 towers. Most of these have now gone, although the ivy-clad keep remains, whose Torre de Menagem offers a view over the wheatlands of the Alentejo.

Immediately north of the castle, on Rua Antero do Quintal, stands the **Igreja de Santo Amaro**, a rare example of a Visigothic basilica (part of it dates as far back as the 6th century). Note in particular the 7th-century motifs carved on to the interior columns. The church also houses a small museum of archaeological finds from the same period. South of the castle lies Praça da República, complete with an old pillory and the **Misericórdia**, the latter a 16th-century church whose cavernous porch was once used as a meat market.

The Torre de Menagem offers sweeping views across the Alentejan plains

The Alentejo

PRACTICALITIES

Elvas's tourist office (tel: 268 622 236) is in the Praça da República, the town's main square, and lies alongside the bus terminal (tel: 268 622 144). Shuttle buses run to the square from the train station (tel: 268 622 816), 2 miles (3.5km) northeast at Fontaínhas. There are trains and buses daily from Lisbon and Évora, as well as many local bus services.

Elvas, huddled within its protective walls and moat

▶▶ **Elvas**   *186C3*

Elvas is one of Europe's greatest walled cities, whose daunting fortifications and strategic position close to the border with Spain earned it the title of *chave do reino*, or the "key to the kingdom." Although its sights are few and the modern outskirts dull, the vertiginous cobbled streets and old houses within the city walls remain laden with charm. Of all the Alentejo's fortified towns, Évora excepted, this is the one to see if time is short. Elvas was recovered from the Moors around 1230 (late by local standards), and thereafter its history was shaped by almost constant friction with Spain, whose mighty fortress at Badajoz lay just 7 miles (12km) away over the border. In 1581 Philip II of Spain briefly set up court here, while at the beginning of the 19th century, during the Peninsular Wars, the Duke of Wellington used the town as a base for his successful sieges of Badajoz (1811–1812).

FORTIFICATIONS Elvas's star-shaped fortifications are the finest piece of military architecture in Portugal. The town's strategic position suggests the site has probably been fortified since time immemorial, although the earliest surviving section of the present walls dates from the 13th century. Most of the defensive system, however, is 17th-century. One of the most accomplished military engineers of the day, the Frenchman Vauban, was commissioned to incorporate the existing walls into a complex system of moats, ramparts, and bastions. The result was the mightiest fortress in Portugal. Its central redoubt was further strengthened by the building of four outlying forts close to the city, one of which, the star-shaped **Forte de Santa Luzia**, lies just to the south of the town and can easily be visited. Another, the Forte da Graça, to the north, is used as a prison and military base.

CHURCHES Of Elvas's many churches, only two demand close attention: the **Igreja de Nossa Senhora da Assunção**

The tiled ceiling of Nossa Senhora da Consolação

(*Open* Mon–Fri 10–1, 3–5:30), which flanks the Praça da República, the town's beautifully paved main square; and the **Igreja de Nossa Senhora da Consolação** (*Open* Tue–Sun 9–12:30, 2–5:30), just a few steps to the north in Largo de Santa Clara.

The former fulfilled the function of cathedral between 1570 and 1882, when the town lost its status as a bishopric. The design (ca1517) was the work of Francisco de Arruda, who was also responsible for the Aqueduto Amoreira just outside the town walls (see below). Subsequent restoration removed much of his original work, however, leaving just the belfry and two side doorways as memorials to the Manueline plan.

Far more scintillating is Nossa Senhora da Consolação, whose plain-faced facade and porch barely prepare you for the beauty and sophistication of the church within. The church's octagonal plan, conceived in 1543, was probably based on the design of a hermitage belonging to the Knights Templars which had been destroyed three years earlier. Pride of place inside goes to the pulpit, graced by a 16th-century iron balustrade, and to an expanse of outstanding blue and yellow *azulejos* (1659), which cover most available surfaces. Outside, in the triangular Largo de Santa Clara, notice the superb 16th-century ***pelourinho*** (**pillory**), its twisted Manueline column still topped by the four metal hooks to which prisoners were shackled.

The arch at the top of the *largo*, flanked by twin towers from the town's original 10th-century walls, leads via Largo da Alcáçova to the **Castelo**, constructed by the Moors on earlier Roman foundations (tel: 268 626 403. *Open* daily 9:30–5:30). The last of the town's major sights, and one you may have glimpsed on the approach to the town from the west, is the **Aqueduto Amoreira** (1498–1622), designed like Nossa Senhora da Assunção by Francisco de Arruda, and paid for by the country's first water tax. The causeway runs for some 4 miles (7km) before emptying into a fountain in the town's Largo da Misericórdia.

FESTIVALS
Elvas's key festival is the Festa de São Mateús, which takes place over the last ten days of September. It sees southern Portugal's largest procession, and also includes bullfights, handicrafts, folk dancing, and a wide range of agricultural activities. If you plan to be in town be sure to reserve your accommodations well in advance. Otherwise, you may enjoy the large weekly market held every other Monday just outside the town alongside the aqueduct.

Market day in the center of Estremoz

PRACTICALITIES

Estremoz's tourist office is in Largo da República (tel: 268 333 541). The bus station (tel: 268 322 282) is in Rossio Marquês de Pombal; its principal services include daily buses from Évora and Portalegre. There is no train service to Estremoz.

ESTREMOZ POTTERY

Thanks to deposits of local clay, Estremoz has long been famous for its unusual pottery and naive ceramic figurines. The former is characterized by its distinctive shapes, simple floral motifs, and the occasional use of marble as a decorative inlay. Much of the work is now ornamental but most early pieces were variations on porous water coolers known as *moringues*, recognizable by their single handle and double spouts.

► **Estremoz** *186C3*

LOWER TOWN Arriving in Estremoz, foremost of the Alentejo's "marble towns," you will find yourself in the lower town close to the atmospheric Rossio Marquês de Pombal. This large, café-lined square contains the **Câmara Municipal (Town Hall)**, housed in a former convent (founded in 1698). Creep inside to admire the lovely 17th-century *azulejos* lining its main staircase. On the square's eastern flank stands the **Museu Rural da Casa do Povo►►**, a small but fascinating museum devoted to crafts, costumes, tools, and other aspects of local rural life (*Open* summer, Tue–Sun 10–1, 3–6. Rest of year, Tue–Sun 10–1, 3–5. *Admission: inexpensive*).

It is worth seeing it in conjunction with the similar **Museu de Alfaia Agrícola**, located on Rua Serpa Pinto to the northwest (tel: 268 339 200. *Open* Tue–Fri 9–12:30, 2–4:30, Sat–Sun 2–4:30. *Admission: inexpensive*). En route to the latter museum, take in the church of **São Francisco**, a Gothic building that dates back to 1213. If you are in town on Saturday be sure to make the most of the superb market that takes place in the Rossio, where stalls selling Estremoz's famous pottery (see panel) stand among the usual colorful arrays of fruit and vegetables.

UPPER TOWN Robust 17th-century ramparts and the inevitable **castle** (Largo Dom Dinis) dominate Estremoz's old upper town. The latter (built in 1258) is now one of the most famous *pousadas* in Portugal (see page 257). You are free to look around; the views, as ever in these lofty citadels, form one of the chief attractions. The main tower, is known as the Torre das Três Coroas, or "Tower of the Three Crowns," after the three kings involved in its construction (Dom Afonso III, Dom Dinis, and Dom Afonso IV). Also be sure to find the castle's Capela da Rainha Santa Isabel, a chapel devoted to Isabel of Aragon, the sainted wife of Dom Dinis: its walls are covered in tiles depicting scenes from her life. Below the castle to the south stands the **Museu Municipal**, worth a quick visit for its displays of historic Estremoz pottery (tel: 268 339 200. *Open* Tue–Sun 9–12:30, 2–5:30. *Admission: inexpensive*).

▶▶▶ Évora

186B2

Évora is one of Portugal's most charming and pleasing cities, graced with lovely buildings, quaint cobbled streets, and tempting medieval nooks and crannies. Pleasant to wander around in for its own sake, it can also boast a series of outstanding monuments and museums that embrace its periods of Roman, Moorish, and Renaissance splendor. These combined attractions draw more than their share of visitors, although despite this the city remains one of those special places whose charm survives the arrival of endless coach parties. Just 13,500 people live within the walls, around a quarter of the city's 50,000 inhabitants. This modest proportion of the total population ensures that life within the walls retains the friendly and close-knit feel of a small town: as a base for the Alentejo and beyond, you could hardly ask for more. Note that Évora's thoroughgoing medieval appearance does bring problems for the modern visitor. If you arrive by car, it's far easier to park on the outskirts and walk rather than trying to negotiate the center's narrow streets and its one-way system.

HISTORY Évora's history dates back at least to Roman times, when it was the political center of Roman Iberia: Pliny gave it the title Ebora Cerealis, an allusion to the vast wheat producing potential of its hinterland. It may also have been the seat of Quintus Sertorius, the infamous Roman governor of Hispania, who around 80 BC foolishly tried to create a kingdom for himself independent of Rome. The city declined in the wake of the Visigoth invasions but recovered under the Moors, who remained its masters from 711 to 1165. Delivery from Moorish occupation was provided by Geraldo Sempavor (see panel on page 198), who turned the city over to the rule of Afonso Henriques.

Évora then became the seat of the House of Avis (see pages 32–33), whose royal connections guaranteed wealth

GETTING THERE

Évora is linked by train to Portalegre, Beja, Estremoz, and other centers, including daily services from Lisbon, Beja, and Faro. The train station (tel: 266 744 541) lies just 0.5 miles (1km) southeast of the center: follow Rua da República north from here to reach Praça do Giraldo and the tourist office.

The bus terminal (tel: 266 769 410) is more central, lying on the southern edge of the old center on Rua da República. Buses converge on the city from a wide variety of places, including Lisbon, Faro, and Beja.

195

The Temple of Diana, Évora's finest Roman monument

The Alentejo

TOURIST OFFICE
Évora's tourist office lies at the heart of the old town at Praça do Giraldo 71 (tel: 266 702 671). To reach the cathedral from the office walk 200 yards (200m) east from the Praça on Rua 5 de Outubro. The office will help with accommodations, which are at a definite premium in the high season (book in advance if at all possible and be prepared to pay slightly higher prices than elsewhere in the Alentejo).

196

and fame that endured until the 16th century. The royal court naturally attracted the country's leading writers, artists, architects, and thinkers, men and women whose legacy accounts for the city's present artistic and architectural riches. In 1559 a famous Jesuit university was founded here by Dom Henrique, a slightly ill-timed venture, for just 21 years later, in 1580, the Spanish seizure of the Portuguese throne precipitated a marked decline in the city's fortunes. This decline continued after 1640, despite the restoration of the Portuguese monarchy, when the country's kings moved their court closer to Lisbon. However, Évora's backwater status stood to preserve much of its charm, recently further secured by a long-term program of restoration and the designation by Unesco of its historic centre as a World Heritage Site.

CATHEDRAL Any tour of Évora should start first with a visit to the tourist office (see panel) and then with the cluster of sights that gathers around the nearby Largo Marquês de Marialva. Chief among these is the **Sé (Cathedral)**►►► in Rua 5 de Outubro (*Open* daily 9–noon, 2–5), a doughty granite construction of fortress-like appearance. It was probably begun in 1186 on the site of a former mosque, 20 years after the Moors had been expelled from the city. Its towers and other external elements display a simple Romanesque bias that was gradually replaced by a more thoroughly Gothic design as building continued into the 13th century. The highlight of the rather plain exterior is the main **doorway**, which is garlanded by sculptures of the Apostles, probably the work of French and Portuguese sculptors working between 1322 and 1340.

Inside, the building's Gothic ancestry becomes more apparent, although both the chancel and high altar were

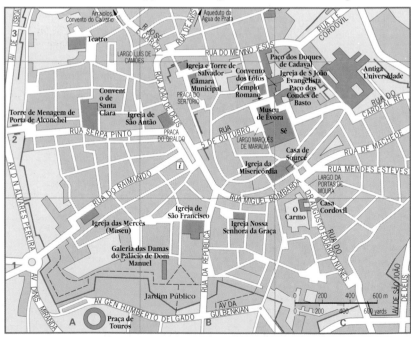

restored in baroque mode in 1718 by Friedrich Ludwig (who is buried here), an Italian-trained German architect also responsible for the Convent at Mafra (see page 69). Pay particular attention to the **Cadeiras do Coro** (**Choir Stalls**), whose oak stalls and beautifully decorated panels were created by Flemish Renaissance artists. Flemish artisans were a common feature of life in medieval Évora, and a major influence in Portugal (and elsewhere in Europe) on the evolution of indigenous Renaissance art. This was partly as a result of their skill in handling new media such as oils, and partly because of the strong maritime and other trading links that existed between Portugal and the Low Countries.

Elsewhere in the cathedral be sure to see the superb Gothic **cloister** (1322–1340), whose four corners are guarded by statues of the Evangelists. Also visit the terrace above the western portal, which offers memorable views over the city and a firsthand look at the building's twin towers. More interesting still is the cathedral's **museum** (*Open* Tue–Sun 9–noon, 2–5. *Admission: inexpensive*), chock-full of vestments, silver plate, and other religious articles. Pride of place goes to the reliquary Cross of St. Lenho, whose silver gilt and enamel is studded with 1,426 precious stones. Equally striking is a strange 13th-century French ivory Madonna whose innards open up to display a triptych of scenes from the *Life of the Virgin*.

The fortress-like profile of Évora's cathedral

MEGALITHIC SITES

Évora's tourist office offers a guide to some of the dozen or more megalithic sites in the town's environs. The closest is the Cromeleque dos Almendres, which consists of some 95 granite stones arranged in a 200- x 100-foot (60 x 30m) oval. It is located in lovely countryside 2 miles (3km) from the village of Guadalupe, which lies just off the main N114 road about 6 miles (10km) west of Évora. If you are prepared to tackle unsurfaced roads, you could make a car tour of many of the sites; if not, the tourist office provides details of organized day trips.

The Alentejo

GERALDO SEMPAVOR

Geraldo, or "Gerald the Fearless" to give him his English name, played a key role in the 12th-century recovery of Évora from the Moors. In 1165 internal divisions among the Moors had allowed Afonso Henriques to take the offensive in his campaign of reconquest. During the attack on Évora, so the story goes, Gerald used lances forced into the town's walls as a makeshift ladder, climbing them to capture one of the towers. He appraised the Moorish garrison of the fact, the result being that the defenders hurried to the tower, leaving Évora undefended. Gerald and his followers then simply walked into the city. Henriques made Gerald castellan of Évora for his pains. Today, the city remembers its hero in its coat of arms, where he is depicted in the company of two disembodied heads.

Chapterhouse door,
Convento dos Lóios

MUNICIPAL MUSEUM The city's excellent **Museu Municipal►►►** stands immediately to the left of the cathedral in Largo do Conde de Vila Flor, occupying the former 16th-century Archbishop's Palace (tel: 266 702 604. *Open* Tue 2–5:30, Wed–Sun 9–12:30, 2–5:30. *Admission: inexpensive*). The lower floor is largely devoted to sculpture and architectural fragments, exhibits that span the city's Roman, medieval, Manueline, and Luso-Moorish periods. The latter, a hybrid style common in the mansions and castles of the Alentejo, combined Manueline and old Moorish motifs: delicate carving and the horseshoe arch are two of its chief characteristics.

Upstairs, the museum's emphasis moves to paintings, and to the work of Flemish and Portuguese artists in particular. The highlight here is the cathedral's former high altarpiece, a 13-paneled polyptych depicting the *Life of the Virgin*, executed around 1500 by anonymous Flemish painters.

ROMAN REMAINS Portugal is not overendowed with monuments from its Roman past, but in Évora's **Roman Temple►►**—the best-preserved Roman fragment in the country—it boasts a building that captures something of Rome's imperial splendor. Built at the city's highest point (Praça do Giraldo), it was raised in the 2nd or 3rd century AD, probably in honor of Jupiter (although local folklore has long associated it with the cult of Diana). Somewhat austere—and rather lost amid its surroundings—the temple consists of 14 granite columns, their bases and Corinthian capitals carved from more easily worked Estremoz marble. The temple owes its relatively fine state of preservation (it survived the 1755 earthquake) to the fact that it was used as a municipal slaughterhouse until 1870.

CONVENT The final component in the cathedral square's ensemble of sights is the **Convento dos Lóios►►►**, a church and monastery dedicated to São João Evangelista (St. John the Evangelist). The church was begun in 1485 on the site of a Moorish castle, and was built for the Canons Secular of St. John, whose nickname was the "Lóios." The building was owned until recently by the dukes of Cadaval, but is now run as one of Portugal's most appealing *pousadas* (see page 257), and so is sadly closed to the general public. No tours are available—you need to be a guest. Visitors can glimpse the dukes' adjoining palace, the **Paço dos Duques de Cadaval**, a 14th-century building, remodeled in the 17th century, which was home at various times to João III and João IV.

The church's facade, rebuilt after the 1755 earthquake, boasts an extravagant Gothic portal. Its coat of arms belongs to the once important de Melo family, several of whom are buried in fine Gothic and Renaissance tombs inside. The doorway provides a fitting introduction to the superb interior, whose floor-to-ceiling display of *azulejos* ranks among the most beautiful in the country. Executed in 1711 by António de Oliveira Bernardes, one of the masters of *azulejo* art, their main panels describe episodes from the life of St. Lorenzo Giustiniani, the patriarch of Venice, whose writings greatly influenced the Canons Secular. Tear your eyes away from these long enough to peer through the pavement's grilles, one of which reveals a cistern from the former Moorish castle, the other an ossuary containing the bones of the monastery's former monks.

The monastery building is rather harder to see, having been converted into a *pousada*, but if you are staying (or eating) here, or are sufficiently brazen to walk in, then do your best to see the superb **chapterhouse door**, whose seminal Luso-Moorish design (see opposite) has been attributed to Francisco de Arruda, the architect responsible for the aqueduct in Elvas (see page 189) and Lisbon's famous Torre de Belém (see page 65).

CHAPEL OF BONES The dos Lóios' rather tame ossuary puts you nicely in the mood for Évora's most popular sight, the superbly macabre **Capela dos Ossos (Chapel of Bones)**, which lies concealed within the **Igreja de São Francisco▶▶▶** in Praça 1° de Maio (*Open Mon–Sat 9–12:30, 2–5:30, Sun 10–12:30, 2–5:30. Admission: inexpensive*).

Created by Franciscan monks between 1460 and 1510 as a particularly vivid memento mori, it consists of the skulls, femurs, tibias, and other bones of some 5,000 monks, all neatly arranged on the walls to produce a fetching decorative effect (see panel right). The inscription over the door is of the joyful variety typical of this sort of place: "*Nós ossos, que aqui estamos, Pelos vossos esperamos*"—"We bones here are waiting for your bones." The braids of hair often deposited at the entrance, disturbing in their own way, are exvoto offerings left by women about to be married.

The church also has more conventional attractions, namely the large main **portico**, graced with rounded, pointed, and horseshoe arches, and its Manueline portal, whose pelican and armillary sphere are the emblems of João II and Manuel I respectively.

For a respite from sightseeing, take time out in the Jardim Público (Public Gardens) which are located just south of the church.

BONES
No one can quite agree on the source of the bones used to such macabre effect in São Francisco's Capela dos Ossos. The most likely story suggests they were exhumed from a nearby Franciscan cemetery. Others claim that they either belonged to soldiers who died in battle or to the victims of a plague epidemic.

ARRAIOLOS CARPETS
The attractive little town of Arraiolos lies 14 miles (22km) north of Évora, and has been famous for centuries for its superlative handwoven carpets. The patterns originally owed much to Moorish and Persian designs, but these days, while still beautiful, they tend to be less complex. Prices are fairly high, but the carpets are still cheaper in the town itself than elsewhere.

199

Évora's macabre Capela dos Ossos

Cork, nothing more than the bark of a tree, is one of Nature's wonders. Tasteless, odorless, and nontoxic, it is also light, impermeable, and an excellent insulator against heat and cold. Portugal's myriad cork trees, most of which are in the Alentejo, make the country the world's largest producer of this extraordinary substance.

NUMBERING
As you drive past groves of cork oaks you may see numbers marked on the recently stripped trees. These indicate the year in which the cork was taken from the tree. More than one number indicates cork was taken in two separate years, a procedure that allows growers to regulate their cash flow over the long cycles involved in cork production.

200

Portuguese trees produce most of the world's cork

Monopoly The effects on the world's wine industry, never mind the Portuguese economy, if Portugal's cork trees were struck by some disastrous blight hardly bears thinking about. The country produces around half the world's cork, but through its long-established consortiums (Américo Amorim in particular) it controls around 80 percent of trade. Much of the allied trade centers on Spain, the world's second largest producer. Total Portuguese production is around 143,000 tons (130,000 tonnes) a year, and to the traveler in the Alentejo it sometimes appears as if every last ton comes from the region, so vast are the swathes of cork oaks that blanket its arid interior. In fact, the trees grow in most parts of the country, but are particularly suited to the Alentejo's hot, dry conditions.

Wonder Removing cork from its source, the cork oak (*Quercus suber*), is a difficult and skilled occupation. The process starts when the bark is thick enough (it can grow

up to 4 inches, or 10cm, thick) and when the weather is right: too dry, and the cork breaks up when removed; too wet, and the tree dies of shock. Bark on the trunk and lower branches is first scored with a light ax in sections of 6–10 feet (2–3m). It is then carefully cut from the tree, the aim being to leave the surface beneath (the cambium) as smooth and unmarked as possible: one deep gash blights a tree for ever and reduces future yields. If well cut, a tree will produce around five or six harvests over about 50 years, each one better than the last.

Uses The pleasing "pop" as a cork leaves a wine bottle is what most of us associate with cork. Portugal produces 30 million bottle corks *a day*, and a staggering 500 million a year solely for champagne. Beyond this most vital of uses, however, the humble bark has a variety of less well-known functions. The external fuel tanks of the space shuttle *Columbia*, for example, were insulated with Portuguese cork, cut, so it was claimed, from over 200 Alentejo cork trees. Cork is also used in aircraft and in the air-conditioning systems of nuclear submarines. Its insulating properties (it can withstand temperatures up to 1,450˚F, or 800˚C) mean that radioactive isotopes and other delicate materials are often transported in cork-lined containers. Cork tiles for floors and walls rely on similar properties, and it is claimed that Marcel Proust had his entire Parisian study lined with cork to produce the calm he needed in order to write. More prosaically, there is cork in shoes, dartboards, fishing rods, ping-pong paddles and much more.

Trees Cork farming is not a "get-rich-quick" business, much to the chagrin of Portugal's new breed of marketing gurus, keen to find a way of turning an old-world agricultural product into a slick commodity suited to Portugal's modern self-image. They are unlikely to succeed. Cork trees must be 20 years old before they are first harvested, and once stripped they must be left another nine or so years before they yield another crop. Nature, in this instance, cannot be hurried. Worse still, many of Portugal's cork oaks are nearing the end of their natural life (around 150 years), suggesting a dip in production is at hand. Cork workers, too, are nearing the end of their working lives. Cork cutting is a skill handed down from father to son, but the country's changing social face—in particular the drift from the land—means that finding skilled labor on a sufficient scale could soon be a problem. In an industry where demand exceeds supply, these are worrying portents.

PRODUCTION
Each cork oak yields anything between 55 pounds (24kg) and 100 pounds (45kg) of cork. Once the curved sheets have been sorted, they are left to dry in the sun for several months. This eliminates the fatty residue which fills the countless air holes that give cork its special properties. The sheets are then boiled in water, which makes them pliable, and are flattened before being left to dry once again. The cork is then graded, for not all is of equal quality—cork from the first cutting of a tree, for example, is inferior to that taken from more mature trees. The poorest cork goes to make wall and floor tiles, while the better stuff is used, among other things, for bottle tops, shuttlecocks, and insulating material.

201

High-quality cork is selected by hand

Évoramonte's mighty fortress dominates the surrounding countryside

TREATY
The treaty that halted the so-called War of the Two Brothers was signed at Évoramonte in 1834. It ended the civil war between Dom Pedro, Emperor of Brazil, and his authoritarian brother, Dom Miguel, whom he had awarded the Portuguese throne (see page 40). The latter was defeated (with British help), and Pedro took the Portuguese throne in his place. Miguel was allowed to keep various personal belongings and was awarded a state pension. In return he was given 15 days to leave the country, and he spent the rest of his days in exile in Austria. The treaty took so long to sign, however, that legend claims only stale bread remained in the castle by way of nourishment. This allegedly led to the invention of the now-common Portuguese dish of *açorda*, a soup consisting of water, bread, cilantro, and olive oil.

▶▶ Évoramonte   186C3

The fortress village of Évoramonte (or Évora-Monte) can easily be visited from Évora (18 miles, or 29km) or Estremoz, but should be treated as a swift excursion as it has little to see beyond its spectacularly sited **castle** (*Open* Tue–Sun 10–12:30, 2–5. Closed Mon. *Admission: inexpensive, free Sun mornings*). Signs lead up from the modern cluster of houses to the old village, threading through groves of cork and holm oaks to the superb-looking fortress crowning the steep 1,555-foot (474m) hill. The magnificent site, laden with defensive possibilities, first attracted the attention of the Romans, who built a fort here. Later the site was fortified by the Moors, and later still by Afonso III. The almost constant unrest which ravaged the area led Dom Dinis to strengthen the fortifications, these eventually embracing a swathe of the hilltop in a ring of medieval walls (more or less those you see today).

The castle later became a favored retreat of the fourth Duke of Bragança, who came to live here in 1512 after he murdered his wife in a jealous rage. In 1531 the whole edifice, walls and all, was leveled by an earthquake, only to be reconstructed more or less immediately by João III. At this point the castle acquired its four distinctive rounded towers as well as the obvious knotted motifs on the eternal walls. The latter were symbols of the Bragança dukes, whose motto *Despois vós, nós* ("After you, us") suggested the motif through its pun on the word *nós*, which has the double meaning of "us" and "knot." The quaint stone motifs have survived a controversial restoration which saw much of the castle rendered in a honey-colored concrete veneer.

Inside, there is little to see in the vaulted interior, but it is well worth climbing the three storys to the battlements, where the superb view is said on clear days to stretch from one side of the country to the other. Whether this is true or not, Évora and Estremoz should both be visible, together with the whitewashed villages and cork oaks that dapple the surrounding countryside.

▶▶ Marvão
186C3

North of Portalegre, hard by the Spanish border, the Alentejo's plains rear up into rugged, tree-covered mountains, the Serra de São Mamede. Along their granite crowns runs a succession of redoubtable upland villages, of which the most enticing is marvelous Marvão. An atmospheric and unspoilt village, it crowns an aerie-like crag (2,837 feet, or 865m) overlooking ruggedly grand countryside. Marvão is quiet, as if forgotten by the passing centuries. Its tangle of little streets harbors dark corners, covered alleys, and immaculately whitewashed houses, a tight-knit ensemble sheltered from the outside world by curtain walls, watchtowers, and massive battlements.

With such a splendid site and a location just 4 miles (6km) from the Spanish border, it is no wonder the village has had a long history. It was probably a Roman and Visigoth colony, although no trace of either remains. A century or so later it was resettled, this time by Moors under the tutelage of Emir Maruan, the lord of Coimbra, whose name (of which Marvão is a corruption) means "mild" or "pleasant." The village was recovered in 1166, and in 1229 acquired a castle courtesy of the tireless Dom Dinis. Thereafter it was a linchpin in Portugal's border defenses.

The village is easily seen. Many streets have Manueline windows or old wrought-iron fittings: Rua do Espírito Santo, in particular, is known for two wonderful **wrought-iron balustrades**. The 13th-century church of Santa Maria houses the tourist office (see panel) and a small **museum** filled with archaeological fragments, examples of traditional dress, and some eye-opening old remedies and medical equipment. Most of your time here, however, will probably be spent in the **castle**, which was captured only once—during the civil war of 1833, when Liberal forces reputedly entered it through a secret passageway. The internal cistern, built by Dom Dinis, held sufficient water for six months, although its engineering is unlikely to distract you for long from the superlative views from the keep and parapet walls.

PRACTICALITIES
If at all possible, you should try to stay in Marvão, preferably in the village's outstanding *pousada* (see page 257). Otherwise, the tourist office in Rua Dr. Matos Magalhães (tel: 245 993 886) should, with forewarning in summer, be able to find a room or furnished apartment in its own Turismo de Habitação scheme. Two buses daily (Mon–Fri only) run here from Portalegre. There are infrequent and slow trains from Lisbon, Elvas, and Portalegre, but the station lies 8 miles (13km) north of the village close to the Spanish border.

HISTORY

Monsaraz was recaptured from the Moors in 1167 by Geraldo Sempavor, hero of Évora (see panel on page 198). In 1232 Sancho II awarded the town to the Knights Templars, and on their dissolution it passed to the Order of Christ in 1319. A concerted effort was then made to promote settlement, to which end a castle was built to afford the population protection. It proved to no avail, however, as the town fell (briefly) to the Castilians in 1381.

▶▶ Monsaraz   186C2

It can be hard in a region known for its picture-postcard villages to decide precisely which one you should visit, particularly when so many have little to offer beyond their intrinsic charm. To avoid wasting time you should make either for Marvão (see page 203) or Monsaraz, whose fortified position and tremendous views certainly rival those of its more northerly neighbor. As at Marvão, the streets (there are just four, all cobbled) have largely ignored the arrival of the 20th century. Pleasure here is to be had from wandering around and soaking up village life, as slow now as it must have been in 1167, when it was captured from the Moors and awarded to the Knights Templars (see panel).

There are a couple of churches, neither with much to detain you except for a 14th-century tomb, decorated with a carved funeral procession and hunting scenes, in the **Igeja Matriz**. Like much else of note in the village, the church sits on Rua Direita, the main street, lined for most of its length by 16th- and 17th-century houses. Some are faced in slate, while others are whitewashed, and many have the external stone staircases and wrought ironwork distinctive to much Portuguese rural architecture. At the street's conclusion in the main square stands an unusual 18th-century *pelourinho*, or pillory, crowned with a sphere of the heavens.

As at Marvão, Monsaraz's most enduring memories are likely to be the views, particularly those from the **castle**, whose parapet walls provide a sublime panorama of classic Alentejan countryside—all checkered fields, cork trees, and olive groves. The fortress was built by Dom Dinis in the 14th century but received additional walls and perimeter bastions 300 years later. Later still, part of its interior was turned into an evocative little bullring.

Monsaraz, a mixture of old and new, is known for its views

► **Portalegre**   *186C3*

Two mighty chimneys, part of a cork factory, stand as sentinels on the western approaches to Portalegre, the attractive northern capital of the Alto Alentejo (population 20,000). Long an important settlement thanks to its strategic position near the Spanish border, it was not cork, however, but textiles that brought the town its period of greatest prosperity. During the 16th century the trade was in tapestries, a craft still practiced in the town's world-renowned factory. Most of the tapestries it weaves are private commissions, often of extant works of art. Designs are projected onto graph paper, and colors are matched to around 8,000 different colored wools. Each square yard of cloth contains some 250,000 knots, which at current prices works out at about 1$00 per knot.

PRACTICALITIES
Be warned that Portalegre's train station (tel: 245 906 121) is 7 miles (12km) from the town center (buses connect the two). The bus station (tel: 245 330 723) lies just west of the Rossio at the northern end of the town; the square also has the Galeria Muncipal, which provides tourist information (tel: 245 331 359). There is a regional tourist office at Estrada Santana 25 (tel: 245 300 770).

205

Tapestry weaving has been a specialty of Portalegre for 500 years

In the 17th century, mercantile interest turned to silk, whose production enriched several generations of local families. Much of their wealth was invested in the mansions and palaces that enliven the town's usual array of whitewashed houses; some of the best are to be seen on the town's main street, **Rua 19 de Junho**. At its southern end stands the **Sé**, one of the area's more downbeat cathedrals but worth a look nevertheless for its side chapel paintings and tile-covered sacristy.

Across the street stands the **Museu Municipal** (tel: 245 300 120. *Open* Wed–Mon 9:30–12:30, 2–6. *Admission: inexpensive*), a former diocesan seminary that now houses a motley but occasionally interesting collection of religious art and other artifacts. Among the high points are a number of works in ivory, several polychrome statues, and a sumptuous ebony and silver tabernacle, reputedly paid for from the proceeds of sweets made and sold by the nuns of the town's Santa Clara convent.

Elsewhere in the town, hunt out the unusual **Museu José Régio** (tel: 245 203 625. *Open* Tue–Sun 9:30–12:30, 2–6. *Admission: inexpensive*), located just south of Praça da República. Régio was a Portuguese poet who came to Portalegre in the 1920s. He intended to stay a year but eventually remained until his death in 1969. During his time in the town, Régio amassed an obsessive collection of statues of Christ, some 40 of which (out of a total of over 300) are on display in the museum.

PRACTICALITIES
The tourist office (tel: 068 881 101) in Vila Viçosa is located alongside the town hall in Praça da República. Be aware that accommodations are fairly thin on the ground, although the office should be able to find you private rooms.

▶▶ Vila Viçosa   186C3

Vila Viçosa is a quiet and pleasant little marble town, nestled on a hillside draped in orange and lemon groves (*viçosa* means "luxuriant"), and topped with a castle and wall-enclosed old quarter. The castle, a slightly over-restored affair with a small archaeological museum, was once home to the dukes of Bragança, who eventually left their hill-top aerie in favor of the vast and plain-faced Ducal Palace that is now the town's main attraction.

DUKES The dukes of Bragança were descended from the illegitimate children of João I of Avis. For two centuries they remained fringe players on the royal stage. Vale Viçosa, as it was then called, became home to the first duke in the 15th century, although it was the second duke, Dom Fernando, who first began to take an interest in the town as the seat of a potential court. Interest waned following the execution of the third duke, picking up again under Dom Jaime, the melancholic fourth duke, who in 1501 began work on the Ducal Palace. Vila Viçosa, as it was soon called, became the focus of a flourishing court.

Bragança claims to the throne, meanwhile, had been cast aside in 1580 by King Philip II of Spain. They remained in abeyance until 1640, when Portuguese resentment at Spanish dominion boiled over. While the Spanish were distracted by a Catalonian revolt, a reluctant João IV, eighth Duke of Bragança, was compelled by public opinion to seize the throne. His descendants were to remain Portugal's kings until the revolution in 1910. Vila Viçosa, however, began to decline almost from João's accession, the palace's treasures being progressively stripped to furnish the Paço da Ribeira (Royal Palace) in Lisbon. Successive kings returned to the town nonetheless, usually to hunt, among them Portugal's last king, Manuel II, who frequented the palace until 1910.

Marble extraction near Vila Viçosa

DUCAL PALACE Many of the rooms of the **Paço Ducal►►** (*Open* Tue–Sun 9–1, 2–6. *Admission: palace moderate; armory and Coach Museum inexpensive*), arranged in two wings over three floors, are relatively dull, their original furniture having long been removed to Lisbon, whence it was either shipped to Brazil with João VI or destroyed in the 1755 earthquake. Rooms worth taking more time in, however, include the **Sala dos Duques**, whose ceiling is covered with paintings of the Bragança dukes, together with a portrait of João I, the distant Avis ancestor from whom the Braganças' royal title derived. The **Sala das Virtudes** features several 18th-century tapestries, and there is an outstanding 17th-century tapestry depicting Alexander the Great in the **Sala de Hercules**.

Perhaps the most interesting parts of the palace are the ghostly private apartments of Dom Carlos and his wife Marie-Amélia, left much as they were on the February morning in 1908 when they departed the palace for Lisbon. Carlos, Portugal's penultimate king, was assassinated later the same afternoon. Uniforms hang in cupboards, changes of clothes are laid out, and the table is still set for dinner. This never-to-be-made meal would have come from the palace's kitchen, a vast affair equipped with an incredible 2.4 tons (2.2 tonnes) of copper cooking pots.

For two small additional admission fees you can also see the palace **armory**, full of weapons and armor, and the **Museu dos Coches** (**Coach Museum**), both of which occupy the vast confines of the former Royal Stables (1752). The latter contains more than 70 beautifully maintained old coaches, landaus, and state carriages, including the one in which Dom Carlos was shot on that fateful February afternoon. The palace's final part is the 5,000-acre (2,000-hectare) **Tapada Real** (**Royal Hunting Ground**), still enclosed within its 11-mile (18km) perimeter wall: it can be glimpsed from the castle ramparts.

HIS AND HERS
The square fronting the Ducal Palace, the Terreiro do Paço, contains two separate mausoleums. One, the Convento das Chagas, was founded in 1530 by Dona Joana de Mendonça, the second wife of Duke Dom Jaime, the palace's founder (he stabbed his first wife to death in front of his court, along with the page with whom he suspected her of having an affair).
The convent became a mausoleum for many of the Bragança duchesses. The dukes, by contrast, are buried opposite in the Mosteiro dos Agostinhos.

The Algarve

▶▶▶ **REGION HIGHLIGHTS**

Igreja de Santo António, Lagos *pages 220–221*

Sagres *pages 224–225*

Serra de Monchique *pages 228–229*

– Silves

Tavira *pages 230–231*

The Algarve

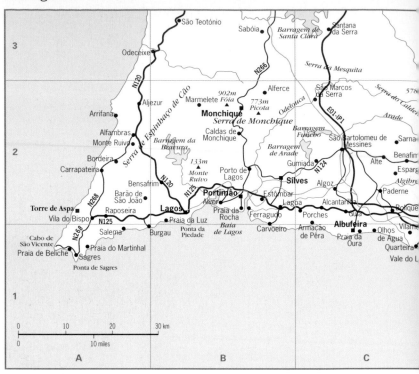

GETTING AROUND
The Algarve railroad runs from Lagos to the Spanish border, a 4½-hour trip in its entirety which links most major centers. EVA and Frota Azul buses run services to most coastal and inland towns and villages. Train and bus staff are used to bumbling foreigners, and make the necessary allowances—a boon to independent travelers. The main N125 east–west road is often busy and jammed by roadworks aimed at "upgrading." Note also that instead of linking coastal centers the road often runs slightly inland, with little feeder roads branching off to the coast. The new IP1–E1 is a good four-lane road running from the Spanish border in the east to Albufeira.

Pages 208–209: Algarve beaches are famous: this one is near Lagos

THE ALGARVE This is the one Portuguese region most people know of—and the one most of them visit. Sandy beaches, idyllic weather in both summer and winter, and a picturesque coastline attract countless vacationers year round. Yet the numbers of visitors and the development provoked by them have in many areas come close to destroying the charms that first attracted tourists to the region. The blight is at its worst in the coast's central reaches—the 50 miles (85km) between Lagos and Faro—where a once pristine littoral is now cluttered with concrete hotels, apartments, shopping malls, modern villas, and water parks (a growing menace). Only at the region's western and eastern fringes, around Sagres and Tavira, can you still find the lonely beaches and little fishing villages of popular imagination, although even here new roads and a burgeoning tourist infrastructure (only now being reined in) threaten the Algarve's last few unspoilt redoubts.

This said, much of the region (notably the interior) retains considerable charm, and many of the resorts, if you can cope with the crowds, are far more amenable than their Spanish equivalents. Not only that, but they are clean—no fewer than 30 of Portugal's 100-plus EU "Blue Flag" beaches are found on the Algarve.

REGIONS The Algarve is modestly sized, its coast stretching for just 150 miles (240km), but within its short span lurks a remarkable variety of landscapes. The coast divides into three main areas. To the east, from Faro to the Spanish border, stretches a region known as the *sotovento*

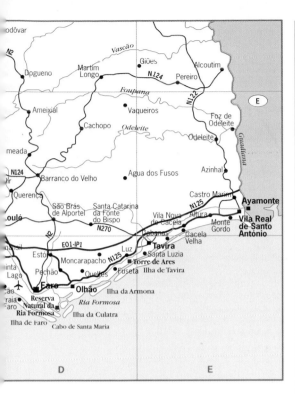

The Algarve's Mediterranean climate guarantees hot summers and mild winters, while its interior mountains shelter the coast from cold northerly winds in winter and scorching noonday heat in summer. Annual rainfall is just 16–20 inches (400–500mm). This makes it a virtually year-round vacation destination, a fact recognized by most hotels and restaurants. Spring and winter are delightful times to visit, partly because prices are considerably lower (luxury and other hotels often offer remarkably reasonable deals), and partly because you can enjoy spectacles such as the almond blossom (mid-January–end of February) and spring flowers (March–May). In July and August, however, reserve accommodations in advance, and be prepared for the highest prices anywhere in Portugal.

(the "leeward"), an area of beaches, salt-marshes, lagoons, and protective offshore sand bars known as *ilhas*. Generally, this is the quieter section of the coast, and in **Tavira**, **Olhão**, and **Faro** (in that order) it has some of the region's nicer towns. It also has the advantage of higher

A boat trip is a good way of admiring the Algarve coastline

The Algarve

NUMBERS

Something of the Algarve's popularity, and the manner in which it has altered over the years, is illustrated in a set of telling statistics. In 1960, before the opening of Faro's international airport, the region offered just 1,000 tourist beds. In 1974, after the revolution, the tight planning regulations imposed by Salazar were quickly relaxed. By 1988 the region had 58,500 beds; seven years later, in 1995, the figure had risen to 82,000. Of the $900 million of foreign investment pumped into Portugal in 1988, over a third went into tourism, an area foreign investors clearly feel is still ripe for exploitation. In 1989 foreign investment was twice the 1988 figure; a year later it had doubled again.

Boats are a way of life in the Algarve

sea temperatures than the area to the west, where the warming effects of the Gulf Stream are offset by a cooling current that washes up from the Canary Islands.

West of Faro, in the *barlavento* (the "windward"), the landscape changes completely, conforming to the classic tourist brochure image of the Algarve: a rocky and cliff-edged coast broken up by sandy coves, small bays, and offshore sea stacks. The area's main resort centers are found here—**Albufeira**, **Praia da Rocha**, and **Lagos**. Beyond Lagos, however, a third region presents itself, namely the wild and rockier coast that culminates in the windswept headlands at **Sagres** and Cabo de São Vicente. At this point you are approaching Atlantic waters, which makes bathing a colder and occasionally more dangerous proposition, although the villages here (notably Salema and Sagres) have largely escaped the development excesses perpetrated farther east.

Inland lies a fourth and largely untouched Algarve, that of the wooded mountains of the **Serra de Monchique**, whose peaks look south to the sea and north to the over-arching skies of the Alentejo. This is a region of small farms, scented pine woods, and remote villages, while the mountains' flower-strewn foothills are clothed in olives, figs, quinces, carobs (see panel on page 223), orange groves, and the blossom-laden almond trees for which the Algarve is famous.

HISTORY Many Portuguese will tell you that the Algarve is not really Portugal at all, largely because for centuries it remained in thrall to invaders and foreign influences that failed to penetrate the rest of the country. The Phoenicians and Romans both maintained a presence here, while around 200 BC Hannibal's Carthaginian armies wintered in the region's mild-weathered enclaves, anticipating the habits of sunseeking tourists by over 2,000 years. The Moors were the next visitors, and left the most lasting

impression, not so much in material remains (which, town walls aside, are few) but in architectural details such as white, flat-roofed houses and their distinctive terraces, patios, and filigree chimneys, and in the groves of oranges, figs, and almonds that the "infidels" did so much to promote.

Even the region's name derives from the Moorish al-Gharb, meaning "Western land," a reference to the most westerly of the Moors' territories. This "western" region also included al-Andalus, or Andalusia, as well as the North African territories of Ceuta, Tangiers, and Fez. In time, "Algarve" came to be used by the Portuguese to describe the lands still under Moorish control. So distinct was this region that when it finally began to fall to the Portuguese—after a Moorish domination which lasted from the 8th to the mid-13th centuries—Dom Sancho I (1154–1211) was moved to declare himself "King of Portugal *and* of the Algarve," a title that endured until the fall of the monarchy in 1910.

The pedestrianized streets of Albufeira, a popular and pleasant package-tour destination

LOCAL STATISTICS
Because visitors focus on the Algarve's coast it is often forgotten that around half of all Algarvios live inland, and that three quarters of the region is agricultural.

PRACTICALITIES

Albufeira's train station (tel: 289 571 616) is at Ferreiras, 3.5 miles (6km) north of the town, to which it is connected by hourly shuttle buses. The bus terminal (tel: 289 586 500) is at the northern edge of town on Avenida da Liberdade, just five minutes' walk from Largo E. Duarte Pacheco. The tourist office is at the southern end of Rua 5 de Outubro (tel: 289 585 279), and the post office (*Open* Mon–Fri 9–12:30, 2–6) is next door.

VILAMOURA

Just east of Falésia is the upscale marina and golf resort of Vilamoura, popular with both Portuguese and foreigners. Enjoy a meal or drink at one of the many bars and restaurants overlooking the extremely chic marina.

►► Albufeira   *210C1*

Resort Albufeira takes its name from the Moorish al-Buhera, meaning "Castle-on-the-Sea." It is the Algarve's premier package-tour destination, a dubious honor that might well have turned the town into a nightmare of concrete high-rises but that has in fact, surprisingly, left it one of the more pleasant of Portugal's resorts.

This said, the whitewashed houses of the old fishing village at its heart, if not exactly overshadowed by tower-block hotels, are still hemmed in by hillsides covered in new apartment buildings. And the streets, while pedestrianized, are thronged day and night with armies of tourists looking for—and generally finding—souvenirs, restaurants, nightlife, and beer, not necessarily in that order. Vacationers, however, among whom the British feature large, are a varied lot and there are restaurants, cafés, and nightlife that cater for all tastes and budgets.

BEACHES Albufeira's town beach is fine but is likely to be crowded. It is reached via a tunnel cut through the rock at the end of Rua 5 de Outubro, Albufeira's main street. Several miles to either side of the town, however, stretches a string of cove beaches, most of them linked to villa and resort developments set back from the lovely rocky headlands that dot this coastline. To the west, the main resorts are Galé, Castelo, and São Rafael; while none of them is directly accessible by bus, taxis will run you out to any of these spots. Public transportation is available to the beaches to the east of the town, notably those at Praia da Oura (1.2 miles, or 2km) and Olhos de Água (5 miles, or 9km). Note that at Falésia, 6 miles (10km) east of Albufeira, the coves usually found on this coast give way to an almost unbroken stretch of cliff-backed sand (see panel "Vilamoura").

Two's company on an empty Algarve beach

► Faro 211D1

Thirty years ago visitors to Faro, as to many of the Algarve's towns, would have found a sleepy fishing community little disturbed by the advent of the 20th century. Today, some 4.5 million tourists a year use its international airport as a point of entry to southern Portugal's resorts, whisked by coach from their charter planes to beach complexes along the Algarve littoral. As a result, the town has become a busy commercial and tourist center, losing a lot—but not all—of its charm in the process. It boasts a fetching harbor area and an inviting little old quarter, while the weight of visitors (some of whom choose to stray no farther than the town in search of sea and sand) guarantees a busy summer buzz and a fair number of bars, restaurants, and nightclubs. The town also has a tremendous beach, although sadly its surroundings have been overdeveloped and during the summer the long strip of sand remains barely visible beneath human bodies. You probably won't want to spend an entire Algarve sojourn here (although some people do), but the beach and town can both be worth a day or two at the beginning or end of a trip.

HISTORY Faro has its roots in the Roman settlement of Milreu, located some 5 miles (8km) from the site of the present city (see panel on page 218). It then rose to prominence under the Moors, for whom it served as a major port and a conduit for trade to the provincial capital at Silves. It achieved still greater fame when the armies of Afonso III defeated the Moors here in 1249, a battle that marked the end of Moorish dominion in Portugal (their power in Spain, by contrast, was to endure another 250 years). Afonso awarded the town a municipal charter and rebuilt its walls, laying the foundations for a period of growth that saw it emerge as one of the most important centers in southern Portugal. By the 1480s the town's

Enjoying the sun on a Faro side street

GETTING THERE
Faro airport is situated 3.5 miles (6km) west of the town center. It has a bank, post office, and tourist office (tel: 289 818 582. *Open* daily 10 AM–midnight), together with the offices of major car rental companies such as Avis (tel: 289 818 538), Budget (tel: 289 818 888), Fixd rent-a-car (tel: 289 818 294), and Europcar (tel: 289 818 316). For flight information, tel: 289 800 800. Taxis to the center of Faro should cost around 1,400$00, plus around 300$00 for any luggage placed in the trunk. A 20 percent surcharge is added at weekends and Mon–Fri 10 PM–6 AM. Check meters are running (or working); if not, agree on a price before setting off. Alternatively, take bus 14 or 16 to the terminal on Avenida da República, around 300 yards (300m) across the harbor from the tourist office and old town.

PRACTICALITIES

Faro's busy tourist office is located just outside the old town at 8–12 Rua da Misericórdia (tel: 289 803 604). Accommodations in Faro are at a premium for most of the year. If you arrive with nowhere to stay, try asking for help at the airport or town center tourist offices. Most hotels and pensions are collected in the streets north of the harbor. When choosing somewhere to stay, insure it does not overlook a street full of noisy, late-opening bars and restaurants. Faro's post office is on Largo do Carmo (*Open* Mon–Fri 9–12:30, 2–6, Sat 9–12:30); it has telephone and poste restante facilities. The police station is in Rua Serpa Pinto (tel: 289 822 022).

Jewish population, together with those of Lisbon and Leiria, had established the country's first printing presses. As a result, Portugal's first published works were 11 Hebrew texts printed by Samuel Gacon in Faro in 1487.

Less happy times were to follow. In July 1596 Englishmen Charles Howard and Robert, Earl of Essex, landed in Faro on their way home from raiding Cadiz. Portugal was then under Spanish rule, and therefore a legitimate target for the buccaneering Elizabethans. Their 3,000-strong army duly sacked the city, which had been abandoned by its population after news of the Englishmen's arrival spread. Essex installed himself in the Bishop's Palace, helping himself in the process to a collection of 200 tooled and gilt-laden theological books. He later presented these works to his friend Thomas Bodley, founder of the Bodleian Library in Oxford, England (the first librarian subsequently complained that various parts of the books had been excised, presumably acts of censorship on the part of Portugal's zealous Inquisition). Essex's parting gift to Faro was to set fire to it, an act of destruction further compounded in 1722 and 1755 by two devastating earthquakes.

In the 20th century destruction of a different kind has been visited on the city: that brought by the advent of mass tourism, a phenomenon unleashed by the building of the international airport. Prosperity has arrived in its wake, however, although scenes of intense poverty still

Faro's peaceful harbor was a bustling port in Moorish times

greet any visitor who wanders to the virtual shanty villages that gird Faro's expanding suburbs.

OLD TOWN GATEWAY Faro's old town, the Cidade Velha, is full of cobbled streets and vividly painted houses, and comes as a pleasant surprise after the daunting concrete high-rises of the outer suburbs. Tucked behind defensive walls, it rises above the harbor area and modern town, its flanks guarded by the *salinas*, or lagoons, that characterize much of the eastern Algarve. The tourist office (see panel on page 216), just off the pleasant greenery of the **Jardim Manuel Bivar**, makes a convenient starting point for a tour of the area, whose tightknit cluster of streets can easily be seen on foot. A stone's throw from the office stands the **Arco da Vila▶**, the finest of the gateways in the ring of 13th-century walls built by Afonso III, and restored in the 18th century. Its Italianate profile is adorned with a white marble statue of St. Thomas Aquinas, added in the 17th century when the saint was called upon to protect Faro from a virulent outbreak of plague.

CATHEDRAL Once through the old town's entrance arch, follow the charming cobbled street of Rua do Município to Largo da Sé, an impressive square lined with orange trees and dominated by the **Sé▶** (tel: 289 806 632. *Open* Mon–Sun 10–5). It also contains a complex of palaces that includes the Bishop's Palace, a descendant of the building

BEACHES
Faro's large beach, the Praia dc Faro, a few miles out of town, is busy and developed. If you want to go there, take the 16 airport bus, which departs from a special stop opposite the bus terminal. Quieter beaches worth considering include those on the sand bars between Faro and Olhão, a large fishing port 5 miles (8km) east of Faro (see page 222). During July and August ferries depart for Ilha Deserta and Farol on Ilha da Culatra from the docks below Faro's old town. Alternatively, take a bus or train to Olhão and then a ferry to Ilha da Armona. Once on the island, a 20-minute walk past the rows of beach huts will take you to a large and relatively uncrowded beach.

217

EXCURSION

The best day trip from Faro is to Estói, located about 6 miles (10km) northeast of the town: regular buses make the 15-minute trip. The main things to see are the modest ruins of Milreu, formerly the Roman settlement of Ossonoba, which lie ten minutes' walk west of Estói's main square. The colony was inhabited from about the 2nd century AD and abandoned some six centuries later. Fragments of a temple, mosaics, a bathhouse, and villa dwellings make up the bulk of the ruins.

Back in Estói, leave time to explore the romantic gardens of the Palácio do Visconde de Estói, a small 18th-century palace (tel: 289 997 282. *Open* Tue–Sun 9–12:30, 2–5. *Admission free*). Palms and orange trees line its terraces and avenues, these offset by pools, statuary, fountains, and decorative tiles.

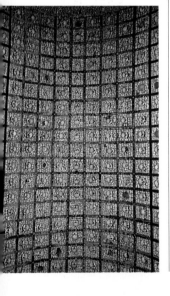

The Capela dos Ossos is decorated with human skulls

appropriated by the Earl of Essex (see page 216). Much of the former Gothic cathedral on the site was laid low by the 1755 earthquake and only the bell tower (worth climbing for views over the town) survives as a memorial. Baroque and Renaissance styles compete for attention to little effect in the new version, and the most interesting parts of the interior are the gaudily decorated organ, an extravagantly fashioned reliquary, and a spread of 18th-century tiles.

MUNICIPAL MUSEUM Behind the cathedral, in Praça Afonso III (the square boasts a bold statue of the former king), lies Faro's **Museu Municipal▶▶**, housed in the 16th-century Convento de Nossa Senhora de Assunção (tel: 289 824 085. *Open* Mon–Fri 9–5:30, Sat 10–1. *Admission: inexpensive*). Archaeological displays form the museum's highlights, many of them Roman remains excavated from local sites. They are housed in the convent's beautiful two-story cloisters, built in 1543. Watch out in particular for two 1st-century AD busts of Hadrian and Agrippina (wife of the Emperor Claudius), part of a 1st-century AD Roman tomb, and the 3rd-century AD mosaic of Neptune and the Four Winds (just two of the "winds" survive, found near Faro's train station). Other exhibits span Faro's Moorish and post-Moorish past, and include weapons, coins, Mudejar *azulejos*, Moorish earthenware, and the Ferreira de Almeida Collections (on the first floor), the last featuring an assortment of paintings, sculptures, and furniture.

HARBOR AREA After the old town you should devote most of your time to dipping into the cafés and gardens that overlook the busy **harbor▶▶**, the bustling heart of modern Faro, and to exploring the backstreets around Rua de Santo António. The main target in these streets is the **Museu de Etnografia Regional** (third floor of the District Assembly in Praça do Liberdade), a fascinating little collection of reconstructed domestic interiors and displays devoted to local rural life (*Open* Mon–Fri 9–noon, 2–5. *Admission: inexpensive*).

You might also want to stop off at the **Museu Marítimo**, a maritime museum housed in the harbormaster's office on the dock close to the Hotel Eva (*Open* Mon–Fri 9:30–noon, 2–4:45. *Admission: inexpensive*).

CHURCHES Also worth looking out for is the **Igreja do Carmo▶▶** on Largo do Carmo, a twin-towered baroque church unremarkable except for its wonderfully macabre Capela dos Ossos (Chapel of Bones), whose walls are decorated with around 1,250 skulls and bones removed in 1816 from the adjacent monks' cemetery. The chapel, in a garden to the rear, is approached via the sacristy, which is entered to the right of the main altar (tel: 289 284 490. *Open* Mon–Fri 10–1, 3–5, Sat 10–1. Closed Sun during services. *Admission: inexpensive*).

A church with more intrinsic architectural interest is the **Igreja de São Pedro▶** in Largo de São Pedro, perhaps built by converted Jews (the so-called "New Christians") in the 16th century. Inside are some beautifully decorated altars and a series of naive but striking frescoes, the author of which remains unknown.

The entrance to the fort at Lagos: the town's first stronghold was built by the Phoenicians

▶▶ Lagos 210B2

Lagos is one of the Algarve's premier resorts, blessed with some of the region's finest beaches, a tempting variety of nightlife and restaurants, and a mixture of visitors that embraces everyone from young backpackers to affluent expatriots. A fishing port and market town, it also retains a life of its own, as well as an old quarter—complete with walls and the inevitable fort—whose charm easily survives the summer onslaught of visitors. This charm, together with the beaches, constitutes the town's main appeal, but there are also a couple of churches and a modest museum to pander to sightseers.

HISTORY The broad bay that embraces Lagos, the Baía de Lagos, is one of the largest in Portugal. Its potential as a harbor attracted attention from earliest times, making the town one of the longest established settlements on the Algarve. The Phoenicians founded a colony here, as did the Lusitanians, who built a stronghold known as Lacobriga. When this was destroyed by an earthquake, the area was absorbed by the Carthaginians, who took possession of the town around 350 BC. The Romans occupied the area afterwards, and since then Lagos has barely looked back.

Many of the great African voyages of discovery in the 15th century embarked from the town's harbor, a refuge that provided one of Henry the Navigator's main maritime bases (see pages 226–227). In 1578 the harbor also witnessed the departure of Dom Sebastião, the doomed 24-year-old king of Portugal, whose voyage marked the last great Mediterranean crusade and prompted a cult that survives to this day (see page 220). Almost his last act

GETTING THERE
Lagos forms the western terminal of the Algarve railroad track and can be reached by train from Faro and all points east. The station (tel: 282 762 987) is a good 15 minutes' walk east of the town center; taxis usually meet trains or can be called (tel: 282 762 469 or 282 763 587). Regular buses also link the town with the region's other main centers. The bus terminal is located a little closer to the center than the train station, one street back from the main waterfront road (Avenida dos Descobrimentos). For bus information, tel: 282 762 944.

The rooftops of Lagos in the early evening sun

PRACTICALITIES
The Lagos tourist office is in Largo Marquês de Pombal (tel: 282 763 031), just to the west of Praça Gil Eanes, the town's main square. Banks are grouped around the *praça*, but the town's streets boast numerous other foreign exchange outlets. The post office (*Open* Mon–Sat 9–6) lies off Avenida dos Descobrimentos just behind the town hall (which is also on the *praça*); there is a Telecom office next door for telephone calls. The police station is in Rua General Alberto Silveira (tel: 282 762 930).

on Portuguese soil was to make Lagos capital of the Algarve, a title it retained until 1755 when the honor passed to Tavira and, ultimately, to Faro.

DOM SEBASTIÃO In 1578, at the age of 24, Dom Sebastião, a weak but headstrong king, led a doomed expedition against a Muslim army in North Africa. On August 4, at the Battle of Alcácer-Quibir, he was defeated and his army destroyed: 8,000 Portuguese soldiers were killed and 15,000 taken prisoner. Sebastião, arrogant and foolish in life, became a hero in death and a symbol of Portuguese spirit and independence. Rumors quickly spread that he was still alive—no body had been found—and a messianic cult, still known as Sebastianismo, grew up. This cast Sebastião in the role of a Portuguese King Arthur, a savior who would rise again in Portugal's hour of need. In the 17th century this meant deliverance from Spain, and four "pretenders" appeared in the 20 years after his death. Even today, the cult is still invoked in times of national crisis. It was ironic that the death of Sebastião without heirs, together with the defeat of his army, should have brought about the extinction of the House of Avis and consigned Portugal to some 60 years of Spanish domination (see pages 36–37).

THE TOWN The Praça da República forms Lagos's appealing focus, its heart dominated by a statue of Henry the Navigator, erected in 1960 on the occasion of the 500th anniversary of his death. On the square's right-hand side stands the former customs house, whose neighboring arcades once housed the **Mercado de Escravos**, Europe's first and Portugal's only slave market. The building was the sordid fruit of Gil Eanes's pioneering expeditions along the African coast in 1434 (see page 34). On the opposite side of the square stands the church of Santa Maria, from whose windows Dom Sebastião is said to have rallied his reluctant troops before their fateful departure for Africa.

Of greater intrinsic interest is the **Igreja de Santo António▶▶▶**, just 100 yards (100m) north of the square, whose plain facade belies the wonderfully sumptuous decoration (1715) of the baroque interior. Among the explosion of gilt and stucco, the woodwork stands out in particular, its carving and capricious details some of the most outstanding in Portugal. Behind the church is the **Museu Municipal►►**, an extraordinary potpourri of weapons, animal fetuses, chimneys, pottery, neolithic remains, statues, religious art, and more (tel: 282 762 301. *Open* Tue–Sun 9:30–12, 2–5. *Admission: inexpensive*). Southwest of the square, on the waterfront, is the picturesque **Forte Ponta da Bandeira**, a neat little fortress that guards Lagos's harbor (tel: 282 761 410. *Open* Tue–Sat 10–1, 2–6, Sun 10–1. *Admission: inexpensive*).

BEACHES The main beaches lie to either side of town, although there is also a relatively uncrowded town beach close to the Forte Ponta da Bandeira. The eastern beaches are dominated by the **Meia Praia**, a broad expanse of sand that stretches for some 2.5 miles (4km), its size guaranteeing space even at the height of summer. Clearly, the farther you travel from town the less crowded things are likely to be; in summer, a regular bus leaves from the Avenida dos Descobrimentos and runs along the entire length of Meia Praia.

To the west of Lagos, in complete contrast, a series of little beaches forms a network of coves and cliffs that riddles the promontory which protects the town's flanks on this side. You can reach most of these coves on foot by walking up Avenida dos Descobrimentos and then picking up the coastal path signposted to Praia do Pinhão, the first of the beaches. The most famous beach here—one of the most photographed in the Algarve—is the **Praia de Dona Ana►►**. A fair few hotels compete for space on the promontory, but with perseverance you can walk (or drive) all the way to the lighthouse at **Ponta da Piedade**, a beautiful viewpoint. Boat trips also provide views of the caves and coast from the sea; for details inquire at the tourist office (see panel opposite).

MAKING A SPLASH
Waterslides are sprouting up the length and breadth of the Algarve. If you want to visit just one, it should probably be the monster Slide & Splash at Vale de Deus, Estômbar, one of the largest of its kind in Europe. It is a half hour trip by road from Lagos along the N125.

221

The caves and cliffs at Ponta da Piedade

Dried fish is a staple food in Portugal

►► Olhão   211D1

Despite its proximity to Faro (just 5 miles, or 8km, to the west), Olhão makes a jumping-off point from which to enjoy the sand-bar beaches (*ilhas*) which characterize the relatively quiet stretch of coast that unfolds east of the town as far as the Spanish border. Only Tavira, another 14 miles (22km) to the east, makes a better overall base for this part of the Algarve (see pages 230–231). The main reason to come here is to visit the beaches on the offshore Ilha da Armona and Ilha da Culatra (see panel on page 217).

The town itself is the region's largest fishing port, which partly explains its rather dingy outskirts—all high-rises and canning factories—but once you reach the old town the place has a fair degree of charm. Its whitewashed houses, flat roofs, and external staircases point to a Moorish influence, but in fact Olhão was founded as recently as the 17th century, its appearance the result of long-established trading links with North Africa. There is next to nothing to see, the most tempting prospects being the view of the rooftops from the belfry of the parish church, Nossa Senhora do Rosário (in the main street), and the vignettes of local life provided by the town's harborfront food and fish market (*Open* Mon–Sat).

► Portimão   210B2

With a population of some 50,000, Portimão is one of the largest towns on the Algarve, a port and industrial center (canning and construction are its staple industries) that is not a place to visit for its own sake. Much the same goes for the string of overdeveloped resorts that clog the coast road west of the town as far as Lagos (11 miles, or 17km, distant). Most people who are forced to make the town's acquaintance do so en route to or from Praia da Rocha, a large and relatively appealing resort just 2 miles (3km) to the south (see opposite). If you do find yourself in Portimão—the town's shops are the most likely reason for a visit—the best thing to do is head for the riverfront

The port and marina at Portimão

The cliffs and sea stacks at Praia da Rocha, one of the Algarve's most popular resorts

behind Rua Serpa Pinto, home to a string of pleasant open-air restaurants. Prices are rock bottom, and there is plenty of streetlife on the quayside to keep you entertained.

The town's tourist office is located at the northern edge of Largo 1 de Dezembro (tel: 282 419 131), but with the far more attractive prospect of Praia da Rocha close by it is unlikely you will need help with accommodations. Potentially more useful, at least in an emergency, is the only British consulate on the Algarve, at Largo Francisco A. Mauricio 7-1° (tel. 282 417 800).

►► Praia da Rocha   210B2

Praia da Rocha was one of the first resorts in the Algarve to attract the greedy eyes of developers, seducing them with its huge beach and its flanking cliffs, russet-colored ramparts that now form the foundations for a panoply of hotels, malls, and villa developments. Prior to its transformation, the village was something of a bohemian enclave, colonized by a group of mainly British writers and artists between the 1930s and 1950s.

For all its present-day crowds and commercialism, however, the resort has something of an upscale reputation and, unlike its newer neighbors, the feeling that here at least is a finished project and not simply a resort-in-progress. If you want a beach vacation with all that that implies, you could do a lot worse than come here. This applies equally in winter, when the area's balmy micro-climate makes it one of the Algarve's most popular spots for an off-season break. Whether you are traveling independently or on a package, be sure to take a room in the resort rather than in the less-than-salubrious town of Portimão (see above).

CAROB TREES
The carob stands out among the Algarve's roster of exotic trees. To the Portuguese it is known as the *pão de São João* (the "bread of St. John"), after the biblical reference to its beans, the "husks the swines did eat," which sustained John the Baptist during his 40 days and nights in the desert. The same beans, which are low in fat and rich in vitamins, protein, and minerals, were also used to feed the Duke of Wellington's cavalry during the Peninsular War. Today they find a variety of uses in health foods, most particularly as a cocoa substitute. The seeds display a remarkable uniformity of size, so remarkable in fact that they were used as a measure called the *qirat*, now better known as the "carat." In all, some 30 uses have been found for the tree and its constituent parts.

PRACTICALITIES

Regular buses run daily between Sagres and Lagos. Information in Sagres is available from the tourist office on Rua Comandante Matoso (tel: 282 624 873). It can arrange accommodations (although rooms are usually fairly easily available), and organizes motor and boat tours. It also rents out mountain bikes, a pleasant way of making the trip out to Cabo de São Vicente.

BATTLE SITE

Cape St. Vincent witnessed a string of major naval battles, beginning in 1693 with an encounter between the French and a combined fleet of British and Dutch forces. In 1759 the British were battling the French again, while in 1780 it was the turn of the Spanish, confronted and defeated by Britain's Admiral Rodney. In 1797 came the most famous engagement of all, when Nelson and Admiral Jervis, outnumbered two to one, inflicted a crushing defeat on the Spanish, a victory that decisively altered the balance of European naval power in Britain's favor.

►►► Sagres   210A1

Sagres village amounts to little—a handful of disappointing streets and a pair of squares—but in historical terms it is one of the most evocative spots in the country. For it was here on a windblown headland in the 14th century that Prince Henry the Navigator created a school of navigation that laid the foundations of Portugal's far-flung empire (see pages 226–227). Today, virtually nothing of the school survives save the ruined outlines of what may once have been Henry's **Fortaleza**, within which temporary exhibitions are occasionally held. These ruins also shelter a large "wind compass," or rosa dos ventos, unearthed in the 1920s and claimed—in the face of a certain amount of scholarly skepticism—to be contemporaneous with Henry's school.

After Henry's death in 1460, much of his school's work moved to Lisbon, precipitating a decline from which Sagres has never recovered. Further damage was inflicted in 1587, when Sir Francis Drake set fire to the town on his return from Cadiz, destroying Henry's matchless library in the process. The present village was raised in the 19th century, built over the earthquake-ravaged remnants of its predecessors. Life of sorts has recently returned to the area, however, most notably in the shape of new villa and apartment developments straggling across the surrounding countryside. More will undoubtedly follow as the new fast road from Lagos brings with it mass tourism's inevitable mixed blessings.

BEACHES Sagres's magnificent beaches, previously the preserve of backpackers and other assorted cognoscenti, will only add to the area's growing popularity. Several lie within easy walking distance of the village. Moving east of the fortress, the **Praia da Mareta** lies just below and to the right of the village's main square; the **Praia da Baleira**, a little farther away, is right by the harbor; five minutes beyond lies the **Praia do Martinhal**, longest and best on this stretch; and beyond that is **Tonel**, which is predominantly a surfers' hang out. Moving west of the fortress, the beaches are more captivating still, if less sheltered, the best being the **Praia de Belixe**, located about 1.2 miles (2km) from Sagres off the road to Cabo de São Vicente (see below). More beaches, most usually almost empty, lie farther along the same road, although many are backed by steep and impressive cliffs, which means care is required when clambering down.

On all the beaches the water is colder than elsewhere on the Algarve, and the currents are strong, so caution is required when swimming. Winds can also be debilitating, in particular the prevailing northerly known locally as the *nortadas*. Belixe is probably the best overall bet, although here as elsewhere the backpacking pioneers are increasingly giving way to families and package-tour visitors.

CABO DE SÃO VICENTE Henry's choice of Sagres for his school was no accident. The nearby Cabo de São Vicente (Cape St. Vincent) is the most southwesterly point of continental Europe and for centuries marked one of the limits of geographical certainty for Western mariners. To the Romans it was a sacred spot, the Promontorium Sacrum, the place where the sun was believed to sink into the ocean each night. Later, the relics of martyred St. Vincent were brought here by boat from Valençia, accompanied by two ravens. The burial place became a Christian shrine, and over many centuries boats dipped their sails in homage as they passed: it was believed that the saint, occupying his throne (one of the sea stacks below the point), blessed each one as it passed. In 1173 the ravens reappeared, when the saint's bones were moved to Lisbon by Afonso Henriques. Vincent is the city's patron saint and the birds feature in the city's crest.

The cape remains a haunting and evocative place, ringed by 200-foot (60m) cliffs and tipped by a lighthouse (one of the most powerful in Europe) built into the ruins of the point's former fortress and 16th-century Capuchin convent. The views are tremendous, particularly at sunset, a fitting climax to a pulse-quickening 3.5-mile (6km) cliff-path walk from Sagres (the walk along the road to the same point is shorter and still offers fine panoramas).

Cape St. Vincent, the most southwesterly point of continental Europe and witness to some of history's great sea battles

Henry the Navigator, the great pioneer of Portugal's medieval voyages of discovery, is one of the most romantic and mysterious figures in Portuguese history. Although not an explorer in the true sense, his energy and vision provided the spur that drove his country's mariners to lay the foundations of a worldwide empire.

CHARACTER

No known portrait exists of Henry the Navigator, which seems somehow apt for a man whose character has so eluded subsequent historians. It seems he had a commercial bent, for he received one fifth of all the proceeds that accrued from his ventures and the trading deals licensed to merchants in Portugal's new lands. Yet he died with huge debts. He was also efficient and farsighted, ably setting about the colonization of Madeira, to which he exported sugar cane, high-quality cattle, vines from Crete, and the best strains of wheat and barley. At the same time he was ascetic and austere, having allegedly died a virgin and worn a hairshirt for much of his life. Worldly in his passionate pursuit of knowledge, Henry was also devout and pious, "his heart," in the words of a chronicler, "knowing no fear other than the fear of sin."

*Right: Henry the Navigator, commemorated on Lisbon's Monument of the Discoveries
Top: giant compass on the cliffs at Sagres*

Talent Henry (Henrique in Portuguese) was born in Porto on March 4, 1394, the third surviving son of João I of Portugal and Philippa of Lancaster, granddaughter of Edward III of England. Like his brothers, Henry was to prove talented and intelligent, and with them, in the words of one historian, he would carry Portugal "to the edge of the modern world." He gained his spurs at the age of 19, when he joined a fleet assembled by his father to take the Muslim port of Ceuta on the Moroccan coast. For all his love of things maritime, however, the Moroccon port (taken in August 1415) would be as far as he ever sailed. Three years later he returned to the scene of his triumph, bewitched by the stories and rumors regarding the mysterious lands and seas that lay beyond the Moroccan hinterland.

School As reward for his part in the victory, Henry was made Duke of Viseu, an amenable region at the heart of the Beira Alta. Rather than settle in his dukedom, however, he turned to the south and to Sagres, a windswept promontory at the southwesternmost point of mainland Europe. There, at what was then the edge of the known world, he founded a center devoted to exploration and maritime research (its precise location remains a matter of dispute). Surrounding himself with the continent's foremost cartographers, navigators, and shipwrights, Henry set about improving maritime navigation and perfecting the design of Portugal's ships (see panel opposite). He also gathered around him the finest sailors in the country, as well as every available chart, map and manual.

Discovery Henry's aim was discovery, and more particularly the discovery of a sea route to the Orient, a passage which was presumed to exist through the uncharted

INNOVATION

Henry's maritime center at Sagres devised improved instruments for plotting course and position, and greatly added to the detail and numbers of maps, charts, and celestial tables available to mariners. One of its most profound innovations, however, was to be a new type of ship, the caravel, a clever amalgam of the *caravelas*, a cargo boat used on the Douro, and the Arab dhow, whose lateen, or triangular sails, made sailing into the wind easier than the square-rigged sails of the old-fashioned *barca*. This, and subsequent improvements to the caravel's masts, stern, and hull, greatly increased the speed and seaworthiness of the boats. These innovations would prove invaluable in the longer voyages undertaken along the African coast after 1440. In 1446, for example, after an encounter with hostile African tribesmen, a crew of just five survivors was able to sail a caravel safely back to port in a voyage that lasted 60 days.

waters off Africa. In 1419 his first ships, crude square-rigged *barcas*, sailed south into the great unknown. All but one returned with nothing to report. The single exception, captained by João Gonçalves Zarco and Tristão Vaz Teixeira, was blown off course in a gale and forced to make landfall at an uninhabited island 400 miles (640km) south-west of Sagres. The pair named the little scrap of land Porto Santo, and later were ordered to return and attempt to settle it. Shortly afterwards, the same pair discovered another island farther to the southwest—Madeira. Henry promptly colonized the wooded paradise.

Progress Eight years later, in 1427, the Açores (Azores) were discovered, adding a wide-arcing archipelago at the heart of the Atlantic to the slow-growing Portuguese empire. More important than the acquisition of territory, however, was to be the rounding of Cape Bojador, or "Jutting Cape," a promontory on the West African coast which at almost 1,000 miles (1,600km) from Sagres marked the limit of charts of the day. Beyond it lay the "Sea of Darkness," an unknown domain wreathed in myth and mariners' tales. Ships had left Lagos, Henry's favored port, in search of the cape for 19 years. In 1434 it was spotted and eventually rounded by Gil Eanes, one of Henry's courtiers, who was dispatched by his master with the words: "There is no peril so great that the hope of reward will not be greater." No prizes or booty accompanied his return, but in the words of writer Marion Kaplan, the "true prize was the breaking of the deadlock of fear and superstition." By 1460, the year of Henry's death, Mauritania, the Senegal river, Serra Leão (Sierre Leone), and the Cape Verde Islands had all been discovered.

PRIME MOVER

"Prince Henry was unquestionably the organizer, the mover, the *impulsionador*—a wonderful Portuguese word—of Portuguese exploration. He was navigator not of any single ship but of the Age of Discovery itself, for above all he kindled a flame that in the years to come would light the path of Portuguese mariners to the far corners of the earth." From *The Portuguese* by Marion Kaplan (1991).

PRACTICALITIES

Just three or four buses (Mon–Sat) run to Monchique from Portimão, some calling in at Caldas de Monchique en route and others stopping on the town's outskirts before continuing to Monchique.

The tourist office in Silves is in the town center at Rua 25 de Abril (tel: 282 442 255).

The train station is 1.2 miles (2km) to the south of the town, to which it is connected by half-hourly shuttle buses. Regular daily trains run here from Faro and Lagos. Buses run regularly from Portimão and drop you at the foot of the town.

Caldas de Monchique

▶▶▶ Serra de Monchique   210B2

The Serra de Monchique rises in a wooded veil behind the Algarve coast, its airy peaks forming a natural barrier between the region's busy resorts and the undulating plains of the Alentejo to the north. The fertile soils of this volcanic massif are nurtured by the high annual rainfall that results from sea mists and onshore squalls being trapped on its slopes as they rise up from the coast. This makes the region both green and fresh, and a welcome summer retreat from the coast's more sultry environs. Walking here is a joy, while most meandering routes traveled by car offer scenic rewards, particularly in spring when mimosa, rhododendrons, and wild flowers gild the lower slopes.

SPA TOWN The enchanting little spa of **Caldas de Monchique**▶▶ lies just 11 miles (18km) north of Portimão, its huddle of houses beautifully cut into a ravine carved through the Serra de Monchique. Its setting, together with the thermal waters, attracts countless coachborne tourists in the summer, the one thing that spoils what is otherwise a delightful excursion from the coast. The only scenic eyesores are the spa and its adjacent bottling plant, the Oficina de Engarrafamento, although a short stroll into the woods quickly takes you away from both the crowds and views of the factory. Lauded since Roman times, the spa reached its apogee in the 19th century, when it became a favorite among the monied middle class.

MARKET TOWN Some 3.5 miles (6km) north of Caldas lies **Monchique**▶, a busy little market town scattered over the emerald slopes of the Pico da Fóia (2,958 feet, or 902m), the highest point in the Serra de Monchique. Newish houses spoil the look of the center, but views from much of the town are superb. The key building is the parish church, the **Igreja Matriz**, which is located at the top of a steep cobbled lane that leads up from the main square. It is known for its Manueline doorway—a caprice of knotted stone columns—and for the tiled facade of its interior chapels. Also worth a look is the evocative **Nossa Senhora do Destêrro**, a Franciscan monastery founded in 1632 and now a roofless and flower-tangled shell that overlooks the town.

A road leads on from Monchique to the summit Pico da Fóia (5 miles, or 8km), but while the views en route are distracting, the summit itself is spoilt by a forest of broadcasting antennas. It is far more pleasant to follow paths from Monchique to Picota (2,526 feet, or 770m), the Serra's second-highest point; the walk takes about 1½ hours.

MOORISH CAPITAL Although not at the heart of the Serra de Monchique, **Silves**▶▶▶ can easily be incorporated into a tour of the mountains or visited by bus or train from Lagos or Faro. Either way it is an essential port of call, and the one inland sight even the most dedicated beach-lounger should make an effort to see. Around 1,000 years ago the town (then known as Xelb) formed the 30,000-strong capital of al-Gharb, the Moors' "Western Land," its cultural and architectural splendor reputed to exceed that of Lisbon itself. Its grandeur, however, did not survive the rapacious attention of 12th-century crusaders, who were responsible for one of the most notorious sieges and massacres in Portuguese history here (see panel).

The former city's only surviving memorials are its tremendous walls and Moorish **Castelo** (tel: 282 445 624. *Open* summer, daily 8–8; winter, daily 9–5:30. *Admission free*), both of which create an unforgettable spectacle as you approach the town. The castle's interior is slightly disappointing (overplanted with gardens and lemon groves), but the views from its walls more than make amends. Below the fortress stands the **Sé** (tel: 282 442 472. *Open* daily 8:30–1, 2:30–7. Closed Sun afternoon), built on the site of a former mosque. Sadly, its 13th-century Gothic nave and aisles have been compromised by later rebuilding, the result—as ever—of the 1755 earthquake. The town was the seat of the Algarve's bishopric until 1580, when the see was moved to Faro. Exploring the rest of the town, which has retained its medieval flavor, is a pleasure, the key target being the **Museu Arqueológico** on Rua da Portas de Loulé (*Open* Tue–Sun 10–6. *Admission: inexpensive*). Its displays trace the town's history from paleolithic times to the present day, the Moorish period accounting for the lion's share of the exhibits.

SIEGE OF SILVES
The fall of the Moors' great capital was precipitated by Sancho I, who in 1189 arrived to besiege the city with a ragbag army of Portuguese soldiers and English "crusaders." The Moors held out for four months, sustained through the summer by teeming granaries and overflowing cisterns. When thirst got the better of them, however, they surrendered, reassured by Sancho's promises of safe passage and respect for their property. Sancho's booty-hungry troops then ransacked the city, torturing and killing 6,000 of its inhabitants. Two years later the city was recaptured by the Moors, but the damage had been done, and in 1249 it fell into Portuguese hands once and for all. By the 16th century, when its river silted up, the population was just 140.

Silves, former capital of the Moorish "al-Gharb"

Tavira harbor and one of its bridges

PRACTICALITIES
Tavira is linked to Faro by regular buses and trains (both 45 minutes). The bus terminal is on the riverfront in Rua dos Pelames, just a minute's walk from the Praça da República, the main square. The train station, which is less convenient, is located about 0.5 miles (1km) to the southwest of the town center. Tavira's tourist office is at Rua da Galeria 9 (tel: 281 322 511), off Praça da República and close to the Misericórdia. As ever, be sure to reserve rooms well in advance in the high season or arrive first thing in the morning to be sure of a vacancy.

▶▶▶ Tavira 211E1

Tavira is widely regarded as the most beautiful town in the Algarve, and it is certainly the most pleasant place to base yourself or break a journey during a tour of the eastern part of the region. The town lies close to some of the area's best beaches and straddles the River Gilão, a watery thoroughfare lined with a tempting succession of gardens, cafés, and old houses. A pair of bridges spans the river, one (with Roman foundations) linking the two halves of the old town, an ensemble of palaces, churches (over 30 in all), and terra cotta-tiled houses that straggles across the surrounding hillsides. One hill holds the ruins of the town's old castle, girdled and half-hidden by the gardens woven into its castellated walls.

HISTORY Legend claims Tavira was founded in 2000 BC by the Turduli, an Iberian tribe of mysterious origin. A more likely date for its foundation is 400 BC, when the Greeks probably created a small colony on the site. Fishing, and tuna fishing in particular, became the town's lifeblood, local fishermen harvesting their catches in July and August when the tuna returned from their spawning grounds in the Mediterranean. Tuna no longer make their runs off the Taviran shore, although the local taste for the fish prevails and a handful of boats still ventures on to the high seas in search of prey. The fishing industry was curtailed by the 1755 earthquake, which not only caused the harbor to silt up but also laid low most of the town's older buildings.

Today, tourism is bringing in increasing amounts of money to the town, along with a certain amount of unwelcome resort development. However, Tavira's council, to its credit, shows a much greater concern than usual for the integrity of its historic town center, and among other measures has produced a *"Guia do Construtor"* ("Builder's Guide") in an attempt to control and direct future growth.

THE TOWN Much of the pleasure in Tavira is to be gleaned from wandering through its old town, surveying the Moorish-era walls, its myriad architectural details, and the small nooks and crannies of its streets. The majority of Tavira's high number of churches are sadly kept under lock and key. One you may be lucky enough to peer inside, however, is the **Igreja de Misericórdia**▶▶, just above the Praça da República, the town's riverside main square. The carvings on its impressive, if somewhat worn, doorway (1541–1551), include a lute-playing couple and corner figures of saints Peter and Paul.

A few steps beyond, by the castle, stands the church of **Santa Maria do Castelo**▶, its Gothic doorway looking out over the Largo de Graça, an attractive and shady little square. Inside is the tomb of Dom Paio Peres Correia, one of the knights of the Order of Santiago, who played a key role in forcing the retreating Moors from Tavira (1224). The town's castle, the **Castelo dos Mouros**, is mostly ruined but offers lovely **views**▶ over the rooftops below. It was one of a string of ancient coastal defenses (an 18th-century map of the Algarve shows no fewer than 46 maritime forts).

BEACHES Tavira's beaches are as appealing as the town itself. In summer, the favorite stretch of sand is the huge beach on the **Ilha de Tavira**, a 7-mile (11km) offshore sand bar with a friendly atmosphere and, as yet, only a modicum of beachfront development. To reach it, drive, take a taxi, or catch a bus from Tavira's bus station to the quay at Quatro Águas (1.2 miles, or 2km) and pick up one of the regular ferries there to the island (May–mid-Oct). In July and August you may be able to find boats leaving direct from Tavira at the quay near the town's fish market; for further details inquire at the tourist office (see panel opposite). Some 2.5 miles (4km) west of Tavira lies Pedras d'el Rei, a holiday village, from where a causeway and small railroad shuttle you to a good beach at **Barril** on the Ilha de Tavira.

The Moorish look lingers even in the churches

UNTOUCHED
Roughly 5 miles (8km) east of Tavira, midway between the town and Monte Gordo, lies the tiny village of Cacela Velha, a pretty ensemble of fort, church, and houses perched on a modest cliff above the sea. Virtually untouched by development, Cacela Velha is one of the less spoiled spots on the Algarve coast. Facilities are few—just a restaurant, a couple of cafés, and a few over-subscribed rooms. The beach is modest but appealing, and in summer it should be possible, for a small fee, to find someone to take you across to the sand bar that protects the village from the open sea. Rather more developed but with another good beach is Cabanas, a short walk from the village of Conceicão, 3 miles (5km) east of Tavira.

Piles of salt, extracted from the seas around Tavira

A picture-perfect day in Vila Real de Santo António

CASTRO MARIM
If you have visited Tomar (see pages 180–183) and the idea of the Knights Templars kindles your curiosity, you might want to visit Castro Marim, 3 miles (5km) north of Vila Real. The vast castle, now just an impressive ruin (the 1755 earthquake the culprit again), was the first home of the Order of Christ, successors to the Knights Templars in Portugal. Despite its role as one of the most powerful castles on the southern Portugal coast, the order eventually gave it up in 1334 in favor of the Templars' old base in Tomar. A small museum fills in some of the historical background, and a tourist office is located just below the ruins (tel: 281 531 232).

▶ **Vila Real de Santo António**   *211E2*

Vila Real is the Algarve's last gasp before Spain, the houses of the Andalusian town of Ayamonte clearly visible on the other side of the Guadiana river. Spaniards flock here to buy local cotton goods and miscellaneous provisions (cheaper that at home), but nothing in the town stands out to delay the passing visitor for more than an hour or so. This said, there are a couple of developed resorts to the west, of which modern **Monte Gordo** (2 miles, or 3km) is the closest. The beach here is reasonable (although the resort is soulless), but perhaps not as good as the one at **Praia Verde**, which is the best local spot to spend an hour or so soaking up the sun.

Vila Real claims the distinction of not having been destroyed in the 1755 earthquake, but only because it had already been flattened by a tidal wave over a century before. The site remained virtually deserted until 1774, when the Marquês de Pombal took it upon himself to create a new model town here, using a grid plan similar to the one he had successfully adopted for the Baixa district of Lisbon. The town was finished in an astonishing five months, and might have been completed even faster had Pombal not insisted on ferrying most of the stone used in the project from Lisbon (equally suitable stone, it turned out, could have been quarried just a mile or so away).

Today, Vila Real prospers, after a fashion, on the back of its border traffic, which is whisked across the river on a new bridge (1992). The town is also one of the Algarve's largest fishing and commercial ports, not to mention one of its main canning centers. If you find yourself here, make for the central **Praça Marquês de Pombal**, ringed by orange and lemon trees and flanked by distinctive low white houses. Then either spend time in one of the square's cafés or head to the public gardens, where a greater choice of cafés awaits you, together with views across to Spain.

Travel Facts

Getting there

Entry formalities

Citizens of countries in the European Union (EU) with a valid passport or national identity card may enter Portugal and remain in the country for up to 90 days before seeking an official extension. Extensions can be obtained from the nearest district police headquarters or the **Foreigners' Registration Service**, Rua Conselheiro José Silvestre Ribeiro 4, Lisbon 1600 (tel: 21 715 5268). Holders of Australian and New Zealand passports may also stay in the country for 90 days; American and Canadian nationals may remain for 60 days before seeking an extension.

Arriving by air

Regular scheduled flights are available to Lisbon, Porto, and Faro: TAP

A street scene in the Alfama, Lisbon's medieval quarter

(Air Portugal), the Portuguese national airline, flies to all three destinations from London Heathrow. British Airways flies to Faro from London Gatwick, and to Lisbon and Porto from Heathrow. Charter flights are available during the peak summer season to all three destinations.
● **TAP** Gillingham House, 38–44 Gillingham Street, London SW1 VJW (tel: 020-7630 0900).
● **British Airways** 156 Regent Street, London W1R 6LB (tel: 0345-222111).

Arriving by train

A daily train service runs from London (Victoria) to Lisbon, Porto, and Coimbra via Paris, Irún, San Sebastian, Vilar Formoso, Guarda, and Pampilhosa. Change in Paris from the Gare du Nord to Austerlitz to connect with the Lisbon train. Changes may also be required at the Spanish border (Hendaye–Irún) and at Pampilhosa (for Porto). The travel time using **Eurostar Channel Tunnel** trains (U.K. tel: 01233-617575) is about 30 hours; using cheaper ferry connections it takes around 40 hours.

Twice-daily trains run from Madrid to Lisbon via Badajoz, Portalegre, Abrantes, and Entroncamento (7–10 hours); change at Entroncamento for Porto. From Seville, services operate via Badajoz or Ayamonte; from Coruña via Valença and Porto; from Salamanca via Vilar Formoso (change at Pampilhosa for Porto); and from Vigo in Galicia to Porto and Lisbon. A daily Motorail service also operates year round between Paris and Madrid. Contact **French Motorail** (U.K. tel: 08702-415415) or **Rail Europe** (U.K. tel: 08705-848848) for details.

Arriving by car

One of the quickest options is to take a **Brittany Ferries** boat (U.K. tel: 0870-536 0360) to Santander in Spain from Plymouth (mid-Mar–Nov). Travel time is 24 hours. From Santander it is around 500 miles (700km) to Porto, 600 miles (960km) to Lisbon, and 800 miles (1,300km) to Faro. Alternatively, take a **P&O European Ferries** service (U.K. tel: 0870-2424999) from Portsmouth to Bilbao in Spain. Or take the Brittany Ferries services from Poole,

Portsmouth, or Plymouth to
Cherbourg, St. Malo, Caen, or Roscoff.
   The least expensive option is to take
a ferry from Dover to one of the
French ports of Calais, Boulogne, or
Dieppe and drive through France (a
distance of some 1,300 miles, or
2,100km). Alternatively, take **Le
Shuttle** from Folkestone through the
Channel Tunnel to Calais. The quickest road route through France is via
Paris, Bordeaux, and the Autoroute
de l'Aquitaine; cross the Spanish border at Hendaye and, depending on
your destination, drive to Portugal
via Burgos and Salamanca.

Customs formalities
Customs procedures in Portugal are
generally simple and problem free.
Note that it is forbidden to bring fresh
meat into the country. There is no
limit to the amount of foreign
currency visitors may bring into
Portugal. Border crossings between
Spain and Portugal are open year
round 24 hours a day at:
Valença–Tui, Vila Verde da
Raia–Verin, Quintanilha–Trabazos,
Vilar Formoso–Fuentes de Oroño,
Marvão–Valencia de Alcántara,
Elvas–Badajoz, Vila Verde de

*The beach at Sagres: road and rail reach
Portugal's remotest corners*

Ficalho–Rosal de la Frontera, Vila Real
de Santo António–Ayamonte.
   "Duty free" has now been phased
out in Europe. In theory there is no
limit on goods imported from one EU
country to another, provided tax has
been paid and they are for personal
use. Authorities have issued "guide-
lines," however, as follows: 10 liters of
spirits, 20 liters of fortified wines,
90 liters of wine, 110 liters of beer, 800
cigarettes, 400 cigarillos, 200 cigars,
1kg pipe tobacco, no limit on perfume.
Duty-free limits for visitors traveling
to/from a non-EU country are:
● 200 cigarettes or 100 cigarillos or 50
   cigars or 250g of tobacco.
● 1 liter of spirits or 2 liters of
   fortified wine or sparkling wine.
● 2 liters of still table wine.
● 60ml of perfume and 250ml of toilet
   water.
● Gifts, souvenirs, and other goods
   up to a value of $220.

Travel insurance
It is highly recommended that
you take out comprehensive travel
insurance, including medical cover.

Essential facts

Climate

Portugal has a reasonably benign climate year round, with warm weather throughout the country between about April and October. Generally, the north is cooler and damper—the Minho in particular can be very wet between October and May—but even here in winter you can expect up to 3½ hours of sunshine daily. Winters in the mountains of the Trás-os-Montes, however, can be bitterly cold. Winter in the Algarve is pleasantly mild (it is possible to swim in the sea from March to November) but, like much of the interior, it is extremely hot and arid here in summer. The northeast can also be hot and dry, in contrast to the cooler

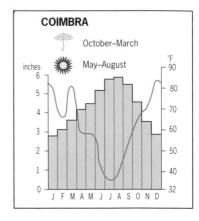

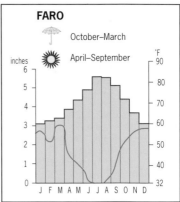

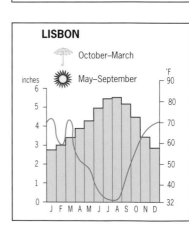

Portugal's fine summers guarantee warm water and sunny skies

coastal and mountain regions of the northwest.

When to go
Spring and fall are the best times to visit Portugal. Spring (late April–early June) would be the first choice if you want to enjoy wild flowers, off-season hotel rates, and a tinge of spring green across the countryside. Fall is especially attractive in the north and the Douro Valley, where the wine harvests and autumnal colors provide appealing spectacles. Reserve accommodations in advance for beach vacations in summer, and be prepared to compete with the crowds. Winter and early spring breaks can also be delightful in the Algarve, particularly in January and February when the almond trees are in blossom. Across the country Easter offers the chance to savor numerous Holy Week festivals.

National holidays
Most things close during national holidays and public transportation services are reduced at this time. The same thing happens during the local festivals held in many towns and cities, notably in Lisbon (June 13) and Porto (June 24). National holidays are as follows:
- **New Year's Day** January 1
- **Carnaval** February
- **Shrove Tuesday**
- **Good Friday**
- **Liberation Day** April 25
- **May Day** May 1
- **Corpus Christi** Late May or early June
- **Camões Day** June 10
- **Assumption** August 15
- **Republic Day** October 5
- **All Saints' Day** November 1
- **Independence Day** December 1
- **Immaculate Conception** December 8
- **Christmas Day** December 25

Time differences
Portugal is five hours ahead of U.S. Eastern Standard Time and eight hours ahead of Pacific Time. It has the same time as Britain, but is one hour behind European time. Clocks go forward one hour on the last Sunday in March and back one hour on the last Sunday in October.

Money matters
The basic unit of currency is the escudo ($), made up of 100 centavos; 1,000 escudos are known as a conto. When writing, place the $ sign between the escudo to the left and the centavos to the right.

Banknotes are issued in denominations of 500$00, 1,000$00, 2,000$00, 5,000$00, and 10,000$00, and coins are issued in denominations of 5$00, 10$00, 20$00, 50$00, 100$00, and 200$00. As an approximate guide, there are usually around 300$00 to £1 sterling, or about 195$00 to US$1. Note that it is normal for stores to round prices up to the nearest 5$00 or 10$00. Try not to present large-denomination notes in rural areas, where stores often have difficulties with change.

Currency During the transitional period for full change over to the euro (December 2001), the escudo will continue to be used as a subunit of the euro and a dual pricing system will operate. In January 2002, euro banknotes and coins will be introduced. The escudo will cease to be legal tender in June 2002.

Foreign exchange Most large towns have foreign-exchange bureaus (*cambios*) or a bank offering exchange facilities. Opening hours are Mon–Fri 8:30–3. Note that commission rates on traveler's checks are especially high in Portugal (anything up to 2,000$00 per transaction); cheaper rates can often be obtained at savings banks or savings and loans (*caixas*).

ATMs All towns and most villages have automatic teller machines (ATMs), called Multibancos, useful for credit card cash advances, while a few places in Lisbon and the Algarve have introduced machines for automatic exchange of foreign currencies.

Credit cards Credit cards are accepted in top hotels and restaurants (Visa, MasterCard, American Express, and Diners Club), and increasingly in establishments in more remote areas. Have some cash just in case.

237

Accommodations

Portugal has many hotels like the Convento São Paolo near Redondo

Portuguese accommodations in most price ranges are divided into a confusing range of categories, each theoretically based on the standards and facilities they provide. In practice, the various denominations in the lower and middle price brackets can bear little relation to what you can expect to find, so treat the various star ratings with a degree of caution. This said, room rates in most hotels are much lower—with the exception of Lisbon and the Algarve—than their equivalent in other Western European countries. And while the least expensive rooms can still be dingy, the standard of state-owned *pousadas* and the ever more popular rural accommodation options can be exceptional.

Private rooms

Rooms in private houses are known as *quartos* or *dormidas*, and offer the least expensive lodgings after hostels. They are often advertised by signs or touted at train and bus stations, but before accepting a room from touts, check its location. Be prepared to bargain over the price, especially if you are staying for a few days.

Pensions

A pension (*pensão*) is the next step up from a private room. These are graded from one to three stars, although often with little discernible difference in the facilities they offer. Less expensive pensions or boarding houses may also be known as *hospedarias* or *casas de hóspedes*. Many *pensões* serve meals, often as part of what can be reasonably priced deals when combined with meals; those that do not serve meals are usually known as *residenciais*.

Hotels

Hotels are graded from one to five stars, a one star hotel usually costing about the same as a three star pension. Note that hotel status does not necessarily mean nicer rooms: better two and three star pensions or *residenciais* may be more pleasant than one or two star hotels. Hotels in the four and five star range are sometimes known as *estalagems* or *albergarias*.

Pousadas

Portugal's 40 or so government-run *pousadas* offer some of the most attractive accommodations in the country, often in converted historic properties or beautifully located rural settings. Most are usually well signposted. *Pousadas* are highly popular, so it is essential to reserve rooms well in advance (either directly or through ENATUR, see below). They are graded into four categories: B, C, C*, and CH. Some are still reasonably priced, but rates have risen sharply recently. All *pousadas* serve food, and their restaurants are open to nonresidents.

Many of the country's *pousadas* are listed in the Hotels and Restaurants section of this guide (see pages 253–260), but a full list of properties can be obtained from Portuguese national tourist offices or from **ENATUR**, Avenida Santa Joana Princesa 10, 1700, Lisbon (tel: 21 844 2001; fax: 21 844 2087).

Solares de Portugal

The increasingly popular Solares de Portugal, previously known as Turismo de Habitação, is a scheme whereby the owners of country (more rarely urban) homes open their doors to paying guests. All properties have been checked by government tourist offices and are graded from A (most expensive) to C (least expensive). Prices are often reasonable.
Properties within the scheme are entitled to display a "green tree" symbol. Properties are further divided into

casas antigas (buildings with historical associations), *casas rusticas* (small rustic country houses), and *quintas e herdades* (farms and large estates). They vary from the baronial to the relatively basic, but standards should approach those of *pousadas* and four and five star hotels. Evening meals are usually provided, and you may often find yourself dining with the owner; where dinner is not available a generous breakfast is usually served.

You should reserve rooms well in advance, either directly or through one of the growing number of marketing organizations (see below). Note that some houses may require a minimum stay of three nights, especially in the high season.
The best-known private marketing organization for Solares de Portugal properties is **TURIHAB**, Praça da República, 4990 Ponte de Lima (tel: 258 741 672; fax 258 741 444). Other well-known agencies include **PRIVETUR** (tel/fax: 258 741 493) and **ANTER** (tel/fax: 266 742 535).

The Flor da Rosa pousada, near Portalegre, was converted from a monastery (see page 257)

Getting around

Portugal is a small country, which makes the business of getting around relatively easy. But, the roads can be poor—and the driving atrocious. Train services are generally slow (but inexpensive) and often require several changes and circuitous routes to reach more rural outposts. Bus services are good, usually quicker and frequently less expensive than trains, often penetrating to the most remote corners of the country.

By air
Train and bus services should take care of most of your public transport needs, but if you have to get anywhere in a hurry then use TAP, the national airline, which runs regular internal flights between the major cities of Lisbon, Porto, and Faro (tel: 21 841 6990). The country's second airline, Portugalia, runs the same routes as TAP (tel: 21 842 559).

By train
Services Portugal's train services are operated by the state-run CP, or **Caminhos de Ferro Portugueses** (tel: 21 888 4025). Services and lines were severely cut in 1990, a year that saw the closure of many scenic

narrow-gauge lines in the north. Timetables are posted on station walls, and for individual routes they should be available from ticket offices. The complete CP timetable, the *Guia Horário Oficial*, can be obtained for a small fee from main train stations.

Trains CP operates four categories of train: *Regionais*, which stop at most stations; *Inter-Regionais* (IRs), which stop only at major stations; *Inter-Cidades* (ICs), or *directos*, which stop at major towns and cities; and *Rápidos*, or *Serviço-Alfas* ("Alfas" for short), which ply the high-speed route between Lisbon, Coimbra, and Porto. CP trains have two classes, first (*primeira classe*) and second (*segunda classe*). Some *Rápidos* trains carry only first-class cars.

Tickets Arrive early at stations to allow for the long lines that develop at station ticket counters. Also allow time to line up for the seat reservations that may be necessary on some faster trains (see below). A ticket (*bilhete*) bought on the train incurs a hefty surcharge unless you board at

Boats are one way of exploring the country's attractive coastline

an unmanned country station. Extra supplements on top of the normal ticket are payable on *Inter-Cidade* and *Rápidos* trains. Seat reservations are also required for these services, adding around 60 percent to the price of a normal ticket. Reservations and supplements should be bought at the same time as your ticket.

Reductions Children under four travel free if they do not occupy a seat. Children under 12 pay half-price. Senior citizens (over 60) receive a 30 percent reduction on the production of a passport or other valid ID providing proof of age. Under 26s get a reduction on production of an "Under 26 Youth card." Train travel is less expensive on main routes on so-called "Blue Days," namely those that avoid the peak periods of Friday afternoon, Sunday afternoon, Monday morning, national holidays, and the days preceding national holidays.

CP sells its own tourist rail pass, or *Bilhete Turístico*, valid for first-class travel for 7, 14, or 21 days on all trains except the Lisbon–Madrid service. It also offers a *Cartão de Família* ("Family Card"), which allows discounted travel at off-peak periods to a married couple and at least one child under 18.

By bus
Services Buses follow many train routes more or less exactly, but are usually quicker and often less expensive than trains. Some local buses have vanished in the wake of privatization, but services still reach most towns and villages. Until recently, most Portuguese bus services were operated by the state-owned Rodoviária Nacional (RN). This has now been privatized, and operates in competition with a growing number of other private companies. With several companies operating over the same route but from different terminals, there may well be confusion and a clash of interests when it comes to proffering information on rival routes and timetabling.

Note that services are often cut back at weekends, especially on Sundays. Many services leave early

Many of Lisbon's historic streetcars are over 50 years old

in the morning to coincide with commuting patterns, while others are tailored to meet the needs of schoolchildren (some services disappear altogether during school vacations). Other buses operate only on local market days. The national network of express buses, or Rede Expressos, survived privatization, and provides fast services between major towns and cities.

While timetables for express services are relatively easy to come by, other timetable information can be elusive; the best source of information is often the local tourist office.

Tickets On rural services tickets can often be bought on the bus. Tickets and reservations for express services must be bought in advance from bus stations—make sure you are standing in the right line for your chosen destination.

Town centers are increasingly being closed to traffic

By car

Documents Drivers from EU countries need a full, valid national driving license, together with the car's registration documents (logbook) and an international insurance certificate ("green card")—third-party insurance is compulsory in Portugal. You should also have a nationality plate of the approved size. License and documents should be carried at all times. If you are driving a car unaccompanied by the owner then you should also have written permission from the owner allowing you to drive in Portugal. A foreign-registered car may remain in Portugal for six months, but note the three-month stopover restrictions that apply to EU nationals (see page 234).

Roads and drivers Improvements to Portugal's notoriously poor roads are continuing apace, but much work remains to be done on many of the country's narrow and cratered secondary roads. Many of the roads in mountainous regions, especially in the north, are full of twisting hairpin bends. Roads in and immediately around towns and cities can be extremely congested.

New expressways are gradually being built across Portugal, spreading from a central spine that connects Setúbal, Lisbon, Coimbra, Porto, and Braga. There have been many recent additions to the network, including the IP1 in the south, linking the eastern Algarve to the Spanish border, and spurs from Porto and Aveiro to Bragança and Vilar Formoso. Tolls are payable on expressways, the relatively high cost restricting much local traffic to minor roads and leaving expressways reasonably empty. As an approximate guide, you will pay around 3,000$00 in tolls to travel between Lisbon and Porto. Tolls are also payable on some bridges.

Portugal has one of the worst accident records in the EU, and Portuguese drivers are widely considered some of the worst in Western Europe. Notoriously dangerous stretches of road include the Lisbon–Porto motorway, the Lisbon–Algarve IP1, and the Lisbon–Cascais Marginal coastal road (IP5). However, considerable care is required at all times, for drink-driving seems to carry little stigma, the rules of the road are widely flouted, and common courtesy and regard for other drivers seem to cut little ice. Note also that the huge rise in the number of cars on Portuguese roads in recent years has resulted in a lack of parking in many large towns and cities: a hotel with its own parking lot can be a considerable boon.

Rules of the road Conventions and rules of the road are the same as in other EU countries, and Portugal uses the international road sign system. Note the following:
● Drive on the right and pass on the left. Stationary streetcars in cities may be overtaken on the right where it is safe to do so.
● At junctions give way to traffic from the right unless there is a sign to the contrary.
● The use of seatbelts is compulsory everywhere.

242

● Speed limits are 31mph (50kph) in built-up areas; 62mph (100kph) on two-lane and four-lane roads; and 75mph (120kph) on expressways.

Breakdowns and accidents If you break down you may seek assistance from the Portuguese Automobile Club, the **Automóvel Clube de Portugal** (**ACP**), which has reciprocal arrangements with foreign automobile clubs such as the American Automobile Association (AAA). The club's head office is at Rua Rosa Araújo 24, Lisbon (tel: 21 318 0100). For help in the north of the country (beyond Coimbra), call the ACP office in Porto (tel: 22 834 0001); in the south, call the Lisbon center (tel: 21 942 9103).

After an accident seek out the nearest SOS roadside telephone (painted orange) and press the button until you receive a reply.

Fuel *Gasolina* (gasoline) is fairly expensive—currently around 23¢ per gallon (170$00 per liter). *Super* is 97–96 octanes. Diesel, unleaded, and lower-octane fuels are widely available. Most rental cars run on unleaded petrol (*gasolina sem chumbo*). Credit cards are accepted in theory in most garages.

Car rental Renting a car in Portugal is less expensive than in most Western European countries, except in the Algarve in high season. However, it may still be cheaper to organize rental before you set off, possibly as part of a fly-drive package. All the big international agencies have offices in major towns and cities, and at the airports in Lisbon, Porto, and Faro. Prices offered by small local companies can be more reasonable, but it pays to read the small print carefully, particularly the sections dealing with extra insurance and damage waivers, the latter well worth paying. It is also worth checking the age, safety, and service records of cars rented from small agencies.

The streets of Monsaraz, still unspoilt by cars

Communications

Newspapers and magazines
Although they are among the most half-hearted readers of newspapers in Europe, the Portuguese have an inordinately large number of titles from which to choose—around ten in Lisbon alone.

Sports newspapers, however, rather than serious dailies, are the most widely read publications, together with frothy women's magazines and salacious tabloids. The leading serious papers are Lisbon's *Diário de Notícias* and the Porto-based *Jornal de Notícias*. Several newspapers are state-owned but generally maintain a reasonably independent editorial line. The main weekly news magazine is the independent *Expresso*. Most towns and regions boast a wide variety of local and provincial papers.

Foreign newspapers can be bought in Lisbon, Porto, and the main tourist areas, usually on the day following publication, although you should find copies of the *International Herald*

The Portuguese read fewer newspapers than most Europeans

Tribune and European editions of the London *Guardian* and *Financial Times* on the day of issue.

Television and radio
Portugal's two state-owned channels have been joined by a number of private and satellite channels, although programs are generally of depressing predictability—game shows, endless sports programs, and a plethora of Brazilian *telenovelas*, or soap operas, that keep millions of Portuguese glued to their sets. Most programs are subtitled rather than dubbed, meaning that British and American imports often show up in the original.

Until 1988 all radio stations were run by the state with the exception of one, Radio Renascença, a station operated by the Roman Catholic Church. Today, the airwaves have been deregulated, ushering in dozens of new and often advertisement-saturated stations.

Postal services

Portugal's post offices are known as *correios*; collection boxes are red. In larger towns they are usually open Mon–Fri 8 or 9–6, although smaller offices may open 8 or 9–12:30 and 2:30–6. City and main post offices sometimes also open on Saturday mornings. The main Lisbon branches have even longer opening hours, typically weekdays 8 AM–10 PM, Sat–Sun 9–6.

Stamps (*selos*) can be bought from post offices or from shops displaying the sign "*CTT Selos*" or "*Correio de Portugal Selos*." The sign has a picture of a red horse on a white circle against a green background. Check you are in the right line when buying stamps. Current prices for postcards and letters are 100$00 to Europe, 140$00 to other foreign destinations. Air mail is *por avião*. The postal service is generally fairly efficient, mail in Europe taking a week or less to arrive, that to North America a week to ten days.

Letters sent poste restante (to await collection) should be marked "*Posta Restanta*" and "*Lista do Correios*" and sent to the main post office of the designated town. Print names clearly. When collecting mail (there is a small fee), head for the desk marked "*Encomendas*" and take a passport as proof of identity. If mail is not where it should be, ask the clerk to check under surname, first name, and any initials.

Telephones

Portugal's telephone system once had a deserved reputation for being antiquated and inefficient. However, as in most areas of Portuguese life, matters are improving, with many new private companies setting up.

Pay phones are found in bars, cafés, tourist offices, and newsagents, usually marked by a sign showing a red horse, white circle, and green background with the words "*Correio de Portugal—Telefone*." They accept 20$00, 50$00, and 100$00 coins, or will often be charged on a meter. Take note of the *preço por periodo* (price per unit used) as this can vary enormously (20$00 to 70$00). The country has many public phone booths, now accepting either coins or phonecards/credit cards. Phone cards can be bought from post offices or often from newsagents in 650$00, 1300$00, or 1900$00 denominations. Main post offices in most towns have phone booths which are ideal for making longer or international calls: join the right line, tell the clerk where you want to call, and then pay him or her for the call afterwards.

For international calls try to find a *credifone* or use a post-office booth. Note that there are no cheap periods for international calls from public phones. For English-speaking international directory inquiries, prices, and time zone information dial 099, or 098 for the international operator. Collect calls abroad can be made by calling the international operator.

Portugal's telephone booths are based on an old British design

Emergencies

Crime
Portugal is still remarkably crime-free, but petty misdemeanours and car thefts may occur in Lisbon and the resorts of the Algarve. Common sense will guard against most eventualities: avoid parks, unlit backstreets, and the areas around the station in towns and cities; never leave any valuables or luggage of any kind in cars; and do not carry valuables or wear expensive-looking jewelry on the street. Also beware pickpockets in crowds, markets, and on public transportation. If threatened, do not try to fight back.

Police
To contact the police in an emergency, dial 112. If you are the victim of a crime visit the nearest police station, where a report will be made (essential for any subsequent insurance claims). Thefts must generally be reported within 24 hours to satisfy insurance claims.

Portugal has two main police forces: the PSP (Polícia de Segurança Pública) deal with everyday police matters, including crimes involving tourists; the GNR (Guarda Nacional Republicana) tend to run highway patrols and oversee the policing of more rural areas.

Embassies and consulates
● **Republic of Ireland Consulate** 1 Rua da Imprensa à Estrela, Lisbon (tel: 21 392 9440).
● **U.K. Embassy** Rua de São Bernardo 33, 1200 Lisbon (tel: 21 392 4000).
● **U.S. Embassy** Avenida das Forças Armadas, Lisbon (tel: 21 727 3300).

Health care
Private medical insurance is essential.

The **International Association for Medical Assistance to Travelers: in the U.S.:** 417 Center Street, Lewiston, NY 14092 (tel: 716/754–4883); **in Canada:** 40 Regal Road, Guelph, Ontario N1K 1B5 (tel: 519/836–0102); **in Europe:** 57 Voirets, 1212 Grand-Lancy, Geneva, Switzerland, offers a free worldwide list of approved physicians and clinics whose training meets American standards.

An historic pharmacy in Coimbra

Doctors

For minor ailments you should first visit a pharmacy (see below), where trained staff may well be able to advise on a suitable course of treatment. If you need a doctor or dentist, inquire at your hotel, the local tourist office, or the nearest police station. Failing that, visit the nearest hospital. Portuguese doctors usually speak some English, many of them having been trained abroad. In the last resort contact a consulate or embassy.

Pharmacies

Most towns and villages have a pharmacy (*farmácia*). In larger towns you should be able to find one where English is spoken. Opening times are generally Mon–Fri 9–1, 3–7, Sat 9–1. Many drugs on sale over the counter are available only on prescription elsewhere. Pharmacists can help distinguish between unfamiliar brand names, but bring a prescription with you if you need to renew your own medication. This will avoid problems at customs and also help the pharmacist.

Health and safety

Upset stomachs and the usual travel ailments are likely to be your biggest health problems in Portugal. Water is safe to drink everywhere, with the possible exception of a few spots in the Algarve in high summer. Bottled water is widely available. Mosquitoes can be a curse for much of the summer, but sprays, coils, and plug-in deterrents can easily be purchased in stores and supermarkets. Also beware of taking too much sun. When swimming, the EU "Blue Flag" indicates water of acceptable quality. Watch out for strong undertows off Atlantic beaches: red and yellow flags indicate that swimming is dangerous. Normal precautions against HIV should also be taken: condoms in Portuguese are *preservativos*, and are readily available in all but the most rural areas.

Vaccinations

Vaccinations are not required for visitors to Portugal from the United States, Canada, the U.K., Ireland, and other countries in the EU. However, vaccinations may be required, together with an international certificate of vaccination, if you are arriving in the country from somewhere with a known problem or epidemic; if in doubt, check with your doctor or the Portuguese embassy before setting out. Polio and tetanus boosters are a good idea, and you may want to consider typhoid and hepatitis jabs (there have been a handful of outbreaks of the latter around Porto).

Emergency telephone numbers
● **Police, fire and ambulance** 112.

Every which way but lost: Portugal's well-signposted streets should get you to your destination

247

Other information

Addresses

Addresses in Portugal consist of a street name followed by a street number. Occasionally the street number is followed by another number indicating a floor or story within the building: thus "Rua Francisco a Maurício 7-2°" refers to an address on the second floor of No. 7. If the floor number is followed by "E." or "esq.," short for *esquerda*, it means you turn left for your destination; if it is followed by "D." or "dir.," short for *direita*, it means you turn right. Numbers before the main town or village—such as 1500 Lisbon—indicate a postal district.

Electricity

Electric current is 220 volts AC, with plugs of the two-pin Continental type, which means that plug adaptors are required for U.S. appliances.

Etiquette

Portugal is a country where old-world courtesies are still proffered and expected. The Portuguese also set great store by the idea of respect—bear this in mind when dealing with the police, officialdom, or other people in authority.

Avoid shorts, skimpy tops, and uncovered shoulders in churches, and do not enter while a service is in progress.

Further reading
History and background

● David Birmingham, *A Concise History of Portugal* (Cambridge

Stores often close for lunch, but bars and cafés stay open all day

University Press). A brief and lucid account of Portuguese history up to 1991.
● A. H. de Oliveira, *History of Portugal* (Columbia University Press). A two-volume study for more detail on Portugal's general history.
● Marion Kaplan, *The Portuguese: The Lands and its People* (Penguin). The best single-volume introduction in English to contemporary Portugal.

Travel and guides
● William Beckford, *Recollections of an Excursion…Travels in Spain and Portugal* (Centaur Press). Lively and eccentric account of travels in Portugal at the end of the 18th century.
● Bethan Davies and Ben Cole, *Walking in Portugal* (Footprint Guides). The best (the only) guide in English to hiking in Portugal's premier natural and national parks.
● Rose Macaulay, *They Went to Portugal* (Penguin). A classic account of visitors to Portugal over the centuries.
● Laurence Rose, *Where to Watch Birds in Spain and Portugal* (Hamlyn). Practical and informative handbook for ornithologists.

Literature
● Luís Vaz de Camões, *The Lusiads* (Penguin). A prose translation of Portugal's best-known epic poem.
● Fernando Pessoa, *A Centenary Pessoa* (Carcanet). An anthology of poetry, prose, and letters by Portugal's most famous poet; see also *Selected Poems* (Penguin).
● José Saramango, *The Year of the Death of Ricardo Reis* (Harvill). Award-winning novel by Portugal's preeminent writer: see also *Baltasar and Blimunda* (Picador), *Manual of Painting and Calligraphy* (Carcanet), and *The Stone Raft* and *The Gospel According to Jesus Christ* (both Harvill).

Food and wine
● Jan Read, *The Wines of Portugal* (Faber). A full and enlightening account of Portugal's wines and wine regions, together with interesting snippets of historical and social interest.

Rural crafts and handicrafts make good souvenirs

● Edite Vieira, *The Taste of Portugal* (Grub Street). An excellent amalgam of recipes, history, and anecdote.

249

Opening times
● **Stores** Mon–Fri from about 9, 9:30 or 10–12:30 or 1, then from about 2:30 or 3–7 or 8. Stores outside the larger towns and cities and traditional commerce within cities tend to close at lunchtime (1 PM) on Saturday and not reopen in the afternoon. Newer shopping malls mostly remain open seven days a week, often until as late as midnight.
● **Banks** Mon–Fri 8:30–3, although some branches in Lisbon and tourist resorts may open in the evening to offer exchange facilities.
● **Post offices** Mon–Fri 8:30–6, and in larger branches occasionally Sat 9–noon. The large Lisbon branches have extended hours.
● **Restaurants** Restaurants usually serve lunch noon–3 and dinner from about 7:30. Outside cities and tourist areas most restaurants take last orders at about 10 PM.
● **Museums and galleries** Most open 10–12:30 and 2–6, although the larger and more important ones may remain open through lunch. Most public museums and monuments are closed on Mondays.
● **Churches** Many churches are open 7–noon and 4–7; others open only for services early in the morning and again in the evening.

CONVERSION CHARTS

FROM	TO	MULTIPLY BY
Inches	Centimeters	2.54
Centimeters	Inches	0.3937
Feet	Meters	0.3048
Meters	Feet	3.2810
Yards	Meters	0.9144
Meters	Yards	1.0940
Miles	Kilometers	1.6090
Kilometers	Miles	0.6214
Acres	Hectares	0.4047
Hectares	Acres	2.4710
U.S. gallons	Liters	3.7853
Litres	U.S. gallons	0.2642
Ounces	Grams	28.35
Grams	Ounces	0.0353
Pounds	Grams	453.6
Grams	Pounds	0.0022
Pounds	Kilograms	0.4536
Kilograms	Pounds	2.205
Tons	Tonnes	1.0160
Tonnes	Tons	0.9842

MEN'S SUITS

U.S.	36	38	40	42	44	46	48
U.K.	36	38	40	42	44	46	48
Rest of Europe	46	48	50	52	54	56	58

DRESS SIZES

U.S.	6	8	10	12	14	16
U.K.	8	10	12	14	16	18
France	36	38	40	42	44	46
Italy	38	40	42	44	46	48
Rest of Europe	34	36	38	40	42	44

MEN'S SHIRTS

U.S.	14	14.5	15	15.5	16	16.5	17
U.K.	14	14.5	15	15.5	16	16.5	17
Rest of Europe	36	37	38	39/40	41	42	43

MEN'S SHOES

U.S.	8	8.5	9.5	10.5	11.5	12
U.K.	7	7.5	8.5	9.5	10.5	11
Rest of Europe	41	42	43	44	45	46

WOMEN'S SHOES

U.S.	6	6.5	7	7.5	8	8.5
U.K.	4.5	5	5.5	6	6.5	7
Rest of Europe	38	38	39	39	40	41

A vacation obligation—the postcard home

Tipping

A 10 percent service charge is usually added to the bill in more upscale restaurants. Where it is not, it is common practice to leave a similar amount as a tip, except in smaller bars and cafés where a quantity of small change should suffice. Around 10 percent is also usual for taxi drivers. Hotels often add a service charge, but cleaners and porters in more upscale places expect something in addition.

Toilet facilities

In more rural areas public toilets (*serviços públicos*)—of which there are few—and those in bars, cafés, and inexpensive restaurants may still be of the "sit and squat" variety. Men's toilets are labeled *"homens"* and women's *"senhoras."* No one should mind if you ask to use café or hotel facilities without being a customer. Otherwise, bus and train stations are the best places to seek out public toilets. To ask "where is the toilet?," use the phrase *"onde ficam os lavabos?"* (*quarto de banho* means "bathroom").

Tourist offices

Before visiting Portugal it is worth contacting the **Portuguese Trade & Tourism Office**, 1900 L Street N.W., Suite 210, Washington, DC 20006 (tel:

202/331–8222; fax: 202/331–8236; www.portugal.org).

In Portugal itself, most towns and many villages have a local tourist office, known as a Posto, Comissão de Turismo, or, more usually, a Turismo; most are unfailingly helpful and welcoming. They supply maps and pamphlets, and all offer some help in finding accommodations: some will make reservations for you, others may supply only lists of rooms and hotels. Most have someone who speaks a little English.

Opening times for tourist offices are supposed to be Mon–Sat 9–6, but in practice you will find times vary from town to town and from season to season. Generally you should assume most offices will open around 10 AM and that many will close for lunch from around 12:30 to 2 or 3; many remain closed on Saturday afternoon. The exceptions, as ever, are offices in Lisbon, the Algarve, and other popular tourist areas.

Travelers with disabilities
Portugal is doing its best to assist travelers with disabilities, but new and special facilities are proving slow to materialize. Individual Portuguese, however, are usually unfailingly helpful.

The Portuguese Railway (CP) has carriages with toilets adapted for wheelchair use and it gives priority to wheelchair users in the reservation of carriages. The best you can expect in some towns and cities are reserved parking spaces (where the "orange badge" sign is recognized), together with specially adapted toilets and wheelchair facilities at airports and major train stations.

Wheelchair hire can be found in most towns at Centros de Enfermagem (Nursing Centers).

Portuguese national tourist offices abroad (see above) provide lists of wheelchair-accessible hotels and campsites. Failing this, try local tourist offices, which should be able to direct you to suitable hotels and restaurants.

Before you travel, contact the **Society for the Advancement of Travel for the Handicapped (SATH)**, 347 Fifth Avenue, Suite 610, New York, NY 10016 (tel: 212/447–7284; fax: 212/725–8253). They can provide information on tour operators and lists of tour operators specializing in travel for the disabled.

Women travelers
Machismo is not as deeply entrenched in Portugal as it is in some countries, but, that said, women can still expect hisses and clucks from men or groups of men in larger towns and cities.

Women should take the usual commonsense precautions in cities and popular tourist areas, namely staying away from backstreets and the areas around bus and train stations (traditional red-light districts). Hitchhiking alone should be avoided completely. Taxis and public transport are generally safe, but beware night and early morning trains: if in doubt, try to travel in a compartment with other women.

Lisbon's Alfama district during the festival of the Santos Populares

251

Language

Portuguese is a Romance language, so a knowledge of French, Spanish, or Italian helps in deciphering the written word. Understanding the spoken word, however, let alone speaking Portuguese yourself, are different things altogether—it is a fiendishly difficult language to deal with, at least at the outset. This said, most Portuguese welcome any attempt on the part of foreigners to wrestle with their vocabulary. English is now the second language and is taught in many Portuguese schools.

Basic rules for pronunciation include the following: **c** is soft before "e"and "i," but hard before "a," "o," and "u"; **ç** is pronounced as an "s," as in *almoço* (lunch); **ch** is soft—thus chá (tea) sounds like "sha"; **e** at the end of a word is silent unless it has an accent, so that *doze* (twelve) is pronounced "doz"; **j** is pronounced like the "s" in pleasure or leisure—*igreja*

(church); **g** is also pronounced as the "s" of pleasure before "e" and "i," but hard, as with "c," before "a," "o," or "u"; **q** or "qu" is pronounced as a "k"; **s** at the end of word or before a consonant is pronounced "sh," as in *inglês* (English), otherwise the "s" is pronounced as in English; **x** is also pronounced "sh"; and **ão**, a common conjunction, sounds like a nasal "ow," as in the English "now."

Basic vocabulary

yes/no sim/não
please por favor
thank you obrigado (spoken by a man), obrigada (spoken by a woman)
hello olá
goodbye adeus
good morning bom dia
good afternoon boa tarde
good night boa noite
excuse me com licença
I'm sorry desculpe
how? como?
where? onde?
here/there aqui/ali
right/left direita/esquerda
near/far perto/longe
more/less mais/menos
big/little grande/pequeno
cheap/expensive barato/caro
today hoje
tomorrow amanhã
yesterday ontem
now/later agora/mais tarde
open/closed aberto/fechado
men/women homens/senhoras

I don't understand não compreendo
at what time...? a que horas...?
please help me ajude-me por favor

do you speak English? fala Inglês?
is there...?/there is há...?
do you have...? tem...?
I would like... queria...
can I have...? pode dar-me?
I'd like a room queria um quarto
with bathroom com banho
for one night para uma noite
for one week para uma semana
can I see it? posso ver?
how much is it? quanto custa?
is there a cheaper room? há um quarto mais barato?

1 um	**16** dezasseis
2 dois	**17** dezassete
3 três	**18** dezoito
4 quatro	**19** dezanove
5 cinco	**20** vinte
6 seis	**21** vinte e um
7 sete	**30** trinta
8 oito	**40** quarenta
9 nove	**50** cinquenta
10 dez	**60** sessenta
11 onze	**70** setenta
12 doze	**80** oitenta
13 treze	**90** noventa
14 catorze	**100** cem
15 quinze	**1,000** mil

Accommodations and Restaurants

ACCOMMODATIONS

Prices for a double room in the following hotels have been given in three categories:

- **budget** ($) = 6,000$00 and under
- **moderate** ($$) = 6,000$00–14,000$00
- **expensive** ($$$) = over 14,000$00

LISBON

As Janelas Verdes ($$$)
Rua das Janelas Verdes 47 tel: 21 396 8143
www.heritage.pt
Almost as charming, and very similar in style, to the nearby York House (see below).

Avenida Palace ($$$)
Rua 1 de Dezembro 123 tel: 21 346 0151
www.maisturismo.pt
The place to come if you want both old-world elegance and a city center location (although the central position means potential noise and bustle).

Britania ($$)
Rua Rodrigues Sampaio 17 tel: 21 315 5016
www.heritage.pt
A traditional hotel with a loyal clientele.

Dom Carlos ($$)
Avenida Duque de Loulé 121 tel: 21 351 2590
e-mail: hdcarlos@mail.telepac.pt
Efficiently run, conservative hotel that offers more competitive rates than others in the area.

Hotel Lisboa Plaza ($$$)
Travessa do Salitre 7, Avenida da Liberdade
tel: 21 321 8218 e-mail: hoteisheritage@.pt
A charming place built in 1953 but very elegantly updated in 1988. Crisp, large, modern-style rooms.

Hotel Mundial ($$$)
Rua Dom Duarte 4 tel: 21 884 2000
www.hotel-mundial.pt
Airy rooms that attract business travelers.

Hotel Tivoli ($$$)
Avenida da Liberdade 185 tel: 21 319 8900
e-mail: business@tivoli.pt
Renovated in 1992, with facilities (including pool) that are generous given the reasonable prices. Modern and traditional furniture and fittings.

Lapa Palace ($$$)
Rua do Pau de Bandeira 4 tel: 21 395 0005
www.orient-expresshotels.com
In a 19th-century palace; has recently challenged the Ritz (see below) as Lisbon's best upscale hotel. Luxurious and stylish, with a lovely garden.

Metropole ($$)
Praça Dom Pedro IV 30 tel: 21 346 9164
e-mail: almeida_hotels@ip.pt
Imposing and elegant building on one of the main squares. Air conditioning and double-glazing.

Pensão Arco Bandeira ($–$$)
Rua dos Sapateiros 226, 4° tel: 21 342 3478
Good fourth-floor pension close to the Rossio.

Pensão Londres ($–$$)
Rua Dom Pedro V 53, 2° tel: 21 346 2203
Friendly and efficient in a former mansion. Smarter than some budget options, and a good location.

Pensão Ninho das Águias ($)
Costa do Castelo 74 tel: 21 886 7008
Plain rooms, but a superb setting near the Castelo.

Residencial Camões ($–$$)
Travessa do Poço da Cidade 38 tel: 21 346 7510
Modestly sized but nicely decorated rooms in Bairro Alto. Amiable atmosphere.

Ritz Four Seasons ($$$)
Rua Rodrigo a Fonseca 88 tel: 21 381 1400
www.fourseasons.com
Lisbon's most famous and highly regarded hotel. Decor is smart 1950s. Suites are superb, but while the overall ambience is excellent, some rooms are not quite worth the high rates.

Senhora do Monte ($$–$$$)
Calçada do Monte 39 tel: 21 886 6002
Lovely but not central hotel, although rooms are attractive, the staff amiable, and the views superb.

York House ($$$)
Rua das Janelas Verdes 32 tel: 21 396 2435
www.cidadevirtual.pt yorkhouse
A first choice among many regulars, thanks to the lovely courtyard, tasteful rooms, and fine service.

TRÁS-OS-MONTES

Bragança

Hotel São Jose ($$)
Avenida Dr. Francisco Sá Carneiro
tel: 273 331 579
e-mail: hotelsãojose@mail.telepac.pt
Comfortable, central, and blandly modern; a professional and reliable mid-price option.

Pousada de São Bartolomeu ($$$)
Estrada do Turismo tel: 273 331 493
www.pousados.pt
Located 0.5 miles (1km) from the town center in a panoramic position. Built as a *pousada* in 1959, so has nothing by way of historic interest.

Chaves

Hotel Trajano ($$)
Travessa Cândido dos Reis tel: 276 332 415
Tidy, modern rooms (some with views). The restaurant is also one of the better in town.

Quinta da Mata ($$$)
Estrada de Valpaços tel: 276 340 030
A 17th-century manor house in a wooded setting just 2 miles (3km) out of town; pool, tennis courts, and just a few rooms. Nice restaurant terrace.

Miranda do Douro

Pensão Santa Cruz ($)
Rua Abade de Bacal 61 tel: 273 431 374
Inexpensive and characterful place in the old town.

Pousada de Santa Catarina ($$)
tel: 273 431 005 www.pousadas.pt
Nine average rooms and three suites just out of town overlooking the local dam and reservoir.

Vila Real

Mira Corgo ($$–$$$)
Avenida 1 de Maio 76 tel: 259 325 001
e-mail: miracorgo@mail.telepac.pt
The smartest hotel in town, with pool and views, but the modern building is a little uninspiring.

Residencial São Domingos ($)
Travessa de São Domingos 33
tel: 259 322 039
The best of several inexpensive options in a little street by the cathedral.

THE MINHO

Barcelos
Albergaria Condes de Barcelos ($$)
Rua Arquiteto António Borges Vingre
tel: 253 811 061
One of the best known (if slightly faded) of the
more upscale modern places.

Braga
Hotel do Elevador ($$)
Bom Jesus do Monte tel: 253 603 400
This large, elegant hotel has a gracious French-
style garden and valley views from some rooms.
Hotel do Parque ($$)
Bom Jesus do Monte tel: 253 676 548
In a fine rural setting with large comfortable
rooms; this is a better bet than the Elevador.
Residencial Inácio Filho ($)
Rua Francisco Sanches 42 tel: 253 263 849
Central, clean, and charmingly eccentric.

Guimarães
Hotel Toural ($$)
Largo A. L. do Carvalho tel: 253 517 184
Comfortable hotel right at the heart of town.
Pousada de Nossa Senhora de Oliveira ($$$)
Rua de Santa Maria tel: 253 514 158 or
253 514 159 www.pousadoas.pt
A wonderful old *pousada* contained within several
linked 16th-century manor houses; retains its
period fittings and an intimate ambience. Situated
at the heart of the old town, and also has the best
restaurant in town.
Pousada de Santa Marinha da Costa ($$$)
Costa tel: 253 514 453 www.pousadas.pt
One of the most fabulous *pousadas* in Portugal. In
a rural setting 1.2 miles (2km) north of the town
center, and housed in a converted convent dating
back to 1154. Ask for one of the older rooms, not
one of the rooms in the newer wing (although
these have more "facilities").
Residencial Das Trinas ($)
Rua das Trinas 29 tel: 253 517 358
Good budget choice. All rooms have private
bathrooms; old-town location.

Parque Nacional da Peneda-Gerês
Pousada de São Bento ($$–$$$)
Caniçida, Vieira do Minho tel: 253 647 190
www.pousadas.pt
A traditional wood and stone house (not historic)
with a pool. Panoramic position overlooking the
wooded slopes of the Caldo Valley.

Rio Lima
Casa do Barreiro ($$$)
São Tiago da Gemieira, Ponte de Lima
tel: 258 948 137
A lovely old traditional house (1652) with just
seven rooms and one apartment. Pool and
terraced garden with pleasant views; located
3 miles (5km) east of Ponte de Lima.
Paço de Calheiros ($$$)
Calheiros, Ponte de Lima tel: 258 947 164
This elegant villa has just nine rooms, plus a pool,
tennis courts, and horse-riding facilities. Located
4 miles (7km) north of Ponte de Lima.

Residencial Morais ($)
Rua da Matriz 8 tel: 258 942 470
Quiet and traditional—a cheap in-town alternative
to the large number of historic Solares de Portugal
properties around Ponte de Lima.

Valença do Minho
Pousada do São Teotónio ($$–$$$)
Balvarte do Socorro tel: 251 824 242
www.pousadas.pt
The rooms are slightly dated but the setting (in the
town's former fortress) is wonderful.
Residencial Ponte Seca ($)
Avenida Tito Fontes 57 tel: 251 822 580
Clean and welcoming low-cost choice on the
eastern flanks of the new town.

Viana do Castelo
Casa Grande de Bandeira ($$)
Largo das Carmelitas 488 tel: 258 823 169
Three rooms in a charming family-run place on a
shady square on the edge of the historic quarter.
Pousada Monte Santa Luzia ($$$)
Santa Luzia tel: 258 282 889 www.pousadas.pt
A large villa on the hill above the town; superb views
from the hotel terrace and many of its rooms.
Modern interior and high-quality rooms.
Residencial Dolce Vita ($)
Rua do Poço 44 tel: 258 824 860
A good budget option. Located above a restaurant;
shared bathrooms.

PORTO AND THE DOURO

Amarante
Casa de Pascoaes ($$$)
São João de Gatão tel: 255 422 595
A beautiful 18th-century house once owned by the
Portuguese poet Texeira de Pascoaes, and still
home to his study and library. There are four rooms,
so reserve ahead. In a hamlet near Amarante.
Hotel Estoril ($)
Rua 31 de Janeiro 49 tel: 255 431 291
Amiable and well-situated hotel by the river.
Hotel Príncipe ($)
Largo Conselheiro António Cândido 53
tel: 255 432 956
An inexpensive hotel near the bus station.

Lamego
Hotel Parque ($$)
Parque Nossa Senhora dos Remédios
tel: 254 609 140
Definite first choice in town. At the top of the hill
by the church, with a garden and views.
Villa Hostilina ($$)
Villa Hostilina, Lamego 5100 tel: 254 612 394
Pleasant farmhouse in a lovely rustic situation out-
side town. Seven tastefully appointed rooms.

Porto
Grande Hotel da Batalha ($$$)
Praça Batalha 116 tel: 22 200 0571
e-mail: h1975gm@accorhetils.com
An old-town location about ten minutes' walk
from the river and business district. Recently
renovated, and less expensive than the Infante de
Sagres (see page 256).

255

Accommodations and Restaurants

Hotel Castor ($$)
Rua das Doze Casas 17 tel: 22 537 0014
Dates from the 1960s, but the small rooms are
tastefully decorated and the staff are friendly. It
has a "pub" and a couple of restaurants.
Hotel Infante de Sagres ($$$)
*Praça Dona Filipa de Lencastre 62
tel: 22 339 8500
e-mail: his.sales@mail.telepac.pt*
This luxurious, elegant, and traditional hotel has
no equal if you want to stay in Porto in high style.
Hotel São João ($$)
Rua do Bonjardim 120, 4° tel: 22 205 6114
Pleasantly decorated and welcoming hotel in the
heart of the city; a mixture of antique and modern.
Pensão Marinho
Praça Carlos Alberto 59 tel: 22 205 4380
Welcoming pension in a reasonably central garden-
square setting. All rooms have private bathrooms.
Residencial Rex ($$)
Praça da República 117 tel: 22 207 4590
Located on one of the city's prettier garden
squares, this excellent low-cost option has
grand old public areas and airy if rather
perfunctory rooms.

Vale do Douro
Pensão Douro ($)
Largo da Estação, Pinhão tel: 254 732 404
One of just two pensions in this little village.
Pousada São Gonçalo ($$)
*Curva do Lancete, Ansiães, Serra do Marão
tel: 255 461 113 www.pousadas.pt*
A superbly situated and remote mountain *pousada*
on the road between Amarante and Vila Real.

THE BEIRAS

Aveiro
Hotel Paloma Blanca ($$)
*Rua Luís Gomes de Carvalho 23
tel: 234 381 992*
Pleasant town center villa with small tropical
garden and reasonable, old-fashioned rooms.
Residencial Beira ($)
Rua José Estevão 4 tel: 234 423 818
Central and popular lower-priced option.

Buçaco
Hotel Palace do Buçaco ($$$)
*Mata do Buçaco tel: 231 930 101
e-mail: almeida_hotels@ip.pt*
One of Portugal's most famous hotels, although
the grandeur in some rooms is (elegantly) faded.

Coimbra
Hotel Astoria ($$–$$$)
Avenida Emídio Navarro 21 tel: 239 822 055
Large, comfortable, and sedate historic hotel in
the town center.
Hotel Dom Luís ($$)
Quinta da Varzea tel: 239 802 120
Modern and tasteful, but located 0.5 miles (1km)
south of the city center.
Hotel Domus ($)
Rua Adelina Veiga 62-1° tel: 239 828 584
Amiable budget place in a quiet street near
the station.

Hotel Oslo ($$)
*Avenida Fernão de Magalhães 25
tel: 239 829 071*
A recently overhauled modern hotel, but avoid
noisy rooms facing on to the street.
Residencial Pombal ($)
Rua das Flores 18 tel: 239 835 175
First choice in the budget range.

Conimbriga
Pousada de Santa Cristina ($$$)
*Condeixa-a-Nova tel: 239 944 025
www.pousadas.pt*
One of Portugal's newest and most impressive
pousadas, with garden, pool, and tennis courts.
Only 9 miles (15km) from Coimbra.

Figueira da Foz
Clube de Vale de Leão ($$–$$$)
Rua da Floresta, Buarcos tel: 233 433 057
A first-rate resort hotel just out of town. A choice of
25 self-contained apartment-bungalows plus pool
and tennis courts.
Hotel Mercure ($$$)
*Avenida 25 de Abril tel: 233 422 146 e-mail:
mercurefigueirah1921@accor-hotels.com*
A big, recently renovated, 1950s-era hotel.
Comfortable but uninspired; popular with upscale
tour groups.
Hotel Pena Branca ($$)
Rua 5 de Outubro 42 tel: 233 434 502
In Buarcos, a fishing village at the northern end of
the town beach. First choice among the mid-priced
hotels; also has a good restaurant.

Serra da Estrela
Pousada de São Lourenço ($$$)
*Penhas Douradas-Manteigas, Estrada da
Gouveia tel: 275 982 450 www.pousadas.pt*
A stone-built *pousada* in great countryside; 8 miles
(13km) from Manteigas on the Gouveia road.

Viseu
Hotel Avenida ($$)
Avenida Alberto Sampaio 1 tel: 232 423 432
A small, pleasant family-run hotel off main square.
Hotel Grão Vasco ($$)
Rua Gaspar Barreiros tel: 232 423 511
Best known of the central hotels; deservedly popu-
lar, but perhaps overpriced for what it offers.
Quinta de São Caetano ($$)
Rua Possa das Feiticeiras 38 tel: 232 423 984
Book ahead to secure a room in this 17th-century
villa 0.5 miles (1km) north of Viseu; pool, garden.

ESTREMADURA

Alcobaça
Hotel Santa Maria ($$)
Rua Francisco Zagalo 20–2 tel: 262 597 395
Friendly modern hotel right by the monastery.

Batalha
Pousada de Mestre Afonso Domingues ($$$)
*Largo Mestre Afonso Domingues
tel: 244 765 260 www.pousadas.pt*
Modern, comfortable but slightly characterless
pousada in the middle of town.

Fátima

Estalagem Dom Gonçalo ($$)
Rua Jacinta Marto 100 tel: 249 539 330
Stands out among the plethora of bland modern hotels in Fátima. Garden setting on the edge of town plus a good restaurant.

Hotel Santa Maria ($$)
Rua de Santo António tel: 249 533 015
Modern and reliable if a trifle uninspiring.

Nazaré

Hotel Praia ($$$)
Avenida Vieira Guimarães 39
tel: 262 561 423
Bland upscale hotel close to the beach; recently renovated.

Pensão Central ($–$$)
Rua Mouzinho de Albuquerque 85
tel: 262 551 510
Good traditional budget option.

Pensão-Restaurante Ribamar ($$)
Rua Gomes Freire 9 tel: 262 551 158
A whitewashed waterfront building with a sprightly yellow trim; modest-sized but appealing rooms, some with balconies. Traditional oak-beamed restaurant.

Óbidos

Estalagem do Convento ($$)
Rua Dom João de Ornelas tel: 262 959 216
e-mail: estconventhotel@mail.pt
Welcoming hotel in a plain-fronted old convent; spacious and appealingly faded rooms.

Pousada do Castelo ($$$)
Paço Real, Apartado 18 tel: 262 959 105
www.pousadas.pt
Smallish but very comfortable *pousada* housed in a converted 15th-century palace.

Rainha Santa Isabel ($)
Rua Direita tel: 262 959 323
Central, modest, and fetching modern hotel behind a period facade.

Tomar

Hotel dos Templários ($$)
Largo Cândido dos Reis 1 tel: 249 310 100
A large 178-room hotel with a wide range of facilities. All the rooms are perfectly acceptable, but those in the annex are more modern.

Residencial Luanda ($)
Avenida Marquês de Tomar 15
tel: 249 315 153
Decent modern hotel; views from some rooms, but traffic noise in others.

THE ALENTEJO

Beja

Hotel Cristina ($$)
Rua de Mértola 71 tel: 284 323 035
A modern if slightly bland hotel on the main shopping street.

Hotel Melius ($$)
Avenida Fialho Almeida tel: 284 321 822
A brand-new hotel on the southern edge of town.

Pousada do Convento de São Francisco ($$$)
Largo do Nuno Alvarez Pereira
tel: 284 328 444 www.pousadas.pt

Recently opened and luxurious *pousada* in a converted monastery, with pool, tennis courts, and garden.

Elvas

Estalagem Dom Sancho II ($)
Praça da República 20 tel: 268 622 686
First choice among the central hotels.

Pousada de Santa Luzia ($$$)
Avenida de Badajoz-Estrada N4
tel: 268 622 194 www.pousadas.pt
Recently renovated *pousada*, but poor location on main road outside city walls.

Estremoz

Hotel Monte dos Pensamentos ($$)
Estrada da Estacaõ do Ameixial
tel: 268 333 166
A lovely, whitewashed Moorish-style hotel a few miles out of Estremoz.

Pousada da Rainha Santa Isabel ($$$)
Largo Dom Dinis tel: 268 332 075
www.pousadas.pt
Among the most grandiose and luxurious *pousadas* in the country.

Évora

Hotel Planície ($)
Rua Miguel Bombarda 40
tel: 266 704 066
Extremely appealing hotel housed in a former ducal palace.

Pousada dos Lóios ($$$)
Largo Conde de Vila Flor tel: 266 704 051
www.pousadas.pt
One of Portugal's best *pousadas*; housed in a 15th-century monastery. Good restaurant.

Residencial Solar Monfalim ($$)
Largo da Misericórdia 1 tel: 266 750 000
Very tastefully converted Renaissance palace. Clean, simple, and traditional rooms with more than a touch of class in the public areas.

Marvão

Pousada Santa Maria ($$$)
Rua 24 de Janeiro 7 tel: 245 993 201
www.pousadas.pt
A small, friendly *pousada* situated in a simple townhouse with exceptional views.

Portalegre

Pousada Flor da Rosa ($$$)
Mosteiro de Santa Maria tel: 245 997 210
www.pousadas.pt
Imposing former monastery near Crato, a village located 14 miles (23km) west of Portalegre.

Vila Viçosa

Casa dos Arcos ($$)
Praça de Martim Afonso de Sousa 16
tel: 268 980 518
Welcoming hotel in an historic 18th-century townhouse.

Casa de Peixinhos ($$$)
Vila Viçosa 7160 tel: 268 980 472
Fine 17th-century building only about 500 yards (0.5km) from the town center, and with eight delightful, elegant rooms.

257

THE ALGARVE

Albufeira
Hotel Villa Joya ($$$)
Praia do Galé tel: 289 951 795
One of the loveliest—and costliest—of the newer
deluxe resort hotels; 3 miles (5km) east of Albufeira.
Residencial Limas ($)
Rua da Liberdade 25–7 tel: 289 514 025
Popular ten-room central hotel.
Residencial Vila Bela ($$)
Rua Coronel Águas 15 tel: 289 512 101
West of the center; airy rooms overlooking the bay
and small pool.

Faro
Hotel Eva ($$$)
Avenida da República tel: 289 803 354
The best hotel in town: an eight-story modern
building overlooking the harbor.

Lagos
Casa de São Gonçalo ($)
*Rua Almirante Cândido dos Reis 73
tel: 282 762 171*
Charming old-fashioned house at the heart of
Lagos; avoid noisy street-front rooms.
Hotel de Lagos ($$$)
Rua Nova da Aldeia 1 tel: 282 769 967
On a hilltop overlooking Lagos. Slighly eccentric
rooms, but still the best in its price range.

Praia da Rocha
Hotel Bela Vista ($$$)
Avenida Tómas Cabreira tel: 282 450 480
Tasteful, recently renovated Moorish-style hotel on
the cliffs above the beach. Attractive bar terrace.

Sagres
Pousada do Infante ($$$)
*Ponta da Atalaia tel: 282 624 220
www.pousadas.pt*
Wonderful situtation with clifftop views; handy for
beaches, plus tennis courts, restaurant, and sea-
water pool. Note the four-room annex 1.2 miles
(2km) towards the cape, also with restaurant.
Residencial Dom Henriques ($$)
Sitio da Mareta tel: 282 620 000
Cozier and cheaper than the Infante. Sea views.

Serra de Monchique
Estalagem Abrigo da Montanha ($$$)
Estrada da Fóia tel: 282 912 131
A lovely mountain retreat with pool and peaceful
gardens; situated 1.2 miles (2km) from Monchique.

Tavira
Convento do Santo António ($$$)
Atalaia 56 tel: 281 325 632
Majestic convent recently converted into a superb
hotel with choice of apartments or small rooms.
Pensão do Castelo ($)
Rua da Liberdade 4 tel: 281 323 942
Central, clean, and reasonably priced.
Quinta do Caracol ($$)
Bairro de San Pedro tel: 281 322 475
Individual whitewashed apartments in a pleasant
complex with garden; located close to the center.

258

RESTAURANTS

Restaurants in most of Portugal are reasonably
priced by European standards; expect to pay
per person for a three-course meal without
drinks:
● **budget ($)** = 1,200$00–2,000$00
● **moderate ($$)** = 2,000$00–3,500$00
● **expensive ($$$)** = 3,500$00 and over

LISBON

A Gôndola ($$)
Avenida de Berna 64 tel: 21 797 0426
A little outlying (by the Gulbenkian), but the place
to go if you develop a craving for Italian food.
Bota Alta ($–$$)
Travessa da Queimada 35–7 tel: 21 342 7959
A rustic, very popular, and tightly packed Bairro
Alto restaurant.
Casa da Comida ($$$)
Travessa de Amoireiras 1 tel: 21 385 9386
Highly rated French-Portuguese restaurant.
Casa do Leão ($$–$$$)
Castelo de São Jorge tel: 21 887 5962
The traditional cooking is perfectly good, but what
you pay for here is the glorious castle setting.
Cervejaria Trindade ($–$$)
Rua Nova de Trindade 20c tel: 21 342 3506
This atmospheric beer-hall and *azulejos*-lined
restaurant has been in business since 1836. The
food is reasonable and inexpensive.
Conventual ($$–$$$)
Praça dos Flores 45 tel: 21 390 9196
Excellent food at lower prices than its rivals.
Antique-filled interior; attractive location.
Gambrinus ($$$)
*Rua das Portas de Santo Antão 23
tel: 21 342 1466*
A smart, central restaurant devoted mainly
to seafood.
Lautasco ($$–$$$)
Beco do Azinhal 7 tel: 21 886 0173
A welcoming courtyard setting in the famed
Alfama district.
O Cantinho do Aziz ($–$$)
Rua de São Lourenço 3–5 tel: 21 887 6472
Rough and ready, but a great place to sample
spicy ethnic Mozambique cooking.
Pap' Açorda ($$–$$$)
Rua da Atalaia 57–9 tel: 21 346 4811
Currently one of Lisbon's trendiest bar-restaurants,
with a young clientele. Built in an old bakery.
Pastelaria Sala de Cha Versailles ($)
Avenida da República 15a tel: 21 355 5344
One of the city's most famous old teahouses
(opened in 1932). Superb period atmosphere and
good for snacks.
Rei dos Frangos-Bom Jardin ($)
*Travessa de Santo Antáo 11–12
tel: 21 342 7424*
A great Lisbon institution, known for its
sensational roast chicken.
Sua Excêlencia ($$–$$$)
Rua do Conde 38 tel: 21 390 3614
An intimate, innovative, and rather trendy restau-
rant with excellent Angolan-influenced cooking.

TRÁS-OS-MONTES

Bragança
Lá em Casa ($)
Rua Marquês de Pombal 7 tel: 273 322 111
Stone walls and pine chairs make for a rustic
charm. Central location, amiable atmosphere, and
tasty fish and beef dishes.
Restaurante Poças ($)
Rua Combatentes da Grande Guerra 200
tel: 273 331 428
Two floors bustling with locals in a restaurant in
the *residencial* of the same name.

Chaves
Carvalho ($$)
Largo das Caldas tel: 276 321 727
The exterior is inauspicious, but the regional
cooking is excellent.
Dionisyos ($$)
Praça do Município 21 tel: 276 332 602
Generous portions, fine food, and a location close
to the castle.

Vila Real
Churrasco ($$)
Rua António de Azevedo 24 tel: 259 322 313
Come here for the town's best BBQ chicken.
O Espadeiro ($$)
Avenida Almeida Luçena tel: 259 322 302
Widely considered the best restaurant in Vila Real.

THE MINHO

Barcelos
Casa dos Arcos ($)
Rua Duques de Bragança 185
tel: 253 811 975
Small, traditional-style restaurant usually well
patronized by locals.
Dom António ($)
Rua Dom António Barroso 87 tel: 253 812 285
Another favorite, with a large, rustic interior.

Braga
A Marisqueira ($$)
Rua Castelo 15 tel: 253 262 152
An old-fashioned, central restaurant whose high
reputation dates back some 60 years.
O Inácio ($$)
Campo das Hortas 4 tel: 253 613 235
A popular local restaurant situated in a rural-style
18th-century house. A little pricier than some.

Guimarães
El Rei ($)
Praça de São Tiago 20 tel: 253 419 096
A local favorite at the center of town: a first choice
if you're not eating at the nearby pousada.
Grelhados do Mar ($)
Largo Condessa do Juncal 27 tel: 253 518 427
A wide range of dishes at reasonable prices. They
specialize in fish and seafood.

Rio Lima
Encanada ($)
Avenida Marginal-Alameda, Ponte de Lima
tel: 258 941 189

Fair prices, a lovely situation overlooking the river,
and wonderful traditional food.
O Brasão ($$)
Rua Formosa 11, Ponte de Lima
tel: 258 941 890
Popular restaurant in traditional stone building.

Viana do Castelo
O Três Arcos ($$)
Largo João Tomás da Costa 25
tel: 258 824 014
Considered the best restaurant in town; seafood.
O Três Potes ($$)
Beco dos Fornos 7–9 tel: 258 829 928
Very popular, and the food is good (if pricier than
the Três Arcos); traditional music and dancing laid
on during summer weekends.

PORTO AND THE DOURO

Lamego
Combinado ($)
Rua da Olaria 84 tel: 254 612 902
Snug and inexpensive restaurant just behind the
tourist office.

Porto
A Brasileira ($–$$)
Rua do Bonjardim 116 tel: 22 200 7146
Old-style café for daytime coffee and snacks; there
is also a good restaurant here.
Aquário Marisqueiro ($$–$$$)
Rua Rodrigues Sampaio 179 tel: 22 200 2231
Widely acknowledged as one of the city's leading
fish and seafood restaurants.
Chez Lapin ($$)
Cais da Ribeira-Rua dos Canastreiros 40–4
tel: 22 200 6418
A large place that appeals to locals, especially on
Sundays, when you should make a reservation.
Majestic Café ($)
Rua de Santa Caterina 112 tel: 22 200 3887
Founded in 1922 and, with the A Brasileira (see
above), the best of the famous art-deco cafés.
Portucale ($$$)
Rua da Alegria 598 tel: 22 537 0717
Porto's top restaurant if you don't mind hotel
dining. This intimate and smart place sits on top
of the Albergaria Miradouro, with wide views
accompanying the quality international cuisine.
Restaurante Escondidinho ($$)
Rua Passos Manuel 144 tel: 22 200 1079
Old-fashioned stone and wooden-beamed room;
Portuguese cooking with a French twist.
Reservations are advised.
Taverna de Bébobos ($)
Cais de Ribeira 21–5 tel: 22 205 3565
Founded in 1876, this is among the oldest and
tiniest restaurants in Porto. Snacks are sold down-
stairs, while the cozy restaurant is housed
upstairs. Very popular, so reserve a table.

THE BEIRAS

Aveiro
Centenário ($)
Largo do Mercado 9–10 tel: 234 422 798
Popular place alongside the town's bustling market.

Accommodations and Restaurants

Salpoente ($$)
Rua Canal São Roque 83 tel: 234 382 674
Stylish fish and seafood restaurant just north of the town center.

Coimbra
Adega Paço do Conde ($)
Rua Paço do Conde 7 tel: 239 825 605
Large, popular, rumbustious, and authentic.
Café Santa Cruz ($)
Praça 8 de Maio tel: 239 833 617
One of the most famous old cafés in Portugal, located in the monastery chapels; snacks only.
O Trovador ($$)
Largo Sé Velha 15–17 tel: 239 825 475
Beautiful old restaurant by the cathedral; occasional *fado* sessions.

Viseu
O Cortiço ($)
Rua Augusto Hilário 47 tel: 232 423 853
First choice for a reliable *tipico* eating experience in the old town.

ESTREMADURA

Alcobaça
Trindade ($$)
Praça Dom Afonso Henriques 22
tel: 262 582 397
Alongside the monastery, and like most local restaurants often crammed with visitors.

Nazaré
Brisa do Mar ($)
Avenida Vieira Guimarães 10 tel: 262 551 197
A good antidote to the town center's preponderance of fish and seafood restaurants.
Mar Bravo ($$)
Praça Sousa Oliveira 67A tel: 262 551 180
Among the most popular of Nazaré's often expensive restaurants.

Óbidos
Restaurante Alcaide ($$)
Rua Direita tel: 262 959 220
Portuguese tavern-style restaurant; noted for its balcony dining area (reserve to secure a table here).

THE ALENTEJO

Beja
Luís da Rocha ($)
Rua Capitão João Francisco de Sousa 63
tel: 284 323 179
Bluff, simple, and popular with locals.

Elvas
Canal Sete ($)
Rua dos Sapateiros 16 tel: 268 623 593
Popular, straightforward place off the main square; rock-bottom prices.

Estremoz
Águias d'Ouro ($$)
Rossio Marquês de Pombal 27
tel: 268 333 326
Reasonable food and prices. Interesting building.

São Rosas ($$)
Largo de Dom Dinis 11 tel: 268 333 345
First choice for good food unless you want to eat in the *pousada*.

Évora
Cozinha de Santo Humberto ($$)
Rua da Moeda 39, off Praça do Giraldo
tel: 266 704 251
A wonderfully rustic and atmospheric restaurant, heavily patronized by locals.
Guião ($)
Rua da Républica 81 tel: 266 703 071
Hearty regional cooking in a family-run place.
O Fialho ($$$)
Travessa das Mascarenhas 14–16, off Praça Aguiar tel: 266 703 079
One of the best traditional restaurants in Portugal.

Portalegre
O Abrigo ($)
Rua de Elvas 74 tel: 245 331 658
Plain but cheerful, plus low prices.

THE ALGARVE

Albufeira
A Ruína ($$)
Praia dos Pescadores, Largo Cais Herculano
tel: 289 512 094
Simple, old-fashioned place by the fish market.
O Cabaz da Praia ($$$)
Praça Miguel Bombarda 7 tel: 289 512 137
In business for 30 years; good food, roof terrace.

Faro
Cidade Velha ($$$)
Rua Domingos Guieiro 19 tel: 289 827 145
Faro's top restaurant: reservations essential.
Dois Irmãos ($$)
Largo do Terreiro do Bispo 13–15
tel: 289 823 337
A seafood restaurant in business since 1925.

Lagos
Alpendre ($$$)
Rua António Barbosa Viana 17 tel: 282 762 705
Rather formal atmosphere; service can be slow, but the food is pleasingly sophisticated.
Dom Sebastião ($$)
Rua 25 de Abril 20–2 tel: 282 762 795
Rustic, popular—the town's best restaurant.

Praia da Rocha
Safari ($$)
Rua António Feu tel: 282 423 540
Cliff-edge location above the beach; Portuguese food with an African twist.

Tavira
Bica ($)
Rua Almirante Cândido dos Reis 22–4
tel: 281 322 252
Cheap, good-quality food. Plain surroundings.
Imperial ($$)
Rua José Pires Padinha 22 tel: 281 322 234
Celebrated locally for its fish and seafood.

Index

Index/Acknowledgments

Acknowledgments

The Automobile Association wishes to thank the following photographers and libraries for their assistance in the preparation of this book.
ALLSPORT (UK) LTD. 24a (S. Munday), 24b (M. Thompson)
ARQUIVO NACIONAL DE FOTOGRAFIA-INSTITUTO PORTUGUÊS DE MUSEUS 59 (Museu Nacional de Arte Antiga, José Pessoa), 62 (Museu Nacional de Arte Antiga, Francisco Matias)
ART DIRECTORS AND TRIP PHOTO LIBRARY 178a
BRIDGEMAN ART LIBRARY 32b Juan I of Avis beating Juan I of Castile I in the Battle of Aljubarotta, Portugal, 1385, Vol. III "From the Coronation of Richard II to 1387," by Jean Batard de Wavrin Chronique d'Angleterre, (15th century), (British Library, London), 33 Duke of Lancaster dines with the King of Portugal, from Vol. III "From the Coronation of Richard II to 1387," by Jean de Batard Wavrin, (British Library, London), 36a The Charles V Tapestry depicting the Marriage of Charles V to Isabella of Portugal in 1526, detail of the cardinal blessing the couple, Bruges, ca1630–1640 (Musée du Temps, Besancon) (Lauros-Giraudon), 37 Portrait of the Empress Isabella of Portugal, 1548 by Titian (Tiziano Vecellio) (ca1485–1576) (Prado, Madrid)
MICHELLE CHAPLOW 228
MARY EVANS PICTURE LIBRARY 29, 35a, 36b, 38/9, 38, 39a, 39b, 40a, 40b, 42b, 172b
GETTY IMAGES 41, 42a, 43, 46/7
MAGNUM PHOTOS LTD. 17 (B. Barbey), 44b (De Andrade), 46 (Jean-Paul Paireault), 178b (B. Barbey)
NATIONAL MARITIME MUSEUM LONDON 227
PICTURES COLOUR LIBRARY 67
REX FEATURES LTD. 47
RIBATEJO TOURISM BOARD COLLECTION 179 (Mauricio Abreu)
SPECTRUM COLOUR LIBRARY 87, 93, 107, 114, 119
SPIX-IMAGENS LDA. 22/3, 31a (Museu Alberto Sampaio), 44a, 45, 88a (Fototeca), 88b (Fototeca), 173a (Fototeca)

The remaining photographs are held in the Association's own photo library (A.A. PHOTO LIBRARY) and were taken by Alex Kouprianoff with the exception of the following pages:
I. BURGUM 34a; M. BIRKITT 12, 138, 220, 223; D. BUWALDA 34b; J. EDMANSON front cover (b), 10b, 16, 18b, 138/9, 139, 192, 202/3, 204, 226a, 233b; T. OLIVER front cover (a); J. A. TIMS 11, 160, 173b; P. WILSON 21, 22, 27, 54, 90/1, 99, 109, 199, 200, 252.

Contributors

Designer: Jo Tapper   Original copy editors: Susi Bailey & Sue Gordon
Revision verifier: Emma Rowley Ruas   Revision copy editor: Sarah Hudson
Indexer: Marie Lorimer   Updated by: OutHouse Publishing Services